A PLUME BOOK

THE MOTHER-DAUGHTER PROJECT

SuEllen Hamkins, MD, was for twelve years the psychiatrist for Smith College. She now has a private practice specializing in women's mental health. She is the mother of two daughters, ages eighteen and twelve.

Renée Schultz, MA, has been a marriage and family therapist for more than twenty years. She is the mother of a nineteen-year-old daughter and a twenty-four-year-old son.

In 1997, the authors created the Mother-Daughter Project with several other women in their community, with the hope of disproving the damaging assumption that mothers and daughters must separate during adolescence. Since 2002, they have presented their work on the Mother-Daughter Project internationally at conferences in the United States, Mexico, Australia, and Hong Kong. There are currently dozens of Mother-Daughter Project groups worldwide.

"Every mother of a girl should read this book, try out some of the exercises with her daughter, and start her own mother-daughter group."

—Sharon Lamb, EdD, coauthor, *Packaging Girlhood: Rescuing Our Daughters from Marketers' Schemes*

"A thoroughly realistic road map for sustaining mother-daughter relationships in a culture that seems determined to undermine them . . . Hamkins and Schultz demonstrate how collective energy and commitment can help mothers and daughters thrive."

—Meredith Michaels, coauthor, *The Mommy Myth: The Idealization of Motherhood and How It Has Undermined All Women*

"A lively and engaging book that offers hope and inspiration as well as practical advice for maintaining and enhancing the mother-daughter connection."

—Jean Kilbourne, author, *Can't Buy My Love: How Advertising Changes the Way We Think and Feel*

"Wise to the ways of girls and the stresses on moms, Hamkins and Schultz bring to life a mother-daughter revolution—a revolution of love and connection during the most difficult transition in a girl's life. This is a practical handbook for an extraordinary transformation, for the next generation of women."

—Elizabeth Debold, coauthor, *Mother Daughter Revolution: From Good Girls to Great Women*

"How I wish *The Mother-Daughter Project* had been around when my daughter was becoming a woman, and I'm thrilled it's here in time for my granddaughter."

—Gina Ogden, PhD, author of *The Heart and Soul of Sex: Making the ISIS Connection*

"An enthralling chronicle of a pioneering community of mothers and their daughters. Here, the generation gap closes, as mothers and daughters join in solidarity, mothers empowering their daughters while having their own sense of empowerment re-charged . . . Invigorating and engaging . . . rich in invention."

—David Epston, family therapist; codirector of the Family Therapy Centre, Auckland, New Zealand; coauthor, *Biting the Hand That Starves You: Inspiring Resistance to Anorexia/Bulimia*

The Mother-Daughter Project

How Mothers and Daughters
Can Band Together, Beat the Odds,
and Thrive Through Adolescence

• • • • • • • • • • • • •

**SuEllen Hamkins, MD
and Renée Schultz, MA**

A PLUME BOOK

PLUME
Published by the Penguin Group
Penguin Group (USA) Inc., 375 Hudson Street, New York, New York 10014, U.S.A. •
Penguin Group (Canada), 90 Eglinton Avenue East, Suite 700, Toronto, Ontario,
Canada M4P 2Y3 (a division of Pearson Penguin Canada Inc.) • Penguin Books
Ltd., 80 Strand, London WC2R 0RL, England • Penguin Ireland, 25 St. Stephen's
Green, Dublin 2, Ireland (a division of Penguin Books Ltd.) • Penguin Group
(Australia), 250 Camberwell Road, Camberwell, Victoria 3124, Australia (a division of
Pearson Australia Group Pty. Ltd.) • Penguin Books India Pvt. Ltd., 11 Community
Centre, Panchsheel Park, New Delhi – 110 017, India • Penguin Group (NZ), 67
Apollo Drive, Rosedale, North Shore 0632, New Zealand (a division of Pearson New
Zealand Ltd.) • Penguin Books (South Africa) (Pty.) Ltd., 24 Sturdee Avenue,
Rosebank, Johannesburg 2196, South Africa

Penguin Books Ltd., Registered Offices: 80 Strand, London WC2R 0RL, England

Published by Plume, a member of Penguin Group (USA) Inc. Previously published in
a Hudson Street Press edition.

First Plume Printing, April 2008
10 9 8 7 6 5 4 3 2

 REGISTERED TRADEMARK—MARCA REGISTRADA

The Library of Congress has catalogued the Hudson Street Press edition as follows:
Hamkins, SuEllen.
    The Mother-Daughter Project : how mothers and daughters can band together, beat
the odds, and thrive through adolescence / SuEllen Hamkins and Renée Schultz.
        p. cm.
    Includes bibliographical references.
    ISBN 978-1-59463-034-7 (hc.)
    ISBN 978-0-452-28916-1 (pbk.)
    1. Mothers and daughters.   2. Mothers—Social networks.   3. Daughters—Social
networks.   4. Parenting.   5. Parent and teenager.   6. Communication in the family.   I. Schultz, Renée.   II. Title.
    HQ755.85.H343 2007
    306.874'3—dc22   2006036591

Printed in the United States of America

To all girls and women everywhere

Acknowledgments

Without a doubt, it takes a community to write a book. To all the mothers and daughters with whom we've spoken and to the women and men whose writing has inspired us, especially the writers of the first, second, and third waves of feminism, we say a heartfelt thank-you. A deep and abiding gratitude to all the mothers and daughters who have participated in the Mother-Daughter Project with us over the past decade: Barbara Allen, Arianna Baum-Hommes, Vicki Baum-Hommes, Addy Berard, Erin Berard, Grace Berard, Susannah Berard, Amy Bowes, Isolina Leiva Bowes, Magali Leiva Bowes, Susannah Brown, Teneya Brown Schare, Diane Fabig, Amy Fabig-Roosa, Anne Fitzgerald Connie Fitzgerald, Franny Hamkins-Indik, Tiama Hamkins-Indik, Kim Holden, Savannah Holden, Robin Jurs, Marcia LaRocque, Hannah Levy-LaRocque, Katrin Lloyd-Bollard, Margaret Lloyd, Jill Mendez, Juliana Mendez, Cindy Parrish, Emma Parrish Post, Fiona Parrish Post, Diane O'Sullivan, Maeve O'Sullivan, Arcadia Rom-Frank, Ronnie Rom, Mia Schultz-Baer, Shoshana Sokoloff, Hannah Sokoloff-Rubin, Paula Swenson, Kira Yoshen, Shino Yoshen, and Victoria Yoshen. Words are insufficient to express the thanks we owe the mothers and daughters of our mom-daughter group with whom, over the past ten years, we have talked, laughed, cried, played, and grown, learning together the true meaning of the word *comadre.* Your willingness to share the intimate details of your journeys is a gift to girls and women everywhere. To our three sister mothers, your skill and commitment to nurturing our group through the challenges of taking our story public and your loving support of us individually and together as authors is a miraculous gift in our lives for which we cannot thank you enough.

We are also grateful to the larger community of people who have supported us in bringing this book into the world. We are grateful for our agent, Nina Collins, for her faith in our project, and to our publisher, Laureen Rowland at Hudson Street Press, for her vision, her brilliant guidance, and her unflagging commitment to bring our message to every mother of a daughter. An extraspecial thank-you to Sarah B. Weir, editor extraordinaire, who played a pivotal role in the shaping of the book, bringing her skills, her compassion, and her deep caring for girls and their mothers to this task, heroically going above and beyond. A thank-you also to Stephanie Golden for her editorial contributions. We are grateful to Danielle Friedman for her graceful editing and for her care in shepherding us through production, and to everyone at Hudson Street Press for their support and enthusiasm.

Renée's Acknowledgments

I am deeply grateful to my partner, Ron Baer, for supporting me every step of the way, from those first moments as a new mother right through the long and arduous process of birthing this book. A big thank-you to my daughter, Mia Schultz-Baer, for her keen observations, her reminders to lighten up, and her own unique voice in the world. (You're the "beast"!) I also thank my son, Ian Schultz-Baer, for being a light in the world and my best teacher. Mothering can be a lonely journey, especially when you have a child with special needs, and a special thank-you to the mothers who have shared those particular joys and challenges. A thank-you also to my springboard, my mother, Virginia Schultz, and to my sister, Carla Laubach, who always knows how to buoy me up. I am grateful to my mother-in-law, Aurelia Baer, who has taught me much about being a loving and supportive mother and an independent woman. Thank you to Lynn Keating and the Westhampton Memorial Library for the steady stream of books and to Manuel Garcia of Core Solution Group for technical assistance and moral support, especially when my "mother board" crashed at a critical moment. I thank my many friends, colleagues, and clients who have generously shared their lives with me and enriched my understanding of mothers and daughters, and of course, myself. Thank you to SuEllen Hamkins for our years at your kitchen table discussing, writing about, and sharing our passion for making the world a better place for mothers and daughters.

A special thank-you to all my writing friends over the years and most especially to Brett Averitt, Rita Bleiman, Penny Cunningham, Carol Edelstein, Cynthia Kennison, Lida Lewis, Tanyss Martula, and Nanny Vonnegut. To Lida Lewis, in particular, I offer a special thank-you, for handholding and encouragement when the task of writing this book seemed too great.

SuEllen's Acknowledgments

The soul of this book has been fed by my experiences as a daughter and a mother. I wish to thank my mother, Monica Hamkins, for the inspiration of her spirit and the depth and tenacity of her love, which has been illuminated to me ever more brightly over the years. I love you. Next I wish to thank my daughters, Tiama and Franny Hamkins-Indik, for blessing my life with joy and love beyond my wildest hopes, for teaching me daily what love between mothers and daughters can be, and for giving me the exact balance of solitude and companionship that I needed for writing this book. I love you each to the sun and moon and back again a hundred million times. Unwavering love and support from my husband, Jay Indik, has been my daily blessing, as has been his steadfast, playful coparenting and his willingness to share his professional acumen as an expert in child and adolescent development, reading every draft of every chapter and being my best critic and cheerleader. Thank you for being a *great* dad.

I am grateful to my teachers, colleagues, and clients and to the worldwide community of narrative therapists for their inspiration and encouragement, especially Norma Akamatzu, Gene Combs, David Epston, Jeff Fishman, Jill Freedman, Farnsworth Lobenstine, David Moltz, Jenifer McKenna, Beth Prullage, Sallyann Roth, Shona Russell, Shoshana Sokoloff, Gerry Weiss, and Michael White. I am indebted to Cheryl White, publisher of Dulwich Centre Publications, and David Denborough, editor, whose early faith in this project was instrumental to the creation of this book. I am grateful to Renée Schultz for her vision and for her care and kindness to me over the years.

I am indebted to the circles of support that have embraced me through the long days of writing, especially Mary Beth Brooker, Susan Yard Harris, and Karen Randall of my writer's group, attentive midwives from the first quickening of tentative musings to the birth of the final draft; my sister doctors, mothers, feminists, and friends Gaylinn Greenwood and Shoshana Sokoloff, from whom I have learned so much; and Janice Waldron-Hansen and the dancing C-students. I offer my heart to Karen Bivona, Melissa Hamkins, Mary Leonard, and Cindy Parrish for their unstinting love and support through sorrow and joy.

Contents

Acknowledgments   vii

Introduction   xv

PART I. Creating a New Vision for Mothers and Daughters

CHAPTER ONE
What Is the Mother-Daughter Project?   3

CHAPTER TWO
Daughters
Helping Our Girls Thrive   13

CHAPTER THREE
Mothers
Confronting the Myth of Supermom   34

CHAPTER FOUR
Preventing Mother-Daughter Disconnection   51

CHAPTER FIVE
Finding a Common Ground
Developing Mother-Daughter Mutuality   69

CHAPTER SIX
Creating a Community for Mothers and Daughters   80

PART II. Mothers and Daughters Banding Together

CHAPTER SEVEN
Celebrating Girls
Seven Years Old—In Love with Mom and the World   95

CHAPTER EIGHT
Fostering True Friendship
Eight Years Old—Branching Out   108

CHAPTER NINE
Welcoming Cycles
Nine Years Old—Big Changes Ahead   120

CHAPTER TEN
Learning to Love Our Bodies
Ten Years Old—Capable and Outspoken   137

CHAPTER ELEVEN
Hanging Out and Having Fun (Shhh!) with Mom
Eleven Years Old—In Transition   156

CHAPTER TWELVE
Cultivating Desire
Twelve Years Old—Curious   173

CHAPTER THIRTEEN
Teaching Safety and Freedom
Thirteen Years Old—Gaining Independence   195

CHAPTER FOURTEEN
Speaking Her Heart and Mind
Fourteen Years Old—Establishing Values   216

CHAPTER FIFTEEN
Earning Money and Wielding Power
Fifteen Years Old—Looking Ahead   232

CHAPTER SIXTEEN

Growing Roots and Wings

Sixteen Years Old—Testing New Boundaries   251

CHAPTER SEVENTEEN

Flying Toward the Future

Seventeen Years Old—Becoming a Young Woman   269

Appendix 1: Creating a Mother-Daughter Group   287

Appendix 2: The Moon Dance of the Body   297

Notes   301

Selected Bibliography   313

Introduction

Ten years ago, watching our carefree seven-year-old daughters riding their bikes through the neighborhood, ponytails flying in the wind, it frightened us to imagine that, someday, they would be teenagers. The possibility that there might come a time when our vibrant and affectionate young girls—girls who shared their every thought with us, whose knees we bandaged when they fell—would want nothing to do with us was painful to consider.

As committed mothers, and as psychotherapy professionals with more than forty years combined experience in the fields of women's mental health and family issues, we, Renée and SuEllen, asked ourselves: How can mothers help our girls make it through adolescence strong, confident, and whole? Is there any way mothers and daughters can sustain their positive and loving relationships beyond childhood, through the teenage years, and on into adulthood? How can women find the support they need to do the tough work of mothering, especially when our girls are teens?

In 1997, we joined other concerned mothers from our local community to try to find the answers to just these questions. Among us were a high school guidance counselor, three teachers, a community organizer and activist, two health professionals, and an artist. We were determined to come up with a plan that would enable our girls to thrive through adolescence, and that would enable us to remain close and connected with them.

We began by reading *Mother Daughter Revolution* (1993)[1] by Elizabeth Debold, Marie Wilson, and Idelisse Malavé, a groundbreaking book that encourages women to join one another in mothering their daughters, while challenging the common expectation of mother-daughter separation. Starting with monthly mothers-only discussions, we explored our own experiences of adolescence and our relationships with our mothers, and brainstormed ways we could stay close to our daughters as we nurtured them through their teen years. Together we came up with the plan of creating a small, supportive community—an extended family of committed mothers—in which mother-daughter connection was the norm. Banding with our daughters, we created an ongoing mother-daughter group that met regularly, and we developed playful but powerfully effective activities that fortified our girls' self-esteem as they explored key issues with us, such as girls' friendships and puberty when they were young, and, over time, more challenging subjects such as body image, drugs, sexuality, and violence against women. As they matured, we marveled at the strength and confidence with which they thrived through adolescence, and found that our group did indeed provide an antidote to the perils of teen culture. We also learned that it *is* possible for mothers to have warm and loving relationships with our teen daughters. Equally important, the group offered us the sustenance we needed as mothers to navigate our daughters' adolescence with integrity and grace.

The Mother-Daughter Project was born.

In our monthly mother-daughter get-togethers, we alternated between addressing age-appropriate topics like learning to be media savvy or stay safe on public transportation with purely enjoyable activities like kayaking and mother-daughter movie nights. One of the secrets to staying close with your daughter as she grows up, we learned, is simply finding ways to continue to have a good time together even when her desire to be with her peers begins to eclipse her interest in being with her family. Our monthly mothers-only meetings—held in the evenings a few weeks before our mother-daughter meetings—supported our relationships with our daughters, as we offered one another encouragement and wisdom and experience on topics from how to help a shy ten-year-old make friends at school to how to effectively respond to a thirteen-year-old's angry outbursts. We also recognized that our worlds as women encompassed more than mothering, and we helped one another over the years in creating more fulfilling lives, by encouraging one another to seek out the best for ourselves, whether it was a more satisfying and better-paying job or a household division of labor that left time for painting. We and our girls thrived with the support of other mothers and daughters. And our meetings weren't a drain or just one more thing to cross off the "to do" list—they were fun!

As psychotherapists, we knew from our work and research that we were breaking new ground in the area of mother-daughter relationships and adolescent development. Excited by our discoveries, we wanted to share them with other mothers and with family therapy professionals. So in 2002, when our girls were twelve years old, and with the blessing of the other women in the Project, we, Renée and SuEllen, began meeting every other week in the couple of hours we could squeeze out of our busy lives to discuss what we were learning, and we began presenting our work at psychotherapy conferences, first in the United States, then in Mexico, Australia, and Hong Kong. The work struck a chord. Many women with whom we spoke—professionals in the field of psychology and mothers themselves—asked how they could join us. Wanting to ensure their daughters' safe passage through adolescence often provided the impetus to get involved, but some hoped to use the concepts we presented to heal rifts in their relationships with their own mothers. Others wanted to have a positive influence on mothers and daughters with whom they worked professionally. Dozens of mothers expressed their intentions to start groups with their own girls. We now know of groups in Tucson; Seattle; Belmont, California; Albany, New York; Amherst, Massachusetts, and other towns in the United States, as well as in Australia, New Zealand, and Mexico.

This book details the success of the Project's innovative model, providing the reader with a clear map for strengthening her bond with her own daughter now and in the future and offering road-tested strategies for helping guide her during her teen years.

Mothers and Daughters Banding Together

The Mother-Daughter Project rests on the conviction that other mothers and daughters are one of the most powerful resources you can draw upon to help you safely shepherd your daughter through adolescence. You may never start a mother-daughter group of your own, but finding one other mother and her daughter to share your journey can make all the difference in the world. At the moments when it seems your daughter is struggling and you're not sure what to do, feeling isolated makes mothering even harder, while getting encouragement and advice from other mothers who share your values can help you and your daughter find your way through the difficulty. By reading this book, you join a global community of mothers who want to stay connected with their daughters and help them thrive.

Why do we talk specifically about mothers and not fathers? Why not focus on parents in general? We appreciate the tremendous support mothers and children get from committed fathers, but women who are parents are subject to powerful messages and constraints that men who are parents are not. What it means to be a good mother is entirely different from what it means to be a good father. While the work of parenting by men and by women is interconnected, and issues related to fathering are important and compelling, our focus in this book is on women who parent—that is, mothers. Likewise, daughters are subject to ideas and situations that sons are not. While we intend our research and findings to stand alongside and support other projects on mothers and sons, and on fathers and sons or daughters, in this book we shine the spotlight on mothers and daughters.

When we say *mothers* in this book, whom do we mean? A mother is any woman who is given or takes on the responsibility of raising a child. We include mothering through adoption, foster care, comothering among lesbian partners, coparenting with divorced spouses or stepparents, sole mothering, biological mothering, grandmothers who are mothering their grandchildren, as well as the many other ways in which women nurture beloved children. We honor the ways in which our opportunities to mother as we would like have been constrained by limited financial resources or by racism, homophobia, classism, or ability discrimination, and we honor our dedication and resourcefulness as we creatively nurture children regardless of the challenges.

In addition to outlining specific activities you can do with your girl, throughout this book we pose questions that will help guide you in finding the unique mothering path that is right for you and your daughter. Questions like *What is my own vision of what it means for my daughter to thrive? What worries me most about her teen years? When do my daughter and I feel closest nowadays? What kinds of support are most helpful to me as a mother?* Inspired by the healing and empowering approaches of narrative therapy[2]—a therapeutic process that helps people cultivate their values and strengths through developing healing life stories, and which we've both used in our practices—our questions are designed to make your own preferences and skills more apparent to you, to aid you in connecting more fully with the people and resources that support you, and to help you overcome the obstacles that stand in the way of achieving your vision of what it means for mothers and daughters to thrive. Our questions honor the diversity of mothers as they help you clarify your personal hopes for your daughter and yourself, framed by the context of your individual lives and cultural environments. While the questions may seem simple, they aim to provide you with a fresh and innovative perspective on your relationship with your daughter and offer solutions for times when the going is rough. The answers they generate are likely to surprise and please you, whether you reflect on them in your journal or discuss them in a group with other mothers.

Meet the Mothers in the Original Mother-Daughter Group

While many women and their daughters are now involved in the Mother-Daughter Project, in this book we have chosen to focus on one of the original mother-daughter groups, of which we, SuEllen and Renée, are members. Affectionately referred to as simply "mom-daughter" by group members, we follow it from the time the girls were seven until they are seventeen (the age most of the girls are at the time of this writing). Along the way, we provide you with a detailed guide for anticipating and tackling the most difficult issues of adolescence. Although we changed names and identifying characteristics (including our own) of the various members to protect the privacy of the girls, the stories are true. Now let's meet the group's members.

Sarah Diamond, thirty-eight at the start of the group, divorced from her girls' dad and remarried four years later, has two daughters, Kay and Maggie Diamond. Maggie, a cheerful cherub at seven when the Mother-Daughter Project started, is now an athletic, outgoing seventeen-year-old young woman. Kay, always spirited and creative, is now, at twenty, working full-time and setting up a home with her boyfriend. Sarah, a nurse, is reliable, capable, affectionate, and outspoken. In the past few years she has moved from simultaneously holding several part-time jobs, in order to have the flexibility to meet her daughters' needs when they were young, to one full-time job that provides more economic security. Sarah has enjoyed a loving and playful relationship with her girls. She is deeply committed to ongoing connection with her daughters and makes attending different intergenerational community events with them a priority, such as contra dances with Kay and mom-daughter meetings with Maggie. When at sixteen, Maggie falls in love and spends more and more time away from home, Sarah learns what it takes to open her heart to make space for Maggie's expanding relational world—while still staying close to Maggie.

Libby Woods, forty-one at the start of the group, has been married for more than twenty-five years, and has one daughter, Vanessa Woods-Rosen. At seven, Vanessa was a quiet, serious child, prone to perch at the edge of the mom-daughter group. Now, at seventeen, she talks with passion about friends, school, and her future. Libby has worked full-time as an attorney with a private practice in family law since before Vanessa's birth through to the present. Libby and Vanessa's relationship was easy and open—until Vanessa reached middle school. Suddenly they seemed to fight about every little thing. Libby worried about what it meant, and wondered whether an ongoing mother-daughter connection would elude them.

Fun-loving and enthusiastic, Maisie Snowden, the youngest mother in the group, was thirty-one and newly divorced when the group started and homeschooling her two girls, Gabriella and April Snowden-Smith (eight and six when the group started). Gabriella, now eighteen, has grown from being a shy girl into a self-possessed teenager who finds her life's meaning in theater and singing, while April, sixteen, has held on to her athletic, spunky nature as her passion developed from playing kick-the-can into basketball. Maisie found it easy to guide and stay close to her girls until they were seven and nine, when she needed to return to paid elementary school teaching, and her girls began attending public school. Her job responsibilities kept her away from home until the late afternoon and her daughters became more influenced by their peers—in ways Maisie didn't always approve of. Maisie drew on the ideas and activities of the mom-daughter group to nourish her loving connection with her girls and to get practical support in setting limits and nurturing them while endeavoring to respect their emerging identities, different as they were from her own.

Quiet, soft-spoken, and artistic, Katy Riverby is the mother of Marisol and Kaili Trias Riverby, now seventeen and twelve. Thirty-five and in the midst of separating from her girls' father at the start of the group, Katy works full-time as a window display de-signer. Easygoing teenage Marisol is busy with school, chorus, musical productions, work, and friends, and has been an active and enthusiastic member of the mother-daughter group since its beginning when she was seven. Kaili, two years old when the book starts, is lively and open with her mother at home, but more quiet with others. From her own experiences with the world of drugs, sex, and rock and roll, Katy knew that when teen girls feel empty and unheard they are more vulnerable to making choices that don't serve them. She was determined to figure out what went wrong in her own life as a teen and to use the lessons she learned to help her girls avoid making the same mistakes she did, drawing on the experience and knowledge of other mothers in the group to help her.

Phoebe Ruzek, thirty-five at the start of the group, is an an-thropology professor, the mother of Amy and Eliza Ruzek-Cohen, now seventeen and eleven, and is married to their father, Paul. Amy, often the quietest member of the group, has a presence that lets us know she's busy absorbing all that's going on. Today, she loves school, dancing, and friends—pretty much just like when she was six. From her teens into her twenties, Phoebe had a stormy relationship with her mother, and she feared that her own daughters would similarly push her away. When the usually even-tempered and loving Amy literally pushed Phoebe out of her room at age eleven and writes her a note at age thirteen that starts with "Dear Mom, I hate you," Phoebe turned to the mom-daughter group to help them find their way through. Phoebe's younger daughter, Eliza, two years old at the start of the Project, is a firecracker of a girl who loves climbing trees, writing poetry, and figuring out hard math problems. When Eliza and Kaili (Katy's younger daughter) reached age seven, Phoebe and Katy started another mother-daughter group with them and other moms, drawing from the successes of their older daughters' group.

The daughters in the original mom-daughter group attend different schools, hang with different sets of friends, and pursue their own particular interests, but feel close and comfortable with their old friends from the group. The mothers have worked to become supportive members of one another's life, although, like the girls, they also have diverse networks of support outside of the group. Katy, Sarah, Libby, Maisie, and Phoebe. Marisol, Maggie, April, Gabi, Vanessa, and Amy. Together they forged into the wilderness of mothers and daughters banding together, beating the odds, and staying connected through adolescence.

The Heart of the Mother-Daughter Project

For many women, our relationships with our mothers and with our daughters are at the core of our emotional lives. As authors, psychotherapists, and founding members of the Project, we've found that our experiences as mothers *and* daughters are integral to our ideas, our therapeutic conversations, and our activism. While our work is supported by reliable data and intellectual rigor, it springs from the heart. Here, in the interest of transparency, we offer you a window into our personal journeys.

Renée: By the time I was in my twenties, I assumed that I would never become a mother. While I had sweet memories of playing with baby dolls as a young girl and rocking my neighbor's infant son as a teenager, my trajectory seemed firmly on the path of career and the life of a single woman. Perhaps my mother's cautionary remarks when any local girl from our small Wisconsin hometown got pregnant, coupled with her own apparent unhappiness with her life, had convinced me that only a fool would get herself pregnant, married or not.

Yet, in my thirties, the joy and success with which my husband and I negotiated an egalitarian marriage made the idea of motherhood seem plausible. We assumed that we would easily coparent, a fifty-fifty proposition. By the time I was pregnant with our first child, I believed I could both have a career and be a mother. But when our son, Ian, was born with Down syndrome, the idea that we could easily split the work of parenting blew straight out the window. Our son's needs were far greater than either of us could have imagined. As a new mother, facing the challenges of raising a handicapped child felt enormous. I feared I would never be the mother I'd hoped to be—patient, fun-loving, engaged— and that I would get stuck in a role I didn't want. When other mothers with handicapped children talked to me about their decision to give up their jobs or careers to care for their children, I knew that decision would not be right for me or him.

Coming to terms with my son's disability was a difficult struggle. The assumptions I carried about being a good mother, that I'd never lose my temper and be unfailingly loving and giving and generous, were impossible for me to live up to, and I constantly felt as though I was failing. I knew I wanted the best for my son. I knew I wanted to nurture and love him. But I also knew I had to take care of myself, or else the challenges of meeting his enormous needs would overwhelm me. Gradually, I settled into my life as a parent while continuing to work outside our home. Ultimately, Ron gave up his work as a ceramic artist to take care of our son, a job he was far better suited to than I, while I became the primary breadwinner.

Deciding to have a second child was almost as difficult as deciding to have the first; however, this time I was motivated by the desire to have a typical child and by the prayer of having a daughter. By the time my daughter, Mia, was born five years later, I'd figured out how to be both a mother and a psychotherapist in private practice, but doubts remained. Was I a good enough mother? Was I failing my children if I took time for myself? Isn't a good mother one who sacrifices herself for her children? While I had successfully challenged the assumptions I had initially had about being a wife (that it would be my job to do all the housework and cater to my husband), confronting the beliefs I had about being a good mother proved to be far more difficult.

By the time Mia started elementary school, I longed to talk with other women who were also questioning their beliefs, and who were challenging the status quo as mothers. Specifically, I wanted to meet with other mothers who had daughters, to explore a new model of connection as described in *Mother Daughter Revolution* (which I had read when Mia was in kindergarten). It had been easy in my twenties to find women who identified as feminists, but as a mother, it was harder to find compatriots. Mothering a daughter amid the challenges of today's world seemed almost as daunting as raising a handicapped child. Would my daughter make it through adolescence unscathed? Even more, would she end up feeling proud of herself and full of her own potential? Would we stay connected? From my work as a psychotherapist, I knew that many, many girls from stable, happy homes get hijacked during adolescence. When the first "mothers of daughters group" gathered in western Massachusetts in response to an announcement I created with my friend Sarah, I felt I had finally found the kind of support that I needed. Ultimately, joining with other mothers is what ensured my daughter's safe passage and bolstered me on this journey we call motherhood.

SuEllen: For as long as I can remember, I wanted to be a mother. I wanted to be a mother—and I wanted to have the kind of life my father had, working at an interesting job outside the home and being a loving and involved parent. I gave birth to my first daughter, Tiama, during my psychiatry residency. I remember vividly how my waters broke at the municipal swimming pool one weekend afternoon, followed by the rapid onset of painful contractions on the way to the hospital. As labor progressed, I soon reached transition, that intense moment just before the cervix is fully dilated when a woman often finds herself facing her deepest fears.

How could I birth a child? I thought as the warm water of the shower in which I was standing coursed over me. How could I, full of faults, selfish, troubled as a daughter myself, possibly be able to be a good parent?

"What if I'm not a good mother?" I wept to my husband, who was standing close by in surgical scrubs. He answered me gently, some solid words of comfort I can't remember now, but which calmed me, and allowed me to go on. Okay. I was going to be me, I told myself, for better or for worse, committed to doing my best as a mother, and I gave birth to my first daughter, Tiama.

Two years later, in the last year of my psychiatry residency, I was working as the breadwinner for my family while my husband, Jay, was pursuing his career as a theater director. One night, I returned to my messy home from my fourth ten-hour shift in a row after picking up a squirmy, exhausted toddler at day care, and had a revelation. If I wanted to be present and caring as a mother rather than cranky and reactive, then I would need sufficient rest, time off, and support to be able to do so. Willpower and intention, although necessary, were insufficient to guarantee my ability to provide calm and generous nurturing. It struck me at the time, between changing my daughter's diaper and throwing together some kind of pasta for dinner, that I was having a somewhat radical thought. I was considering *what I needed* as a mother to be the kind of mother I wanted to be.

I was grateful for the privilege of having that flash, a thought inconceivable to my mother, for example, when she was raising my five siblings and me. I credit her, however, with my ability to have this thought, because she directed me to feminist ideas ever since I was young, and supported me becoming everything I could dream of, even though the same opportunities had not been open to her. Born to first-generation Polish-American parents, she followed their path of hard work and devout Catholicism, sacrificing her career hopes to expectations of domesticity. My father, of Austrian- and German-American ancestry, put himself through college at night during my childhood, and even-handedly encouraged my sister, my four brothers, and me to pursue higher education. Despite the family division of labor, my parents enjoyed an unusually egalitarian marriage.

I credit them both with my ability to not only imagine that what I needed as a mother was important, but also to be able to negotiate with my husband to get it. It wasn't easy for us to challenge gender expectations among other challenges of married life in 1989, but we did it. Our shared feminist values inspired us then and still inspire us now. I am grateful that I could ask for what I needed and get it and still be happily married to the same man. We found ways to equitably share parenting responsibilities, including taking turns doing the laundry and reading stories at bedtime, while supporting each other to also pursue our artistic dreams.

My feminist stance brought me comrades in college and ostracism in medical school. I slogged through my psychiatry residency dodging criticism from sexist supervisors. After one memorable lecture entitled "Why Women Are Inherently Masochistic," I disagreed with the speaker, who in turn suggested I might have to repeat my training since I didn't understand the basics of psychoanalysis. Ultimately my commitment to feminism brought me home: Smith College Counseling Service was specifically looking for a feminist psychiatrist. In 1993, I began as the college psychiatrist at the oldest college for women in the country, and for twelve years I had the privilege of nurturing the well-being of more than a thousand college women in an explicitly feminist institution.

Although I had many sources of feminist inspiration, it was when I read *Mother Daughter Revolution* in 1993, while pregnant with my second daughter, Franny, that I understood most thoroughly what I was up against as a mother and why connecting with others for support was essential. The three authors described, for the first time, how patriarchal forces in our culture separate daughters from their mothers so as to effectively disempower both. I knew that my daughters would face sexism in their lives, but I had not considered the idea that damaging their bonds with me would be one of its effects. I believed that maintaining a solid, healthy connection with my daughters would best help them grow into empowered women. I knew that I was the person most dedicated to helping my daughters become fully themselves, and this dedication is what led me to join other mothers in cocreating the Mother-Daughter Project.

....

The ideas we present in this book are not about achieving some impossible parenting perfection. Rather, they show how we can come together to think about mothers and daughters and expand the tools and practices available to us in ways that ease and support the work of mothering and help our daughters grow into whole, healthy women. The Mother-Daughter Project is not a final vision set in stone, but a living, collaborative work-in-progress.

PART I

Creating a New Vision for Mothers and Daughters

• • • • • • • • • • •

CHAPTER ONE

....

What Is the Mother-Daughter Project?

The only thing *worse* than hearing the pernicious refrain "She loves you now, but just wait till she's a teenager," is the day your adolescent girl screams "I hate you!" and slams her bedroom door in your face. While a situation such as this may be excruciating to contemplate, it's not inevitable. There *is* a better way. Imagine instead:

Five mothers and five twelve- and thirteen-year-old daughters are gathered around a low coffee table in Libby and her daughter Vanessa's living room, nestled in a small town in the hills of western Massachusetts. Several girls and mothers snuggle side by side on a comfy couch, others sit on the floor, and two mothers relax in chairs. It's September, and we are all excited to begin our sixth year of monthly mother-daughter meetings.

"Imagine a day you would love," Libby begins. "Just think of a day that would make you feel really happy."

The coffee table is covered with hundreds of slips of paper, each printed with a word or phrase: *climbing a tree, dancing, cheesecake, ocean.* The faces of the girls and women are intent as they read the words and phrases, and with Libby's encouragement, we begin making selections, going around the circle. We help one another find words on the table that describe our perfect day, trading when copies of a word are gone. Smiling, laughing, and grimacing, we watch one another choose *chocolate, rainy day, roller coaster, fresh vegetable juice.*

"Fresh vegetable juice? Ugh!" Vanessa groans when Libby picks it.

After choosing all the words we want from the table, we pass out paper and pencils. For the next ten minutes all the mothers and daughters each write a description of a day we would love, incorporating these words, then read them aloud.

Twelve-year-old April reads: *I have just woken up from a very long nap. It is three o'clock in the afternoon and I am about to go rollerblading. I look outside and there is thunder and lightning but no rain . . . I rollerblade for about an hour. I am about to go inside when one of my good friends comes up to me and asks if I want to go to an amusement park. Of course, I say yes. . . . At the amusement park I make sure I go on every upside-down ride they have.*

Her mother, Maisie, reads: *I stay in bed all morning, reading and dozing until noon at a cottage near a lake where I'm all alone. The air is still and quiet. I am far away . . . I take a walk around the lake and rest a lot. I climb a tree and think for a long, long time. When I am just starting to feel lonely, I blink my eyes and I am in the kitchen singing a song with my daughters and all the people I love. Good thing someone brought homemade bread, pesto, sun-dried tomatoes, and mozzarella. Oh, and look! There's roast chicken and pie for dessert.*

One by one, we read our descriptions, each as richly unique as the girl or woman sharing it. Together we then consider questions such as *What are the feelings that guide you toward what you want? How did others' choices influence your choices?*

Desire. What do I truly want? For many of us women, raised to consider the needs of others before our own, it's a provocative question. Yes, we are hanging out and having fun with our girls, but we are also enhancing their awareness of one of the most significant and complicated aspects of being female—one that informs so many of their later choices—knowing what makes you happy, and being able to express it clearly, to yourself and to those around you.

We are fascinated by what the girls and the other mothers have to say, but the quality of our conversation is equally compelling. Our daughters, our young teenagers lounging unselfconsciously in their low-riders with the requisite strip of belly exposed, actually want to talk with us, their mothers, about what they desire, why they desire it. They feel comfortable sharing things that are different from what we, their mothers, want, and even from what the other girls in the group say they desire. In this snug house, in this warm, easy moment, we are practicing a new way of being together as mothers and adolescent daughters.

Welcome to the Mother-Daughter Project.

Building a Pro-Girl Community

Have you ever wished you and your precious girl could climb into a bubble and float right over adolescence? Perhaps you are, like we were, concerned that your daughter will become one of the girls who gets ambushed by anorexia or trapped in an abusive relationship. Maybe you worry about depression, alcohol and drug abuse, STDs, or teen pregnancy. As much as we want to protect and shelter our daughters, dire warnings abound, insisting that our daughters must reject us and tear away just as they are entering a teen culture that can be cruel and dangerous.

The Mother-Daughter Project presents a model of prevention. By engaging in developmentally appropriate activities with our girls and finding methods of keeping channels of communication open with them as they become teens, we have discovered how mothers can help their daughters thrive during adolescence. Together we challenge the current popular ideas about girls, mothers, and mother-daughter relationships that typically harm our daughters as they pass from childhood to adulthood. We have found, backed by the latest psychological research, that the commonly held notion that daughters need to separate from their mothers during adolescence in order to grow into healthy, independent adults is misguided and counterproductive. Instead, by teaming with other mothers and their daughters, we have created a community that supports us as mothers, empowers our daughters, and strengthens our mother-daughter bonds. While there is no magic bullet to guarantee any girl's safe passage through adolescence, we know from our experience with our own daughters that the precepts on which the Mother-Daughter Project is based provide a strong and sturdy ship for the ride.

This book tells the story of the Mother-Daughter Project and invites you to join us. The hopes that we put forward in our original mission statement are the same hopes we now extend to you as we bring our work into the world:

> *We want to join with other women in exploring how we can continue to nurture our daughters through preadolescence, adolescence, and into adulthood. We want to find ways to support one another as mothers and support our daughters as they are challenged by the restrictions placed on them by our culture. We want to explore ways that we can welcome our daughters into the powerful community of women.*

In this safe haven, we have addressed with our daughters the most important issues girls and women face today. At the same time, in our mothers-only meetings we have offered one another the solace, comfort, and practical advice all mothers need. Our group, which we simply call mom-daughter—one of the dozens of groups worldwide, inspired by the work of the Project—has been meeting in western Massachusetts for the past ten years and continues to flourish. Our teenage daughters take time from their busy schedules to tackle such critical adolescent topics as violence and sexuality and to just enjoy the girlfriends and mothers with whom they have grown up. The closeness among us is what allows us to reach our daughters. Two years ago, at a slumber party of mothers and their fifteen-year-olds, we circled around one of the girls as we unbraided her hair, talking into the wee hours about work, money, romance, and hopes for the future. The fact that our teenage girls were not only willing—but excited!—to spend time with us is, as you may know, a monumental departure from the norm.

Why does the Mother-Daughter Project succeed at empowering both mothers and daughters and cementing mother-daughter relationships? First, we create a place where it's okay to love your mom. One of the secrets we have learned through our work with mother-daughter groups, as well as from our research and observations as therapists, is that teen girls are desperate to be close to their mothers—as long as they can still be cool in front of their peers. Girls do best when they can explore who they are *in the context of loving relationships with their mothers and families* as well as out in the wider world.

Second, we take Supermom off her pedestal and get her to put her feet up during regular mothers-only time when we share the realities of too little time and too much to do, how crazy we are about our kids and how crazy they can make us. The companionship of other mothers gives women what they need to make motherhood really work: an embracing community.

Third, we address the big issues with our girls early, before they become too hot to handle—not through lectures but through humor, play, and personal stories. Later, when our daughters are faced with trying on their first bra they know that their friends and other mothers in their group believe in the beauty of every body type. When they go out with their first boyfriend, they have already thought about how to know what they want in a relationship—and what they don't want. Our book provides ideas for how to get the support you need to do the work of mothering and the tools to help you stay close to your girl as she grows up. And while you may choose to start a mother's group of your own, you can also find the help you seek through this book by using the Project's methods and becoming a part of a worldwide community of women who not only want the best for their girls but are taking the steps to make a real difference.

Finally, we offer mothers the win-win situation they have been waiting for. We support the needs and hopes and dreams of women as fully as the needs and hopes and dreams of their daughters. The solution is not about you doing more. Instead, it's about getting the encouragement and companionship you deserve as you do one of the hardest jobs in the world.

Our lives are not perfect, nor are our daughters' lives, and we've experienced our share of difficulties along the way, as you'll learn from our personal experiences and those of other mothers and daughters in the chapters to come. But through the Mother-Daughter Project we've been strengthened by a family of girls and women who promote self-awareness, confidence, and a deep sense of belonging at the time when girls are most prone to low self-esteem, depression, and a loss of connection from who they really are.

What Are Mothers and Daughters up Against?

Life is full of challenges for mothers and daughters, particularly during adolescence. Why is this? First, the demands on us today as mothers are contradictory and overwhelming. *The Mommy Myth* and *Perfect Madness: Motherhood in the Age of Anxiety* concur: Over the past twenty years, the expectation of what our job is as mothers has been growing, while support for us has been shrinking. Twenty-first-century mothers are supposed to maintain constant vigilance against our newborn rolling onto her tummy or her back or whichever is the wrong sleeping position of the day while we keep up a constant stream of stimulating conversation with our two-year-old for optimal brain development as we bake organic cookies for the fourth grade last-day-of-school party. All this while living far from Grandma and Grandpa in neighborhoods where no one knows our name and decent day care costs more than half our salary.[1] Inevitably, we fail to measure up to the ideal of Supermom. Rhetoric that promotes the so-called Mommy Wars pits mothers against one another when what we really need is friendship and compassion, and to learn from one another in the ways that generations of women who came before us shared their knowledge. Women value giving support to other mothers and, of course, we all love receiving it. Although most of us are working harder than ever to be good mothers, not to mention partners and providers, when our daughters have difficulties, we are often the ones most likely to be blamed, and the ones most greatly affected.

The fact that girls growing up today enter a teen culture in which the rates of anorexia, bulimia, suicide, depression, self-injury, relationship violence, and sexual assault are among the highest ever can be both terrifying and overwhelming.[2] The path to healthy, wealthy, and wise is rife with quagmires, dead ends, and misinformation. Many girls make it through safely, but casualties are high and there is no sure road.

To make matters worse, as we mentioned earlier, just when a girl is facing the dangers of adolescence, she is pushed to tear herself from the one person who may be her most committed and knowledgeable ally: her mother. In the past decade, the erroneous expectation that daughters will and should hate their mothers has been practically raised to a cultural imperative. Girls trying to appear grown-up comply with popular depictions of mother-bashing. Women trying to be "good mothers" pull back from their daughters because they believe that it is normal and healthy for adolescents to reject and separate from their parents—causing both to suffer unnecessarily. As psychotherapists, we subscribe to the growing school of thought that believes healthy maturity is based on the ability to create mutual relationships, and daughters do best when they have close and loving relationships with their mothers right up through adulthood.[3] Individuation, the forming of one's unique sense of self, occurs best not through separation, but in the context of loving connection. The capacity for true autonomy grows out of a sure sense that one is lovable and loved.

Any one of these problems is hard enough, but it is the three together that make mothering a daughter and growing up as a girl so confusing and difficult today. Through the Mother-Daughter Project, we have found that mothers and daughters can do together what one mother alone cannot: create a lively subculture that simultaneously nurtures mothers, girls, and mother-daughter connection.

As a result of hearing the stories of thousands of girls, women, and families in our professional lives and through our involvement with these early groups, we distilled three ideas that became the underlying principles of the Mother-Daughter Project and continue to guide us:

Supporting girls is implicitly connected to supporting mothers, and vice versa.

Mothers and daughters can *sustain close relationships though adolescence and beyond.*

Mothers and daughters need the support of other mothers and daughters in order to thrive.

Why We Wrote This Book

For the authors, coming of age during the women's liberation movement, our lives opened up for us in ways that our mothers' lives had not. The arrival of our daughters was thrilling, in part, because we thought life was going to be different for them, an easier journey. And it is different in many wonderful ways. Girls today, especially before they hit the teenage years, take it as a given that they are as valuable as boys, that they have choices. They look around and see that their doctor, their mayor, their coach, is a woman.

At the same time, we were shocked by how the world isn't so

different. In some ways it is worse for our girls, particularly during adolescence. The cult of thinness, the sexual objectification of girls, even the social acceptability of surgical "enhancements" and procedures such as breast implants for teenagers, are unrelenting. Likewise, as mothers we are bombarded with unrealistic expectations of mothering. The requirements of mothering today go beyond what one actually does: for example, from getting up in the middle of the night to comfort and feed a crying baby, to feeling guilty if you aren't unequivocally happy about doing so. One slip and you're a "bad mother." Although men are taking a greater role in active parenting than ever before, the standards are dramatically lower for fathers. (One evening after a particularly gratifying day with their daughters, SuEllen's husband, Jay, turned to her and said, "You know, I'm a great dad. And yet, I'd only be considered an average mom.")

Our ultimate dream is to one day see all daughters and mothers thriving. By sharing what we've learned as psychotherapists and as mothers whose daughters have benefited from the Mother-Daughter Project, we hope to show you that mothering an adolescent daughter doesn't have to be so hard. You don't have to do the work of mothering alone.

This Book Is Both a Story and a Map

This book tells the story of what is possible for mothers and daughters, despite the challenges they may face, and offers a map of ways to get there.

Chapters Two through Six make plain the obstacles teen girls, mothers, and mother-daughter relationships face in today's world. We provide therapeutic questions and innovative tools to help you take on those challenges so you can nurture both your daughter and yourself through her preteen years and adolescence.

Chapters Seven through Seventeen offer field-tested, detailed, age-appropriate activities mothers and daughters can do together, designed to be fun for girls while strengthening their resistance to the dangers of teen culture and supporting mother-daughter relationships. These activities have been created to work for you and your daughter alone, or for a pair of moms with their daughters, or for a group.

Throughout the book we share our adventures of creating a mother-daughter community as our daughters have grown up from age seven to seventeen. You will meet one mother-daughter pair from our group at a time in Chapters Two through Six and then follow them all as they participate in various Mother-Daughter Project group activities the next ten years.

As you embark on your mother-daughter journey, we encourage you to remember that a map is not the land itself. The landscape of women and girls is infinitely wider, richer, and more varied than can possibly be captured in these pages. We intend to make the sparkling moments of your own journey more apparent to you, but we do not imagine that we can encompass all the ingenious ways you have found to challenge taken-for-granted notions about mothers and daughters, not to mention the new discoveries you have yet to make. Beautiful, unexplored regions await you in every direction.

CHAPTER TWO

Daughters

Helping Our Girls Thrive

For many girls, the switch from happy child to intense teen seems like it happens overnight. One day, your daughter is bouncing off to school or softball practice, and the next, it seems, she hates algebra, has quit the team, and is sneaking out to get her navel pierced. For other girls, the transition doesn't happen so dramatically—instead she may start spending most of her free time in her room with the door locked, or picking fights with unpleasant frequency. Either way, witnessing these changes can make mothers feel shut out and concerned. As mothers, we all know from talking to other parents and educators and reading the newspaper and watching television that the world can be an unsafe place for teenage girls, and the suddenness with which they enter that world can feel overwhelming. We worry, *What's going on here? Is there anything I can do to help?* As therapists and founding members of the Mother-Daughter Project, we have worked with hundreds of girls, young women, and mothers in order to identify and overcome the obstacles our daughters are most likely to face as teens. What we have learned is that mothers really *can* make a difference.

In this chapter we'll broadly discuss the challenges girls are up against in adolescence, and the concrete ways mothers can help their daughters to make it through (we offer many more directed, age-appropriate tools and activities in Chapters Seven through Seventeen). In the next chapter we look specifically at why life can be so hard for *moms* today and what holds us back. In Chapters Three through Six we bring mothers and daughters together and consider how to make mother-daughter relationships work for the benefit of both. Let's first examine why the developmental shift from child to adolescent often occurs so rapidly and with such turbulence.

It's no coincidence that the transition from child to teen is often rockiest around the time our daughters enter junior high or middle school. The developmental task of an adolescent is to work toward creating an adult identity and find her place in the world. Up to about age ten, girls primarily rely on their parents and teachers to understand how the world functions, hence they generally trust their moms and dads and stay close, wanting to learn from them. At adolescence, however, during the same period when they are going through puberty, girls typically turn their gaze outward, toward their peers and the wider world. Around this time, many girls leave a relatively nurturing, closely monitored grade school environment for the more depersonalized sphere of junior high or middle school—where what they see in the hallways and schoolyard doesn't always line up with their parents' lessons and values. It's normal for kids in early adolescence to desperately want to fit into their crowd of friends, so it isn't surprising that some of them begin to challenge their parents at every turn. Meanwhile, a girl's hormones are firing and emotions are surging while the brain and body undergo the monumental changes that will transform her into a young woman in the short space of a few years. It's no wonder this is such a turbulent period for our children.

According to Craig Winston LeCroy and Janice Daley, experts on children's mental health and founders of the Go Grrrls program to empower adolescent girls, girls who leave elementary school after sixth grade to go to middle school for seventh grade experience a significant drop in self-esteem, in contrast to girls who stay in a K through 8 elementary school, who generally experience an *increase* in self-esteem between sixth and seventh grades.[1] This research corroborates what many of us know from experience—the middle school years are often demoralizing and painful for girls. While there are many wonderful, enriching schools across the nation, researchers observe that "typical middle schools, with their larger size, greater departmentalization, and decreased student-teacher contact, are not a good match for the developmental tasks of early adolescence."[2] In our work with adolescent girls, we've observed that too much of the time, the only institutional effort toward encouraging basic civility in middle school is the punishment of gross breaches of conduct while lesser forms of disrespect such as sexual harassment, name-calling, and bullying are tolerated with the attitude that "kids will be kids."

At the same time that a girl may be confronting a less-than-optimal social environment at school, she is trying to figure out what it means to be a young woman. On top of that, she is being hit with the increased expectation that she should strive to become what *Mother Daughter Revolution* refers to as the "Perfect Girl."[3] Expectations of perfection have haunted girls and women for generations—think of the 1950s debutante or ideal housewife—but the characteristics that define the Perfect Girl change over time, and the millennial version seems particularly daunting. Although many of us women remember feeling decidedly imperfect at some point as teens, at least we weren't coming up against the stunning ubiquity of digitally or surgically "enhanced" skin, breasts, thighs, and teeth that girls witness today on their female icons and idols. As therapists, we've seen that in today's world, there is also more anxiety about success and money generally among teens and society as a whole. Over the past decade working as a college psychiatrist, SuEllen has noted more stress over pressure to succeed academically at her institution and others. Finally, although it's too early to conclusively analyze the impact of technology on today's teenage girls, we suspect that the interactions involved through instant messaging, e-mails, and cell phone text messaging are ultimately less sustaining than communicating directly with a friend in person or even by telephone.

In their immaturity, it escapes most adolescent girls' notice that the Perfect Girl's requirements are contradictory: being sexy but virginal, accomplished but uncompetitive, gorgeous but down to earth, energetic but ultrathin. The Perfect Girl icon is prevalent in both contemporary consciousness and the popular media, and without a consistent alternative vision (such as one you have the power to provide, and which we'll discuss throughout the book), girls may internalize that it is she whom the world, including their families, wants them to be.

One of our concerns at the Mother-Daughter Project has been that the image of the Perfect Girl is now in circulation among eight- to eleven-year-olds, influencing them to turn their attention from jumping rope and climbing trees to focusing on their appearance. We surmise that one reason for this is that, over the past decade, a profitable new marketing group has been identified: tweens. In our opinion, this label is harmful to girls. Many people mistakenly believe it represents a bona fide psychological stage of development when it was actually created by the business world to carve out a new marketing niche.[4] The term is applied almost exclusively to girls, not boys, and implies that girls ages eight to eleven are "between" childhood and their teen years, rather than the young children they still are, with children's needs to be protected and guided by their parents. When younger girls are directly targeted by the media, they are that much more susceptible to messages that negatively influence their self-regard and distract them from more important developmental tasks, such as learning how to act kindly toward their peers, write a proper paragraph, or imagine their future as a novelist or astronaut. We worry that the positive self-image characteristic of eight- to ten-year-olds will erode, leaving a flimsy foundation for adolescent identity development. Mothers now routinely tell us that their seven- and eight-year-old daughters complain that they are "ugly" or "fat," statements that just five years ago were rarely heard from girls younger than age eleven. In the chapters to come, we detail how to counter these kinds of negative messages and foster strong, resilient girls.

What does it mean for girls to maintain an unhealthfully low weight, attempt to look beautiful all the time, and strive for unrealistic ideals of perfection? In our experience, it means a lot of girls are hungry and tired, and may become unhappy, unmotivated, and unable to live up to their potential, too drained and distracted to fully commit to positive self-development activities such as academic achievement, cultivating nurturing relationships, figuring out her purpose in life, or being creative. And yet, resisting perfection comes at a high cost, too, which is the catch-22. Unless a girl has a community that supports her for who she really is, rejecting the pursuit of the Perfect Girl ideal can lead to ostracism. Through example and instruction (which we will discuss in detail in the coming chapters), mothers can play a vital role in countering the damaging expectations of the Perfect Girl and guide daughters to aspire to fulfilling themselves as girls and women. Our experience in the Project teaches us that drawing on other mothers and daughters who share these intentions as a resource is particularly effective in providing girls with a positive view of what it means to be a successful girl and offers them a supportive peer group at a time they need it most.

What It Means for Girls to Thrive

The first aim of the Mother-Daughter Project is helping girls to thrive through adolescence (and beyond), despite the challenges we've outlined above. We can start by defining what this means to us and for our individual daughters. For mothers, defining what we think it means for preteen and adolescent girls to flourish is an incredibly powerful tool. As our girls grow up, we'll get plenty of advice from sources ranging from grandparents to talk show hosts to advertisers and we need to be able to critically appraise what is good for *our own* daughters in order to find ways that directly support them and their individual needs.

When Katy's daughters, Marisol and Kaili, were eight and three, Katy separated from their father. (Katy was thirty-six at the time, and a talented window display designer.) As a newly single mom, she struggled to make ends meet. A colleague at one of the stores where she worked as a window display artist offered to introduce her to a friend who owned a modeling agency in New York City. He said that her lovely, dark-haired, brown-eyed girls had "just the look that's big right now." Wanting to start a college fund for her daughters but finding that rent and other basics claimed her entire paycheck, Katy was intrigued—but not completely sold on the idea.

She brought it up at mothers' group, where we discussed the pros and cons of what commercial modeling could mean for her daughters. Katy was an accomplished painter and respected the need for artists' models—she herself had modeled for life drawing classes to help pay for art school. Although she loved photography, she didn't like the way girls and young women were generally presented in popular magazines. We asked the question *Who is telling this story, and why?* She answered that the story in most ads is told by people who want to make money. The effect these ads have on many young female readers is to make them feel like their material possessions and their looks are more important than who they are inside, which is the opposite of the vision she had for her daughters. Katy realized that she didn't want her girls to even look at such ads, let alone model in them, and she decided that she didn't want to send her beautiful, healthy daughters into a profession where the typical body type was unnaturally thin. Grounded in her own values, she politely declined her colleague's offer, and now, even as Marisol is planning for college and they are figuring out loans and financial aid, she is glad she did.

For any age girl, you can create a vision of thriving that will truly work for her as a unique person by recalling her actual experiences of feeling happy and well, and building from there. In a journal or in discussion with other mothers, you can ask:

Can I think of and describe a time when my daughter seemed happy and healthy?

How would I describe the kind of well-being she had then?

Are there moments from another period in her life when I could see that kind of thriving?

Is that aspect of well-being important to me? Is it part of my vision of what it means for girls to thrive?

What helps me provide this kind of well-being for my daughter? What or who else nurtures it?

To generate a wider vision of your hopes for your girl and a deeper understanding of what encourages her well-being, you can respond to these questions multiple times, seeking other elements that support her or starting with a different time when your daughter was happy and healthy. At the Mother-Daughter Project, our broad vision of well-being for girls means they are safe, healthy, loved, and free to determine who they are and what they care about most. We also hope that girls will value themselves as much as they value others.

Girls Have Their Own Vision of What It Means to Thrive

Thinking about what it means to thrive at seventeen, Marisol, Katy's daughter, says, "Balance. I like when my life feels balanced and there isn't any friction." What it means to thrive is different for every girl and will change as each grows up. Periodically, you can check in with your daughter to help figure out how she is doing and what she might need by asking questions like:

When do you feel the best nowadays?

What about those times feels good to you?

Are there times when you don't feel well or happy? What is it about those times that you don't like?

What's the hardest part of those times?

Who or what helps you get through the difficult moments?

What do you think helps you stay true to yourself when times are hard?

Is there anything I can do to help?

Whatever their ages, some girls will love answering questions like these, and others will not, preferring us to discern indirectly how they are doing and what they need. Younger girls' answers are usually frank, brief, and focused on the present. Responses of eleven- to fifteen-year-olds (if they respond at all) are often self-conscious and changeable. Girls sixteen and older can find these questions intriguing. Even if girls act annoyed or as if they don't want to talk about personal subjects, most will appreciate your direct engagement and concern.

As the questions above can help reveal, mothers already know a great deal about what helps our daughters thrive, as do our girls themselves. As our daughters grow into their teens, we can build on and expand the knowledge, skills, and resources we have already developed by keeping the lines of communication open with our daughters, reaching out for advice from other mothers, and by drawing from current research on adolescent girls. Throughout the book we will present more sharply focused findings as they apply to specific ages and topics; here we briefly outline key research.

The Facts: What Research Reveals About Raising Girls Today

It can be reassuring to know that research consistently shows that "parents remain a powerful influence in fostering healthy teen development and preventing negative outcomes."[5] Based on analysis of hundreds of research articles, the Harvard School of Public Health's 2001 consensus report *Raising Teens* concludes that active parental involvement in schools is linked to better grades and behavior, and parents are particularly important in helping teens in "understanding and challenging negative experiences based on race, ethnicity, family structure, sexual orientation, class, immigrant status, emotional and physical health and disability."[6] Along with food, clothing, shelter, and access to health care, teens do best when parents also provide them consistent love, connection, guidance, and access to other caring adults. The report concludes: "If they have strong bonds with their parents, teens tend to choose friends with values that are consistent with those of their parents, when such peer choices are available."[7] Adolescent girls' well-being is also fostered when they can express their authentic selves in mutual relationships. World-renowned psychologist Carol Gilligan, who has been studying adolescent girls for decades, writes in her 2002 book, *The Birth of Pleasure*: "One confiding relationship, meaning a relationship where one can speak one's heart and mind freely, has been found to be the best protection against most forms of psychological trouble, especially in times of stress." Authentic relationships are particularly critical for girls at adolescence. Gilligan continues, "The evidence of my research identified the risk girls face in adolescence as a risk of losing a confiding relationship. In adolescence, girls often discover or fear that if they give voice to vital parts of themselves, their pleasure and their knowledge, they will endanger their connection with others and also the world at large."[8] Over the past decade, we have seen how girls participating in the Mother-Daughter Project draw comfort and strength from their strong relationships and open communication with their mothers, especially when negotiating intimidating developmental tasks such as transitioning to middle school or standing up to peer pressure.

It can be hard not to feel anxious about what our girls are up against in the wider world. It is comforting to keep in mind, however, that despite the challenges, the majority of teen girls with at least one supportive parent successfully navigate the developmental tasks of adolescence.[9] In the educational realm, girls consistently get higher grades than boys from first grade through high school and often graduate at the head of their classes.[10] Compared to previous decades, teen girls today have unprecedented opportunities to pursue fulfilling relationships, family roles, educations, athletics, and careers—but they also have less day-to-day support and guidance while being exposed to graver dangers.[11] This is where mothers can make a critical difference. A mother's awareness and involvement can help prevent a temporary difficulty in her daughter's life from becoming an entrenched and debilitating problem.

What Are the Challenges Our Daughters Face?

Understanding what forces may work against our daughters' well-being helps us take concrete steps to minimize their influence. If we are aware, for instance, that girls and boys have similar math and science proficiency scores but that women constitute a much smaller percentage of the workforce holding jobs in engineering or science (it's theorized that many girls lose confidence in their math and science abilities around eighth grade), we can encourage our math- or science-loving daughter by helping her find peer support in a local science or chess club, introducing her to a woman engineer or computer programmer, or providing her with biographies of pioneer physicist Lise Meitner, Marie Curie, or Sally Ride.[12] The same is true for the problems that may frighten us, such as some teen girls' vulnerability to eating disorders or sexual coercion. The Mother-Daughter Project is a preventive model: If mothers know the facts, including the ones that can be difficult to think about, it gives us a greater opportunity to directly engage with our daughters in ways that will bolster them and help them resist.

A mother knows and loves her daughter as deeply as anyone; by staying connected, she can help her girl hold on to her true voice and resist sacrificing precious parts of herself on her journey of growing up. Most of us are aware that the adolescent years pose dangers for our daughters, but it can be hard to know what is fact and what is fear-mongering. Here we take an evidence-based, in-depth look at exactly what our daughters are facing today, so that we can be more prepared to aid them. It can be upsetting and painful to begin to explore the harsher side of girls' lives, and we recommend doing so with a friend or in a mothers' group.

More than a decade ago, Mary Pipher, in her landmark book, *Reviving Ophelia*, exposed the "junk values of mass culture" and their damaging effects on the psyches of adolescent girls.[13] Likewise, Carol Gilligan, in a series of books from 1982 through the present, describes how the spirits of adolescent girls are diminished and their voices silenced by the sexism that confronts them on the road to adulthood.[14] As the modern dangers of girlhood were brought to light, girl-empowering initiatives were created in response, such as the magazines *New Moon*, *New Moon Networker*, and *Daughters*, and the national club Girls, Inc. Throughout the 1990s, parents, educators, and counselors took up the task of supporting girls' self-esteem and healthy body image. But despite these efforts, girls today are just as likely to experience anorexia, bulimia, sexual assault, depression, and abusive relationships now as they were ten or twenty years ago, and they are even more likely to experience suicidality, alcohol and drug abuse, and self-injury. While poverty and racism can exacerbate the effects of these problems, the problems are prevalent among teen girls of every race, ethnicity, and income level.[15] The fundamental fact remains: Over the past decade, the social and cultural milieu in which teen girls exist hasn't become any kinder and, in some ways, has become more difficult.

Junk culture values, peer pressure, and puberty combine with the acute sensitivity of the adolescent psyche and, along with the effects of poverty and racism, may form a perfect storm within some of our girls, rendering them vulnerable to risky situations and self-destructive behaviors. Virtually all girls hit a rough patch at some point on their journey through adolescence; as mothers, we don't want our daughters to respond to the pain of that moment with choices that can be harmful. For the most part, teenagers have not yet developed the wisdom, common sense, or experience to fully apprehend and counter the most damaging influences they may come up against. Our daughters need adult guidance and support from their parents to find their way through.

Sexual Risks for Today's Girls

Being aware of the sexual risks our daughters may confront guides us in teaching them how to stay safe and make healthy, positive choices. We live in a highly sexualized world. According to the 2005 Kaiser Family Foundation study, the amount of sex on television has doubled since the late 1990s.[16] The Internet poses dangers that today's mothers did not face as girls. If unmonitored in their use of the Internet, not only do kids have access to X-rated Web sites, but to chat rooms where, between sharing song files, kids often brag about their latest "hook-up," making such behavior seem the norm. Talking with other parents can help you keep abreast of the latest developments in safe, age-appropriate Internet use.

Many girls choose to become sexually active at some point in their teens. At what age and with what motivation they do so influences not just their sexual lives, but their sense of self. The reassuring news is that in 2005, most girls waited until age seventeen or older to have intercourse, but it's disquieting that among those who didn't, more girls had intercourse at age fourteen or younger.[17] Younger teens are vulnerable to coercion and more likely to regret engaging in sex.[18] If a girl habitually consents to sex to please her partner, it erodes her self-regard and sense of personal agency. We have found that thoughtfully communicating with our daughters about sexuality (which we cover fully in Chapter Twelve) helps them make the choices that serve their best interests.

One of the most critical issues to be aware of as a parent is sexual assault. The statistics are sobering. Girls ages twelve to eighteen are the most likely of all females to be sexually assaulted. One out of four teen girls is raped, the vast majority by boys or men whom they know.[19] According to a 2001 study by the Harvard School of Public Health published in the *Journal of the American Medical Association*, 20 percent of high school girls have been physically or sexually assaulted by someone they were dating.[20] (In Chapter Fourteen, we outline many ways to teach your daughter about personal safety and risk while bolstering her self-esteem.)

Compassionate understanding from her mother is one of the most powerful healing forces in a girl's recovery from trauma. We hear many stories of abuse and violation from our young psychotherapy clients. The psychological wounds of a survivor can take years to heal, especially if she has to see the boy who assaulted her every day in geometry class. In our experience, girls who feel they can share the story of a trauma with their mothers and receive their loving support have a much fuller and more rapid recovery.

Self-Injury

Although upsetting to contemplate, knowing the facts about self-injury prepares us as mothers to help our daughters. The majority of girls who self-injure are not trying to end their lives, but to manage their emotions. Karen, a seventeen-year-old college student, confessed to SuEllen in psychotherapy that she had been secretly cutting her arm with a razor. She was an eloquent young woman from a loving family, a good student, and the former captain of her high school track team. Nevertheless, she had been injuring herself almost weekly for four years. Karen explained: "I felt I deserved it for being stupid. . . . It helped me get through times when I hated myself."

Over the past twelve years, we have heard more and more stories like Karen's from our female psychotherapy clients. The physical pain of cutting or burning gives momentary but powerful relief from emotional pain. It also causes the brain to release opiate-like chemicals, which can be addictive and draw a girl into more frequent and severe self-injury.

Previously a rare phenomenon, self-injury is prevalent among teen girls and young women today. Thirteen percent of adolescent girls and at least 25 percent of college women deliberately cut or burn themselves in response to stress.[21] Sociologists are currently trying to figure out why. In her 2005 doctoral dissertation for the Smith College School of Social Work, Efrosini Kokaliari proposes that self-injury is increasing in response to the stress girls experience from maintaining vigilance over their bodies and behavior to meet ever more exacting social standards. She also suggests this stress is compounded by the sensory deprivation of e-mail, blogging, and net surfing compared to the comfort offered by more intimate relationships and pastimes with friends and family. What is clear is that girls engage in self-injury as a way to deal with depression, loneliness, shame, and anxiety. Self-injury is a sign that a girl is experiencing unmanageable stress and would benefit from compassionate support and consultation with a knowledgeable psychotherapist.

Depression and Suicide

"It feels as if nothing I do matters," said nineteen-year-old Claire to Renée in a therapy session. "I don't want to leave my room or even see my friends. I can't concentrate on my assignments, and I've stopped going to class. I'm in a constant state of emotional torment that I can't escape." Claire first began experiencing depression when she was fifteen, and at one desperate moment thought of killing herself by taking a handful of aspirin. She did not seek help for her depression until she was a sophomore in college.

Claire's experience is typical for teens with depression. At least one in five teen girls experiences depression and suicidal urges, which is twice the rate for adult women.[22] Depression makes ordinary tasks seem grueling, interrupts sleep, and impairs concentration. Adolescents with depression argue more and lose their tempers more easily. Often girls themselves don't know that what they are experiencing is depression. Instead, they conclude they are worthless failures or feel completely misunderstood and enraged by those closest to them, including their mothers. If untreated, depression can bring thoughts that life isn't worth living.[23] Knowing that depression is common among teen girls helps you keep an eye out for it if your daughter seems to be struggling. The "sullen teen" we've come to think of as normal may actually be suffering from depression. Treatment is very effective and helps prevent ongoing debility.

Eating Disorders

At a mothers' group meeting when our girls were thirteen, Phoebe (forty-one at the time, an anthropology professor, and mother of Amy and Eliza) said, "I was looking through photos last week, and a photo from Amy's tenth birthday party stopped me short. In the picture, six girls are standing in front of our porch, wearing swimsuits and shorts. They're all smiling, and they look so healthy and vibrant. Now, three years later, two of them have anorexia."

There is consensus among experts that the cultural obsession with thinness in women is the most powerful factor contributing to anorexia and bulimia. Leading anti-anorexia psychotherapists Rick Maisel, David Epston, and Ali Borden express the view in their landmark 2004 book *Biting the Hand That Starves You: Inspiring Resistance to Anorexia/Bulimia* that today's high prevalence of anorexia is caused by a warped cultural environment—not by bad parenting, nor by any defect in our daughters.[24] SuEllen's experience treating hundreds of young women with anorexia or bulimia corroborates their perspective. In the 1950s and early 1960s, when leading screen goddesses like Marilyn Monroe typically weighed 120 to 140 pounds, the incidence of anorexia was extremely rare, less than 1 in 200,000. Rates of anorexia steadily increased through the 1960s and 1970s as models got thinner, and now, when it is common for models and actresses to weigh closer to 100 pounds, anorexia is 1,000 times more prevalent than it was fifty years ago: 1 in 200 women has full-fledged anorexia.[25] According to a study by anthropologist Ann Becker and colleagues, anorexia was virtually absent from the remote Fiji Islands until the arrival of satellite TV. Rates of anorexia and bulimia among islanders suddenly skyrocketed, and are now comparable to those of the rest of the world.[26]

As mothers, we all need to know about anorexia because it is very dangerous. It is often the girls we worry about *least* who end up in anorexia's clutches, girls who are agreeable and successful and get good grades and have loving families. Dieting and being thin have come to be powerfully aligned with the moral high ground in contemporary culture: We call declining dessert "being good" while eating a slice of cheesecake is "being bad." Girls who are striving to be "good" are especially vulnerable to believing the lie that goodness equals thinness.

The message we get from television, movies, magazines, and the diet industry is that weight loss will bring happiness. As psychotherapists, we know from our work with thousands of women that this has no basis in reality. Happiness is not linked to dress size. Once it has taken hold, anorexia takes on a life of its own within a girl's mind as an unrelenting taskmaster. Every time a girl reaches a low weight goal, anorexia besieges her with thoughts that she needs to lose even more.

Bulimia tells the same lies as anorexia. Bulimia invades girls' lives when they feel hungry from dieting, eat more than they think they should, and then purge hoping to avoid weight gain. A girl might skip breakfast and lunch and feel hungrier and eat more for supper. That is the crime, and throwing up is the punishment.

According to the National Institute of Mental Health, anorexia is currently controlling the lives of more than 500,000 girls and women in the United States. They estimate that 1 to 4 percent of all girls and women in the United States are experiencing bulimia; that's more than one million people.[27] Five percent of girls with anorexia die by starvation.[28] While most of our daughters won't get drawn into full-fledged anorexia or bulimia, many are negatively affected by the current preoccupation with thinness. A study published in the *Journal of Pediatric Psychology* found that 50 percent of girls in the United States ages twelve to eighteen are unhappy with their weight and more than a third of normal-weight girls say they are dieting.[29] At the Mother-Daughter Project we have witnessed that mothers can effectively help daughters resist the impulse to focus their energies on becoming ultrathin. Chapter Ten offers many ideas for teaching your daughter to love and take care of her body.

Alcohol and Illegal Drug Use

It used to be boys who turned most frequently to drugs and alcohol; now it is girls. In 2004, approximately 17 percent more girls than boys started using alcohol and marijuana and 29 percent more girls than boys started smoking cigarettes.[30] According to the National Center on Addiction and Substance Abuse at Columbia University, girls get addicted faster and suffer negative consequences sooner than boys and young men.[31] They are also more likely than boys and young men to abuse substances in order to lose weight, relieve stress or boredom, improve their mood, reduce sexual inhibitions, self-medicate depression, and increase confidence.

Many girls lose their virginity while drunk. Drug and alcohol use is associated with increased sexual activity and decreased contraceptive use. Of unplanned pregnancies in fourteen- to twenty-one-year-olds, one-third of the girls who had gotten pregnant had been drinking when they had sex; 91 percent of them reported that the sex was unplanned.[32]

In monitoring and guiding our teenage daughters, parents can have an impact on their alcohol and drug choices. The National Institute on Drug Abuse reports that "positive family influences such as family bonding and consistent rules appear to reduce the risk of tobacco, marijuana, and other drug abuse among teens."[33] Working with young women in our therapy practices and with mothers and daughters at the Project, we have also witnessed that the example of other families that share our values (and set similar limits) increases our influence and eases our relationships with our girls as they see our attitudes and rules being verified.

Helping Our Daughters Find Their Way

As we prepare to aid our daughters, it is useful to acknowledge the issues that particularly concern us as they enter adolescence in order to clarify what they as individuals might need to resist and overcome these challenges. What has helped a girl in the past points us toward solutions for the future. Using an example of a time your daughter was happy and healthy that came to you from the questions in the beginning of the chapter, ask:

Was/is there a time in which this kind of well-being was scarce or absent in my daughter's life? What let me know how hard it was for her then?

What worried me most about her well-being at that time? What dangers on the road of growing up was she facing?

What helped or is helping her get through the difficulty and regain her well-being? What else would have been helpful to her?

Looking into the future, what challenges to my daughter's well-being worry me most?

Who and what could support her in resisting or overcoming those challenges?

For Katy's daughter Marisol, during seventh grade, her well-being hit an all-time low. Like many children, she went from a small nearby elementary school into a regional middle school. None of her old friends were in any of her classes or shared her lunch period. Although she didn't experience frank bullying or ostracism, she felt isolated and vulnerable during the day, especially since the materialism, superficiality, and disdain for scholastic achievement that dominated her new social scene contrasted sharply with her own values of kindness, friendship, and commitment to academics. Throughout the year, she became increasingly withdrawn and stopped speaking up in class. She seemed tired all the time and didn't want to get up in the morning. When Marisol told her mother frankly, "I hate school," Katy knew something was really wrong.

Katy worried that this transition would "crush her interest in learning and her faith in school, and that she would look for other things to feed herself like drugs and boys." Katy's own experiences of alienation at thirteen had led her away from education into drug use and romantic attachments to the wrong men—a lifestyle from which it took her years to extricate herself. "Thirteen is when I fell off the edge. When I was pregnant with Marisol, I was already worried about her teenage years."

Katy's awareness of how sensitive girls are at adolescence prompted her to pay close attention to how Marisol was doing and try to figure out what she needed to feel better. Katy felt her parents didn't make an effort to understand what she was going through as a teen. She was determined to keep lines of communication open with her own daughters and to reach out for advice from other mothers. When reflecting on what helped Marisol hold on to her positive sense of self during that hard time, Katy said, "Knowing she could talk to me and that I would listen and take her seriously. Another thing that sustained Marisol was our mom-daughter group. It gave her a special place where she was entirely safe to be herself." Marisol agreed. Looking back from the perspective of seventeen, Marisol recalled, "I threw myself into my schoolwork, so I still got good grades even though I was unhappy. But really, it was having good talks with my mom that helped." With Katy's involvement, Marisol made it through a tough year without being drawn into harmful behaviors. In eighth grade, the results of the randomized scheduling lottery at her large school were more in Marisol's favor. She shared her lunch hour and had classes with her close friends again and was much happier.

In addition to their individual needs, our daughters also have many things in common: It benefits every girl to be held in a circle of love while she grows into her adolescent and adult self. Having a solid bond and good communication with her mother supports a girl during adolescence, as does having a parent who is aware of the dangers she may face and who is prepared to help her find her way. A mother-daughter group can offer additional support, providing a community that nurtures both her and her relationship with her mother. While no girl passes through adolescence completely pain free, mothers do have the power to help their daughters survive the difficult times and make it back to a place where they can thrive.

In the next chapter, we'll consider what supports *mothers'* well-being while they stand by their daughters.

CHAPTER THREE

Mothers

Confronting the Myth of Supermom

Concern for our teenage girls tends to come naturally. Mothers automatically think, *What's good for her? Is she happy? Does she have what she needs?* And typically, *What more could I be doing for her?* It is far rarer but equally important to ask, *How am I feeling? Am I getting what I need?* In order to foster healthy daughters, mothers need to take care of themselves, too. The myth of the Supermom contends that women should possess a kind of infinite maternal energy like the sun, which allows them to give twenty-four hours a day without replenishment. We all know this is impossible; nevertheless many of us continue to place the needs of others before our own until we are utterly depleted— and then berate ourselves for not doing enough (while feeling quietly resentful of our partners and kids). Do fathers feel guilty if, after a full day's work plus errands, housework, playing Candy Land fourteen times in a row with the little one, and checking the teenager's physics homework they don't have the energy to cook dinner? No. Fathers order pizza.

When Renée's first child was a newborn, she would occasionally find her husband, Ron, who was very involved in caring for the baby, staring out the window. "How can you be doing that?" she would ask in an unfriendly way. "I'm taking a break," was his response. It took Renée months to realize that she felt envious because she didn't know how to give herself those small moments of replenishment. What seemed totally reasonable to him came only with conscious effort to her. It may seem strange to have to remind ourselves that *mothers are people with needs, too*, but it is necessary.

In *Perfect Madness: Motherhood in the Age of Anxiety*, Judith Warner writes that "millennial motherhood" is dominated by "the ideal of the sacrificial mother."[1] In other words, the well-being of mothers has become optional and certainly secondary to the well-being of their children. In reality, the needs of mothers and their children are entwined. To support our daughters, especially when they encounter the challenges of adolescence, mothers must feel strong and supported themselves. As any mother knows, one is much more likely to yell at or even slap a kid who is acting up or teasing a sibling when we are tired or stressed.

At the Mother-Daughter Project, we believe it is healthy for our daughters (and others) to understand that the expectations placed on mothers are often unreasonable. When a mother who has just spent a rainy weekend taking care of three feverish kids retreats to her room visibly burned out or snaps at her fourteen-year-old to clean up her dirty dishes, her daughter may feel unloved if she doesn't comprehend that mothers are not bottomless wells of nurturance. Regularly stating with calm conviction, "All moms need breaks to recharge their batteries" before retiring for a nap or going out to visit a friend gradually helps teach this truth to one's children (and partner).

It's important to remember that daughters look to their mothers to learn what it means to be female. What do they see? It's hard for girls to hold themselves and their gender in high esteem if they see their destiny as women is to sacrifice their health and happiness for the wants of others. Your daughter might be momentarily annoyed when, at 9 p.m., you don't instantly drop the newspaper to jump up and help her wash the exact T-shirt and jeans she just decided she *has* to wear tomorrow. However, the deeper message being sent is that she, as a woman, will also have a choice in how she prioritizes what she accomplishes in a day. When girls witness their mothers taking care of themselves, even in small ways, and trying to live their lives based on their own aspirations, they see that their destiny as women is to do the same. Isn't that what we wish for our daughters?

After moving twice in one year, first to an apartment and then to a house closer to town, following the break-up of her second marriage, Maisie, mother of Gabriella, seventeen, and April, fifteen, and usually full of spark and energy, realized that she was running herself ragged fixing up her new house by herself, working full-time as a teacher, helping Gabriella plan for college, trying to keep April away from kids who were smoking marijuana, and coping with the pain of her separation. She told the mothers in our group, "I don't have anything left for mothering. I can't even manage to go grocery shopping." The other mothers reassured her that her kids would survive a few months of sandwiches and take-out Chinese food while she focused on her priorities: the family's emotional well-being and creating a comfortable home. With the encouragement of her friends and the other mothers in her group, Maisie let go of her Supermom ideals and accepted offers to help paint the house and also to pitch in with the girls, chauffering them, speaking with them about their futures—and reminding them that Maisie was doing a great job as their mom. We can get so caught up in the stresses and busyness of our daily lives and also in trying to be a "perfect mother" that we forget (or feel too embarrassed) to stop, evaluate who might be able to support us, and ask for assistance.

What Does It Mean for Mothers to Thrive?

There are two components to taking care of yourself when you have children: taking care of your needs as a mother *and* taking care of your needs as a person. Remember what life was like before you were a parent? At that time, you probably enjoyed some activities and routines that you felt were important to your well-being, ones that you have now given up. Maybe more social-izing with friends, more sex with your partner, the focused pur-suit of your career, an occasional Sunday devoted to sleep, brunch, and reading the paper. Of course parenting takes time, and the love and effort we spend on our children is returned a hundred times over, but it is essential to periodically reconnect with our needs as individuals.

As mothers, many of us have lost touch with our own desires. You can start to reconnect with yourself by vividly bringing to mind a period in your life when you felt particularly healthy and happy, then asking:

What felt best to me in that time?

How important to me is this kind of well-being? Would I say that it is an important part of what it means for me to thrive?

What made that period possible? What, in addition to my own efforts, supported my well-being?

The answers to these questions can show us one facet of what it means for us to thrive and what we need to get there; answer-ing them again about a different time in your life reveals addi-tional possibilities.

Breaking Down the Myths

After thinking about what could improve your well-being as an individual, it's important to consider what you might need as a mom and why you aren't getting it. Just as we exposed the dan-gers girls are facing today in Chapter Two, a key goal of the Mother-Daughter Project has been to analyze the problems that prevent women from thriving in their role as mothers. Fundamentally, today's ideal mother, Supermom, is the Perfect Girl all grown up and being hit with a new set of contradictory standards. Look at any newsstand for evidence. At the same time one celebrity magazine complains that actress Julia Roberts looks "frumpy" just two months after delivering twins, the cover of a popular parenting magazine instructs, "How to Be a Better Mommy in 2006: Step 1: Chill Out." (In the United States, it's particularly hard to achieve chilled-out, frump-free motherhood: According to the U.S. Bureau of Labor Statistics, in 2000, a majority of mothers with children under age *one* worked outside the home, most with no paid maternity leave and no subsidized child care.[2])

Supermom is a cultural icon so dazzling that she can blind us to what our real needs are, as mothers and women. Let's put on some sunglasses and take a good hard look.

Myth #1: A good mother is never tired of mothering.

And why would she be, with such a cush job? She's only working about fifteen hours a day, seven days a week. When mothering is seen simply as an act of love, the *work* of caring for our children is rendered invisible. In fact, it is so invisible it isn't even considered in the U.S. Gross National Product, where we account for the labor and goods it takes to make our country. It's easy to get sucked into believing that if we truly love our children, taking care of them isn't really work. In *Perfect Madness*, Judith Warner corroborates the power of this myth by describing how pleasant it was to mother young children in France, where both the work of mothering and the needs of mothers are respected and it's the norm for both stay-at-home and wage-earning mothers to use subsidized day care. She contrasts this with the struggle of mothering in the United States, where day care is expensive, "good mothers" supposedly don't need lives of their own, and mothering isn't thought of as work. In reality, stay-at-home and wage-earning mothers put in equally long and tiring workdays. The dinner shift and bedtime can be as grueling for the woman who has spent her day nurturing children at home as for the woman who has been glued to a computer screen in an office for eight hours. On top of that, in the 2003 edition of *The Second Shift*, Arlie Hochschild confirms what most mothers know from personal experience: On average, women (wage-earning or not) still work two hours a day more at child care and homemaking than their male partners.[3]

Myth #2: A "good mother" is happy to sacrifice for her children.

If you're happy to do it, it's not even a sacrifice, is it? In fact, a "good mother" has no needs of her own, because *all* her needs are fulfilled simply by loving her children. Both *Perfect Madness* and *The Mommy Myth* (Susan Douglas and Meredith Michaels, 2004), a lively scholarly analysis of societal mothering trends,[4] report that, in the eyes of our culture, a "good mother" supposedly gives up her own interests—from a daily walk to a chance to get a college education—without any regrets to do even the most boring and irksome tasks for her children, such as laundering clothes they haven't worn but are dirty from lying on their bedroom floor all week. (One year, when her children were age two and seven and SuEllen was trying to "do it all," her New Year's resolution was to exercise once a *month*.)

Myth #3: A "good mother" raises perfect children.

And it's all mom's fault if they aren't perfect. This variation of mother-blaming masks serious social problems such as unsafe schools or the widespread use of drugs and alcohol. As psychotherapists, we regularly see mothers so full of shame when their children have problems that they postpone getting help for them, which can lead to issues like learning differences, depression, or an eating disorder becoming more entrenched. While fathers are also reluctant to reach out for assistance, they usually do not engage in this type of self-blame.

Myth #4: There is one ideal way to be a mother.

Which changes year to year. According to *The Mommy Myth*, the new pink at the turn of the millennium is full-time, stay-at-home, intensive mothering—a 1950s mom in the 2000s economy. Well, we'll see how this one works out. Most mothers in the new millennium need or prefer to work outside the home for pay. According to Hochschild, in 2000, 73 percent of women with children under eighteen worked outside the home, as did 61 percent of mothers with children under three, two-thirds of whom worked full-time.[5]

Myth #5: Women are the natural caregivers.

This myth implies that if you happen to have a penis attached to your body, then you aren't required to comfort babies who won't stop crying for hours or skip an important day of work because your kid is home sick or be calm and nurturing to your hormonal teenager. That is what mom is for. However, if you want to watch the World Cup on television with your soccer-loving daughter, then that's okay.

Myth #6: Questioning what it means to be a good mother is a sign of inadequacy.

Isn't that evidence right there that you don't stack up? Shame on you!

....

At the Mother-Daughter Project, we created our own set of guidelines to head off these myths, based on the reality of our experiences as mothers. You may have a few of your own to add to the list. Post it inside your closet or on the fridge if you need the occasional reminder.

Reality #1: Parenting is hard work.

We do it because we love our children so much, but it's still work, and to do the job well, we need support, resources, and time off. All mothers get tired of mothering sometimes; it's both a reality and nothing to be ashamed of.

Reality #2: Every family member counts.

In a family, everyone's needs are important and can be honored at the same time. The needs of mothers are as important as the needs of fathers and children. Taking care of one's self as a mother benefits the whole family.

Reality #3: Communities are responsible for the well-being of all of their children.

How well any child is doing is a reflection of her school, neighborhood, the commitment of local, state, and national governments to provide children with the resources they need, fathers, relatives, and others—not just a sole mother. As the saying goes, "It takes a village to raise a child," and not just a "village" that women of means can buy for themselves.

Reality #4: There are many good ways to parent.

As many good ways as there are parents.

Reality #5: Parenting is a natural role for both men and women.

To thrive in this role, men and women both need good training and ongoing resources and support. Many men are wonderful, dedicated parents.

Reality #6: Questioning what it means to be a good mother is a gift to both ourselves and our daughters.

At our initial mother's meeting in 1997, we opened the discussion by asking, "What is a good mother?" Sarah, thirty-seven at the time, a nurse, and the mother of Kay and Maggie, then ages seven and eleven, read a passage from *Mother Daughter Revolution.* "This really struck me," she said. "The desire to do right . . . makes mothering incredibly pressured. Messages about 'good' mothering and necessities of providing for children often conflict, leaving mothers guilty and torn. Mothers can't afford to fail; failure would damage their daughters."

"I'm homeschooling my six- and eight-year-old daughters, April and Gabriella," responded Maisie, who was thirty-one and taking care of her kids full-time. "I know I do so much for my girls, but I still feel like it's not enough. I'm not much of a cook and I never bake, so I feel bad because on some level I think a 'good mother' always has milk and homemade cookies ready and available for her kids."

"If you don't feel like a good mother, then I don't stand a chance," said Katy, Marisol and Kaili's mom, then thirty-seven. "My own mother stayed home and cooked four-course meals every night, plus she sewed and canned and took care of the house and five kids. But I have to go to work, which leaves me feeling as though I never have the time and energy my kids deserve."

"Once in a while I feel like a good mother, but most of the time I feel pretty crummy—like I should be more patient, funnier, and more inventive," added Vanessa's mom, Libby, then forty-one. "I feel terrible saying this, but I find playing with kids for hours on end boring—and who's got the time?"

As each woman shared the issues that made her feel inadequate as a mother, we began to laugh as we uncovered some of the absurd preconceptions we had about being a "good mother": making great home-cooked meals every day, always having the kids clean and impeccably dressed, never losing our tempers, never getting tired, having loads of free time to spend with our children, creating days packed with enriching but leisurely activities, being a full-time stay-at-home mom while simultaneously working full-time in an interesting career to be a good role model, keeping the house immaculate, looking stylish and acting *chilled out.* . . .

Getting the Support You Need to Do the Work of Mothering

Mothering is hard work, and to do any job well you need resources and backup. The questions below can help you clarify what you, personally, need to do your job as a mother, without sacrificing yourself as a human being. Taking care of yourself will better enable you to take good care of your daughter, which, in turn, will help her to thrive. Understanding what you need as a mother can guide you in negotiating more satisfying ways to share parenting responsibilities with your daughter's biological father or other partner.

Think of a time when you felt particularly good as a mother, then ask yourself the following questions:

Why did that time bring me a sense of well-being as a mother?

What name would I give to what felt best to me in that moment?

How important to me is this kind of well-being?

What made that moment possible? What did I do that supported my well-being at that time? What, in addition to my own efforts, supported my well-being?

Has there been a time in my life when I didn't feel good as a mother? What was the hardest part about that time?

How did I get through it? What other kinds of support would have helped me?

As with the previous questions we've posed, answering the questions again about a different moment will generate more ideas about what might help you thrive as a mother.

. . . .

Like all of us, Maisie has moments when she feels good as a mother and moments when she feels rotten. Seeing the fruits of her labor as a parent is particularly satisfying to her. When her daughter Gabriella was a preteen, she felt self-conscious about being plump and wore big, baggy clothes. Maisie, with the assistance of Mother-Daughter Project activities, tried to consistently convey to her daughter that she had a beautiful, healthy body and didn't need to change a thing about it. During a recent conversation with other mothers in our group, Maisie recalled, "Finally, at about age thirteen, she felt better about letting herself be seen. She wore tighter clothes, cut her hair short, held her head high, and said 'Okay world, here I am.'" The first time Maisie went on a date after separating from the girl's stepdad, David, Gabriella offered that lesson back to her mother. "She helped me get dressed up and was like, 'Wow, Mom, you look great!'"

"But there are lots of moments nowadays when I don't feel so wonderful as a mother," Maisie continued. "There was one time recently when my kids and I were in a big fight, and I almost hit Gabriella. I hadn't felt that bad in years." Maisie went on to describe how upset and vulnerable she felt when only two months after their breakup, the girls' former stepdad, David, had a new girlfriend and invited Gabriella to join them for dinner. Maisie told Gabriella that she wasn't comfortable with her going, which made Gabriella upset. Then, as siblings often do, Gabriella transferred her anger and started shouting at her younger sister, April, for using her computer.

"Gabriella was yelling and swearing at April, who swore right back and said she wouldn't get off the computer because she was waiting for an e-mail from their biological father in California (whom they only see a few times a year). Gabriella snarled that if he really cared he would send her a letter since he knows she doesn't have her own computer. April blew a gasket, she was cursing and yelling, 'Don't you say that about dad, who do you think you are?! He does care about us!'

"I started yelling at them, 'Stop it! Just stop swearing!' and then there we were all screaming—literally screaming in each other's faces. When Gabriella said, 'I can't stand this family!' it stopped me cold." Maisie described how she felt even worse because she thought the neighbors had heard them fighting. She was ashamed that "my children were behaving so horrendously and that I was behaving horrendously. I felt like, if I were a 'good mother' I would have been able to de-escalate the whole thing."

Psychologically speaking, the leap from cultural trends in mother-blaming to blaming ourselves as mothers is a short one. When we fall short of parenting in the way we would like and feel terrible for it, however, identifying what made a moment particularly difficult can help us regroup. Like Maisie, our lowest moments of parenting often occur when we don't have the emotional reserves we need to be able to respond to our children in the ways that we would ideally like. Maisie values being able to help her children cool down during emotionally charged fights, and most days, she succeeds.

Maisie said, "Basically, I felt unsupported and undermined by the men in my life at that time. Both the girls' father and their former stepfather were off with their younger girlfriends and there I was, alone, trying to hold everything together. I try to make my choices in life based on what's best for the kids, but I'm just one person and, as their mom, I'm held totally accountable. Everyone excuses the dads: 'Richard needs to be across the country to earn money' and 'David, he's just being David.' No one says to them, 'Hey, you left your family. You should be taking care of your kids.'"

Maisie concluded, "At least in that awful moment, I knew I was going to have the chance to sort it all through with my friends. My mothers' group helps me remember it's not completely personal—there are lots of other forces at work when we run into trouble as mothers."

Compassion for Our Mothers, Compassion for Ourselves

As part of our preparation for staying connected to our daughters and guiding them as teens, we have examined the myths that impede feeling good about ourselves as moms and getting what we need to do the job of mothering. Another important element in finding compassion for ourselves is by looking at our first mother-daughter relationship. We're not just mothers, we are also daughters. Do you remember what it felt like to be a teenager, recognizing that someday soon you would be a woman? Did you want to be like your mom when you grew up? Most of us would answer with a resounding "No!"

At one mothers' group gathering, Maisie put it this way: "Being a woman looked like the booby prize. It appeared to me that men got most of the rewards while women did the work to keep it all going." Dark-haired, quiet Katy, who usually waited for everyone else to speak first, jumped in, "I hated my mom. I felt like she was trying to control everything about me: my clothes, my friends, my activities, and I rebelled big time. That's probably been my biggest motivation for joining this group. I'm terrified that I'll screw up and Marisol (and Kaili) will end up hating me. That's so painful to even contemplate." We are often motivated to analyze our relationship with our own mothers out of fear and concern for our teenage girls; we seek a way to make adolescence better for them than it was for us.

Some of the troubled feelings women experience toward their mothers are the result of their separation from them at adolescence, something we will discuss in the next chapter. However, much of the disdain arises out of the tendency to blame our mothers for the difficulties we might have encountered as teens. When we were younger, we couldn't see that, perhaps, our mothers were simply women doing the best they could while struggling with unreasonable expectations, just as we are now. How do we move from blaming them to giving them a little slack? One way we can do that is by exploring the complexities of our mothers' lives—from their socioeconomic realities to the power dynamics in their relationships to thinking about our fathers' roles in raising us.

Developing a greater compassion for our own mothers is critical for us as mothers ourselves. Without it, we can think, "She did it wrong! I'll do it right!" Here we're planting the seeds for trying to be Supermom and chastising ourselves when we inevitably fail. Understanding how much effort our mothers put into trying to meet our needs, often in difficult circumstances, lets us experience our mothers' love for us in profound new ways and opens our eyes to how hard and with how much love *we* are trying to meet *our* daughters' needs now. Women report that responding to the questions we pose about their mothers and speaking with other women about their responses are among the most helpful and transforming experiences they have with the Mother-Daughter Project.[6]

Begin by thinking of a specific incident or aspect of your life from when you were nine to seventeen years old that was difficult, then ask the following questions:

What did you need then?

What difference would it have made to you, and in your life, at that time if you had what you needed?

What difference would it make to your parenting of your daughter now if you had what you needed then?

What would your mother have required to have been able to provide you with what you needed at that difficult time?

(First consider what she needed in her life at that time as a mother. Next consider what she might have needed when she herself was nine to seventeen years old to have later been able to provide you with what you needed as a teen.)

In one of our early mothers' meetings, we all wrote and shared responses to these questions. Libby, Vanessa's mom, wrote from the perspective of herself at nine years old:

> *Momma says her daddy didn't believe in sending girls to college. "Just a waste of money." She spent the year after high school teaching piano, saving money, but Momma only had enough to pay for one year of college. If my momma had gotten what she needed, she might have made those fingers that liked to dance across the keys dance their way to Carnegie Hall, but instead, she found herself a husband, an older man who made her do what he wanted. If my momma had gotten what she needed, it would have started with her voice. My momma had a voice as pure as crystal water and she would have let it soar to the heavens, but my momma's voice got stuck in her throat. It got so stuck she lost her song and her stories. If she'd gotten what she needed, my momma would have given me a history, stories to tell myself and my daughter, stories to nourish, to inspire.*

After doing this exercise, each woman in our group expressed a new awareness of the vast extent to which her mother did not have what she needed to thrive as a girl, as a woman, or as a mother—and the impact that had on each of us as daughters. Sarah, a nurse and Kay and Maggie's mom, described the contempt she felt for her mother, but not her father, as a teen. "There was a lot of alcohol flowing in my house and whenever my dad got drunk he would verbally attack my mom. I thought she was weak and wanted her to leave him. I got mad at her, but why didn't I get mad at him?" Maisie listened to Sarah and then responded with stories of her own parents where every weekend was a party, also with lots of drinking. When Phoebe, an anthropology professor and Eliza and Amy's mom, imagined what it would really be like to take care of six kids while stretching every dollar, like her mother had done, she was overcome by emotion. We could all suddenly see, in a way that touched us personally, that when a mother's needs aren't met, she cannot fully take care of her daughter, no matter how valiant her efforts.

With rare exceptions (such as outright abuse or neglect related to mental illness, drug abuse, or other factors), all mothers want what is best for their children. While it is not a straight path from hurt and anger to compassion and forgiveness, it is freeing to acknowledge and accept our mother's shortcomings, even when those shortcomings were significant. Do we long for more? Absolutely. Do we sometimes feel we got dealt a bad hand? You bet. But, when we consider how things might have been if the loving intentions of our mothers had the opportunity to manifest more fully, we acquire respect for their plight. What's more, we are fortified to obtain what helps each of us thrive as mothers—not only for our own sake, but for our daughters.

It takes time, energy, and resources to be able to nurture our daughters and our relationships with them. It's easy to fall into the trap of thinking that anything short of Supermom means we have failed as a mother. Our daughters pick up on this, too, and may feel resentful and angry when we don't live up to the ideal. Consequently, mother-daughter relationships suffer. At the Mother-Daughter Project, we've found meeting the needs of mothers to be one of the most important ingredients to a thriving mother-daughter relationship. The next chapter invites you to determine what kind of relationship you want with your daughter and helps you to identify and counteract the other forces you may need to overcome to achieve it.

CHAPTER FOUR

······················

Preventing Mother-Daughter Disconnection

"You have a teenage daughter?" asks Jolene, SuEllen's new neighbor. It is a sunny fall morning, and the sugar maples arching over the quiet street cast orange and red leaves onto the sidewalk. Amber, her three-year-old, leans against her mother's legs and beams up displaying a leaf in each hand.

"Is it as terrible as they say?" Jolene asks quietly, caressing Amber's hair. "I can't bear to think that someday Amber is going to hate me."

Jolene voices the fear that we hear over and over from mothers around the world: The daughters we love so dearly will not only pull away from us, but will come to despise us. No matter how strong and supported we feel ourselves as mothers and how committed we are to mothering our daughters wisely, if they disconnect from us, our power to help them evaporates. Over the past decade, one of the missions of the Mother-Daughter Project has been to analyze the questions *Is separation natural and necessary? Is it good for daughters? Is it good for mothers?* From our observations in the Project, from our review of research, and from our experiences as psychotherapists, we now know unequivocally that girls do best in loving, supportive relationships that foster both individual autonomy and mutual respect and connection.

Daughters Are Driven to Disconnect

"I'm a teenager. I'm supposed to hate you," fifteen-year-old Vanessa said to Libby one morning during their commute to school in the car. Vanessa articulates what every teen girl seems to know: Cool kids hate mom.

It is important not to be categorical. The world is big and diverse, and alongside stories of mother-daughter disconnection, young people also absorb messages of loving mother-daughter relationships. The movie *Spanglish*, which shows a mother and her teen daughter staying close despite the culture shock of immigrating from Mexico to the United States, and the remake of *Freaky Friday*, which opens with mother-daughter disconnection but ends in mutual empathy, are two positive examples. Girls from families that emphasize and nurture close mother-daughter bonds from generation to generation, or from cultures that celebrate strong mother-daughter ties also learn the value of staying close. That said, backed by the psychological theory of separation, which purports that a primary task of adolescence is to emotionally separate from one's parents, popular culture's loudest message is to reject mom, and many girls comply.

Unfortunately, some ethnic cultures that previously emphasized close mother-daughter relationships have seen their value eroded by the popular media and psychology professionals alike. From a global perspective, mother-daughter disconnection has until recently been the exception, not the rule—that is, until countries become influenced by American and Anglo mores and values, according to researcher Monica McGoldrick, editor of *Ethnicity and Family Therapy*.[1] Psychologists around the world are, for the most part, now trained to tell mothers and daughters that they need to separate to be whole, healthy individuals. When we presented our work in Oaxaca, Mexico, in 2004, a school psychologist approached us and said with chagrin, "I work with girls at a high school in Mexico City. I've been telling them that their problems stem from the need to separate from their mothers.

Now after hearing about the Mother-Daughter Project, I'm going to bring them back in and tell them that I was wrong."[2]

Another reason many adolescent daughters push their mothers away is that they view their mothers as the ones directly constraining their freedom—not letting them go where they want with whom they want. Mothers, often from their own life experience, understand the reality of needing to keep girls safe, and impose realistic limits. Teenage girls feel angry about having their freedom curtailed, and that anger is often directed at the person who is making the rules: Mom. The average girl doesn't see past her frustration with a 10 p.m. curfew to understand that the real problem is that even today, the world can be an unsafe place for girls and women and especially for an unsupervised young teen late at night. When a girl believes that all of her pain and frustration is her mother's fault, pulling away or hating her mother can appear logical and necessary. Meanwhile, mothers are walking a tightrope: not wanting to scare their daughters and not wanting them to be harmed.

Suppose a mother strictly enforces an early curfew for her fourteen-year-old, discourages her from leaving the house showing her cleavage and belly, and doesn't let her go to parties with kids whose parents she doesn't know. The daughter fights about these restrictions, but the mother holds firm. The daughter is angry and unhappy because, in her eyes, her mother is overprotective and out of touch. It is her fault they don't get along.

At the same time, teenage girls are also encouraged by the society-wide influence of talk show therapists like Dr. Laura (as well as some teachers, counselors, and other adults) to rage against their mothers' *failures* to protect them. Another mother takes a different approach. After a forthright conversation about making good choices, the mother lets her daughter go to a party even though she hasn't been able to speak with the host's parents first. She decides that skimpy clothes are just the style and not worth warring over. The parents aren't home, and some kids raid the liquor cabinet. The daughter gets drunk, passes out in a back bedroom, and wakes up half naked with no memory of what happened. She is frightened and upset. She fumes: Her mother should have been more on the ball. Doesn't she care? The painful truth is that there is no perfect mothering zone between being underprotective and overprotective that can guarantee our daughters' safety and happiness in a world with risks. What we can do is support our girls' self-esteem and work toward keeping our relationships with them open and positive.

Mother-blaming is not a new phenomenon. When girls hit puberty, they make the painful discovery that the world can be unkind and unfair to young women. In our mothers' or grandmothers' lives, expectations of girl-subservience were no less excruciating for being explicit. The widespread assumption that education was wasted on girls did not erase the pain of a young woman finding out she couldn't go to college because all the money was being saved to send her brother to school. In our daughters' lives, expectations of girl-subservience are no less painful for being *implicit*. The vague idea that a girl could grow up to be president doesn't nullify her inchoate anger when she turns on the TV to see a bunch of teenage girls in microminiskirts flashing their thongs while they gaze adoringly at a boy who shouts back that they are "bitches." Nor is it a palliative if she rudely discovers that an A in calculus is the scarlet letter of the new century, damning her to isolation as an undesirable geek. Once again, girls direct their subliminal rage at their mothers and at themselves.

At the Mother-Daughter Project, we believe that the myths of the Perfect Girl and Supermom contribute to the chasm between teenage girls and their mothers. When mothers fail to live up to impossible expectations, daughters often feel hurt or cheated. "Why can't you be like Clare's mom?!" they shout, idealizing their friends' mothers while bitterly ruing the perceived deficiencies of their own. As we have discussed, girls also are inclined to blame their own failures and difficulties on their mothers. Now enter the Perfect Girl. The impossible demands of Perfect Girl mean that too many girls feel like a failure much of the time. As the authors of *Mother Daughter Revolution* put it: "Because we are urged to direct our anger toward and hatred of women's oppression at our mothers, something like the San Andreas Fault forms between each generation of women."[3]

To help girls resist the demoralizing effects of the anti-girl messages she will undoubtedly encounter as she grows up, mothers can teach their young daughters that they *can* be president (or a science whiz or skating star or whomever they want to be), that it may not be easy, but that mothers will be there to support them every step of the way. In the same manner that most African American parents explicitly teach their young children to identify and resist racism,[4] mothers can teach our daughters to identify and resist sexism. You can begin at any age by telling your daughter that all women and all men (all girls and all boys) are equally valuable and equally worthy of respect.[5] At seven or older you can tell her that the unfair idea that boys and men are more valuable than girls and women is something with which you completely disagree. It benefits her to learn you disagree with this type of unfairness *before* she has much exposure to it personally, as often happens at around age eight, when girls and boys can get drawn into believing and enforcing negative gender stereotypes. (Chapters Seven to Seventeen are full of many more specific, age-appropriate ways you can band together with your daughter to bolster her sense of pride as a girl.) Girls of all ages have a great sense of fairness, and your daughter will enthusiastically join you in believing in equal rights and opportunities for girls and women (although when she reaches the idealistic mind-set of thirteen to seventeen, she may not believe that sexism still exists, or if it does, it certainly won't ever affect *her*).

Mothers Are Pushed to Push Away

Tragically, mothers teach the mantra of disconnection to their own girls. "Now you say you love me, but you'll hate me when you are a teenager," a mother tells her disbelieving nine-year-old, subconsciously trying to brace them both for the suffering this will entail. The psychological language of separation has so infiltrated our cultural attitudes toward adolescent girls that mothers believe it's inevitable, no matter how painful it feels.

The week before our first public presentation about the Mother-Daughter Project in 2003, we opened the newspaper to find an interview with Susan Borowitz,[6] a Hollywood writer and producer. She had just published a book offering her suggestions for how to mother a teen daughter called *When We're in Public, Pretend You Don't Know Me*. In the interview, Ms. Borowitz says, "We as mothers should be uncool in our daughter's eyes because they need to have their own lives and be the cool ones. In order for them to separate successfully, they're going to want to reject us. If we bend over backwards trying to be cool in order to prevent that rejection, we're standing in the way of a very important psychological stage of development."

This interview is poignant and shows the lengths a mother will go to do right by her girl. But the most poignant and telling comment came from her daughter Lexi, who said, "I'd say [my mom] is definitely more fun since she started writing the book, because now we do more things together, like all these interviews and articles. It's pretty fun." If we listen carefully over the clamor for mother-loathing and rejection, we hear a different story, about what teenage girls really want: togetherness with a mom who loves and respects her as a maturing individual and who presents herself with honesty to her daughter. With the pressure to disconnect taken out of the mix, girls and moms participating in the Mother-Daughter Project feel comfortable showing each other their authentic selves, which better enables them to have open communication and face the challenges of adolescence head on.

Looking Back: Our First Separation

Why do mothers fall into the trap of believing it is good to cut off from our daughters just when they need us so much? Most of us were raised on the lie of separation ourselves. That was certainly the case for the women in our mothers' group. As teens, we had all wanted our independence and fought with our mothers to get it. Later, the theory of adolescent separation dominated SuEllen and Renée's training as psychotherapists. When, as adults, we read in Jean Baker Miller's 1976 classic *Toward a New Psychology of Women* and in *Mother Daughter Revolution* that disconnection was unnecessary and harmful, we hoped it could be true. Now mothers ourselves, we knew that ongoing connection with our young daughters was what *we* wanted—but only if it was best for *them*. Finding a way to stay close to our daughters was the impetus for embarking on the Mother-Daughter Project, and in fact, *staying close* proved to be the key to helping our girls. For the women in our group, understanding that connection could actually benefit our daughters began with an exploration of our relationships with our own mothers. One evening, during the first year of the Project, we wrote about and shared our answers to the following questions:

What was my relationship like with my mother when I was a young girl?

Did my relationship change during adolescence?

What was my understanding of that change?

As an adolescent?

Now, as an adult?

Recollecting our distress over the separation from our mothers at adolescence was a revelation for all of us. Here is what Phoebe wrote and read aloud to the group:

> *When I was little, I loved time with my mother. We sewed doll clothes and baked together. At fourteen and fifteen, I fought with my mother frequently; long yelling episodes. I experienced myself as fiercely independent and wanting to do things my own way. I wanted to speak in my own voice and hated anyone, especially my mother, telling me what to do. Yet even when I was fighting with her, I was longing for something different.*
>
> *My longing was so intense that when I was fourteen-and-a-half, I started writing letters to my own future daughter and wrote one a year until I turned twenty-eight and my daughter was born. I told her about my boyfriends, my relationship with my mother, my questions about religion, and many other elements of my emotional and intellectual life as a young woman. The letters came from my desire, starting when I was fourteen, to have an authentic relationship with my daughter. The kind of good relationship I wished I had had with my mother.*

Now that Amy is seventeen, Phoebe is profoundly grateful that they do have the warm, open relationship that she had dreamed of.

One after another, every woman in our group told a story of closeness in childhood followed by a painful rift at adolescence. Many of us had completely forgotten the sweetness of our early relationship since it had become so clouded over with profound sadness and anger about the disconnection we experienced later. Looking back as adults, we could see how much we wanted to stay close to our mothers, even if we were in conflict with them at the time. We wanted our mothers to learn from us how different our generation was from theirs, to listen to us and to take us seriously. When we were young, we thought we were mad at our mothers because we wanted them to leave us alone, but actually, we ached for them to love, understand, and support us as we grew into women.

The Psychological Shift Toward Intimacy and Identity

This new understanding galvanized our commitment to foster ongoing relationships with our daughters, and prompted us to seek out further verification of how connection might be good for them. We found that while psychologists around the world still promote separation and assert that mother-daughter division is necessary for healthy development, there is a growing consensus that healthy development actually entails getting better at connecting. According to the Harvard School of Public Health's 2001 report *Raising Teens*, "Although the task of adolescence has sometimes been described as 'separating' from parents and caregivers, it is more widely seen now as adults and teens working together to negotiate a change in the relationship that accommodates a balance of autonomy and ongoing connection, with the emphasis on each depending in part on the family's ethnic background."[7]

The old school of thought claims that separation is synonymous with the transition from adolescence to adulthood, and a primary task of growing up is getting better at separating from others. The new view proposes that maturity means developing identity *and* intimacy. Both schools concur that an important and ongoing task of growing up is the forming of one's unique sense of self, known as *individuation* or *differentiation*. The key question is *What process promotes healthy individuation?*

Carol Gilligan and her colleagues from the Harvard Project on the Psychology of Women and the Development of Girls, Jean Baker Miller and others at the Stone Center for Developmental Services and Studies at Wellesley College, and narrative therapist Michael White are some of the researchers who have found that girls can best discover who they are and what they are capable of in the context of supportive and loving relationships.[8] Barbara Turnage's 2004 study of African American teen girls demonstrated that a girl's attachment with her mother and her belief in her mother's willingness to protect, soothe, and prepare her for life is linked with an increased sense of how lovable and capable she feels and higher self-esteem.[9] Lori Lobenstine, Yasmin Pereira, and their colleagues in CADRE (Compañeras Arising to Develop Researchers Everywhere) found in 2004 through their in-depth interviews with Puerto Rican mother-daughter pairs that teen girls share their mothers' most important values and have similar goals for what it means to create positive futures for themselves, and that both benefit from greater opportunities for communication and connection.[10] In *Making Connections: The Relational Worlds of Adolescent Girls at the Emma Willard School,* edited by Carol Gilligan, Nona Lyons, and Trudy Hammer, psychologist Sharon Rich concluded, from serial interviews over three years with predominantly European-American teenagers, that girls want close and loving relationships with their mothers, and that such relationships foster healthy differentiation.[11] And finally, our interviews with and observations of girls participating in the Mother-Daughter Project suggest similarly positive self-regard and robust individual identity among girls who are able to sustain close relationships with their mothers.

Loving relationships are the playgrounds and workshops of differentiation. The creation of one's self is a tender and difficult task; positive relationships offer a safe place to experiment with different ideas of who we are. Intimacy and autonomy are linked, and our most satisfying relationships have both. Realizing the ways we are different from someone with whom we are close does not require pulling away from them. As Kathy Weingarten, a clinical psychologist, suggests in *The Mother's Voice,* "Naming adolescence as a phase in which parents and children, mother and adolescent son and daughter, are freer to know each other" provides an avenue for increased intimacy. Learning from each other offers the possibility of *greater* understanding and provides *more* space to explore our unique identities.[12] Girls blossom when they are simultaneously loved and encouraged to pursue their lives independently. When they have good relationships at home, they are able to move more confidently out into the wider world.

When we grasp that mother-daughter connection does not hinder maturity, we can see clearly the ways that disconnection is bad for our daughters. Predators divide and conquer: Girls cut off from loving adults are more vulnerable to physical and sexual abuse. Sexual predators seek out teen girls who are alienated from their families and alone, often luring them into liaisons with promises of love. Girls are at greater risk of intimate partner violence if an abuser can physically and emotionally isolate them from the friends, family, and others who care about their safety. Girls without mature guidance get fooled more easily by the impossible expectations of the Perfect Girl.

In their hearts, it wracks daughters to lose their mother's closeness. Girls can be screaming "I hate you!" as they stomp out of the house to spend the night with a friend, but they miss their mothers intensely. *They* pulled away, but they're mad at *us* about it. Like a baby who saves up all her tears for after day care, teenage girls often yell at their mothers *because* they miss us. Yelling may be a sign they want more connection, not less. It's hard for girls to deal with the emptiness of losing love, and sometimes they try to fill the hole with unhealthy things, like drugs, unwise sex, or destructive friends. For mothers, the separation is excruciating and can cause them to withdraw emotionally, too.

Mothers also shut down because they can't bear to witness their daughter's distress. According to Janet Surrey, a psychologist and professor at Harvard Medical School and the Stone Center, "Learning to tolerate and bear painful or 'unacceptable' feelings in ourselves and those we love is one of the most difficult trials of life and relationships. It is one thing to desire another's happiness, it is another to deny their pain. Often, mothers try to defend against or deny their daughter's pain or anger because they have not had a relational context which allows them to know and to act on their own painful feelings."[13] Survival for some mothers has meant denying our own troubled experiences or, if we have had the courage to speak of them, having them minimized or distorted by others. When our daughters are expressing their pain, even directing it at us, it can be difficult to remember that they still love us intensely and that we are not to blame. The challenge is to keep listening.

From speaking with other mothers participating in the Mother-Daughter Project and from the research we reviewed, we came to understand that mothers must audaciously assume that our daughters love us and want to be loved by us throughout the tumult of adolescence, and our job is to dedicate ourselves to staying close to them despite the difficult emotions that might arise in us. When your two-year-old is screaming in a temper tantrum, you take a deep breath and remind yourself that she still loves you and needs you to parent her. The same is true of your seething teenager when she gives you the silent treatment over a meal you just spent two hours cooking—yes, it's tremendously unpleasant and upsetting, but, underneath, she also needs you and wants to have a good relationship with you. At the Project, we have seen that holding fast to this idea is essential for remaining connected and responding to her in a way that supports your relationship. In the heat of a difficult moment, sometimes the most helpful thing to do is simply to say, "I'm sorry you are so upset. I really love and care about you. Right now, let's give each other some space, and we can talk later."

Neither passive-aggressiveness nor direct anger is a sign that your daughter has already disconnected. And, as painful as it may be to argue or fight with her (or anyone), don't believe that an absence of fighting equals connection. Fights can be intimate. Conflict arises from the desire to have meaningful, mutual relationships and a willingness to stay engaged despite disagreement. The emotional intensity comes from how much mothers and daughters *care what the other thinks about them.* Underneath the details of arguments that start with "I thought you said you cleaned your room!" or "You're so mean! Jenna's mom lets her go downtown by herself!" mothers and daughters are trying to communicate "I want to trust what you say" and "I want you to recognize my growing ability to be independent."

However, yelling is not the most efficient, effective, or pleasant way to communicate. If you want to de-escalate a fight with your daughter, it helps if you have already developed some phrases that will allow you to pause graciously. You could say, "I really care about you and I know this is important to you, but I don't like arguing, so I'm going to go for a walk (lie down, listen to music, etc.) and talk about this with you after supper (name some specific time)." Say it and mean it, and don't say it as a punishment. Then, during your personal time-out, turn to the Emergency Guide for Fostering Mutuality on page 76 to help guide you back to a less heated form of engagement.

Sometimes talking is not the best way to foster connection with a particular adolescent girl. In our mother-daughter group, Sarah, who works full-time as a visiting nurse, discovered early that low-key physical connection helped keep her and her eldest daughter, Kay, close. When Kay was in grade school she could be emotionally reactive. Sarah would organize her mornings so she had time to snuggle with Kay to wake her up before school. "I found that just lying there quietly next to her helped her relax and reduce her tendency to struggle and get mad at everybody."

Kay and Sarah also both love to dance. "Any time I dance with her, it's like heaven. We both feel present and connected and alive. It's our place of . . . *delight.*" When Kay became a teenager she continued to have a fiery temper and she and her mother regularly fought about things like the dirty dishes stacking up in Kay's bedroom. Supported by the ideas of the Mother-Daughter Project, Kay and Sarah both recognized that the arguing did not mean they had a bad relationship, but sometimes it made them feel miserable. Sarah used dance to soothe them both. "We could have weeks of fighting, but afterward we made sure to go out and take a dance class together." Now that Kay has moved out on her own and is working full-time, they don't have as many heated discussions, but dance is still a pleasurable way they nurture their relationship. Sarah said recently, "I know she is proud that she has a mom who can dance. Last week at a local contra dance she introduced me around, 'This is my *mom!*' That was so cool."

Finding another mother who supports your aim of staying connected to your teenage daughter can offer a safety valve to ease the pressure when tensions arise with your daughter. Another mother can validate how difficult it is to hear harsh criticism from your daughter and help you figure out your way back toward calmer relations. A mother-daughter group can provide a regular way for you and your daughter to maintain your connection; even if you are barely speaking to each other, she'll still come with you to be with the other girls and moms in the group. During Vanessa's early teens, the group was a place of calm where she could connect with her mother, Libby, a lawyer with a thriving practice in family law, during their busy lives and occasional rough patches. Inspired by the other mothers, Libby made sure to have regular dates with her daughter where they did an activity of Vanessa's choice. Now, at seventeen, as Vanessa gathers courage to apply to competitive colleges, she draws strength from Libby's commitment to stand by her through thick and thin. The goal is to make it through the tough spots without cutting off emotionally.

What Is My Vision of a Thriving Mother-Daughter Relationship?

In Chapter Two, we posed questions geared toward helping your daughter thrive through adolescence; in Chapter Three, we presented questions geared toward helping you, as a mother, thrive. Here we suggest exploring what your vision of a thriving mother-daughter *relationship* might look like. It's much easier to respond effectively to difficult mother-daughter moments if we have thought ahead of time about what kind of relationships we want with our daughters, and have identified who and what supports us. To start creating that vision, ask yourself:

Can I describe a moment that I shared with my daughter that felt good to me?

What quality characterized how we were relating at that time?

Is that quality important to me in my ongoing relationship with my daughter? If so, why?

Who or what nurtures that quality in my relationship with my daughter?

Was there a time when that quality was elusive or hard to find in our relationship?

Through that challenging time, is there something or someone that helped me hold on to my vision, so that we could find this quality again in our relationship?

Have we succeeded in bringing that quality back into our relationship? How did we do it? If not, what or who might help us now?

As with the previous questions we've posed, asking these questions again about a different moment of connection generates a fuller vision of what a thriving mother-daughter relationship means to you. Creating a list of the qualities you hope to nurture in your relationship with your daughter—from consideration and honesty to thoughtful communication and playfulness—is an invaluable resource during times of volatility. It can help you find inspiration and center yourself. Talking about your ideas with a friend can be especially comforting when you face the inevitable difficult moments. Creating another list of what and who nurtures your connection with your daughter shows you exactly the steps you can take to help your relationship thrive.

Accepting Girls' Relationships with Others

A time comes in almost every daughter's life when spending time with friends and intimate partners seems more compelling than time with families. This often leaves mothers feeling bereft. What happened to that little girl who thought hanging out with mom was such a treat? Sometimes we mistakenly interpret this shift as a daughter's need for separation instead of an exciting and positive development in her autonomy. Negotiating and accepting our daughter's new connections can be a difficult process, as it was for Sarah and her daughter Maggie, when Maggie was sixteen.

Right up through the teen years, Sarah and Maggie almost never fought. Maggie is adventurous and independent but very easygoing and gets along well with just about everyone, including her mother. Sarah and Maggie could talk about anything and enjoyed learning new things together. As Maggie got older and wasn't home as much, Sarah looked for fresh and more mature ways for them to have satisfying times together. She taught Maggie to drive and traveled with her to explore new places, like the fantastic day trip they took to Boston to visit an MIT exhibit on artificial intelligence.

The biggest challenge to their relationship occurred when Maggie had her first serious boyfriend, Simon. Sarah said, "I never had to share Maggie before—I was used to being *major* in her world." It's not uncommon for mothers to feel left out or jealous when their daughters have strong relationships with other people. However, relationships with coaches, teachers, friends, and others don't take away from the love a girl has for her mother. It is important to see each positive relationship as an opportunity for your daughter to learn more about her self. Sarah mustered up her faith in her ongoing connection to Maggie, despite the change, and, as she put it "realized I had to str-e-e-e-tch to make room for him—without pulling away from her." Sarah's commitment to Maggie allowed her to make room for her daughter to fall in love without having to let go of mom.

Giving space to our daughters while still remaining emotionally close, in contrast to the theory of separation, is a central value of the Mother-Daughter Project. When girls say "I want my space," they don't mean distance. What they are asking is for us to make space in our hearts and in our lives for them to develop in new ways and try new things. They still want us to be there, noticing, supporting, and cheering their development into adults. Hundreds of college women have reported to SuEllen that they deeply appreciated when their mothers allowed them as teenagers to explore new facets of their identity while still staying connected.

In general, our contemporary society does a poor job of creating this kind of positive space for teens. Instead, as Elliot Currie writes in *The Road to Whatever: Middle Class Culture and the Crisis in Adolescence*, youth are banished to a teen world that "combines harshness and heedlessness in equal measure."[14] Mothers can help create a more nurturing place for teenage daughters to grow. By staying close with our daughters and being open to their increasing maturity, we give our girls the space they need without bowing to the widespread presumption of mother-daughter antipathy and disconnection.

In the last three chapters we have explored the difficulties girls encounter in today's world, as well as what we moms are up against, and offered tools that you can use to support your daughter and yourself. We've also investigated the forces that drive mothers and daughters apart. Healthy daughters, healthy mothers, and healthy mother-daughter relationships: It's the three in sync that truly make life better for adolescent girls. In the next chapter, we'll show you how to put the lessons and methods of the Mother-Daughter Project into action so you and your daughter can work together to move from the expectation of separation toward a thriving relationship characterized by mutual understanding, empathy, and well-being.

CHAPTER FIVE

....

Finding a Common Ground

Developing Mother-Daughter Mutuality

Our friend Amelia is the mother of a one-year-old daughter named Anya. "Anya has been waking up to nurse at 3 a.m. every night," she tells us, shifting Anya from one hip to the other. "I know she doesn't really need to nurse then. But if I don't get up to nurse her, she cries. If I do, then I'm exhausted the next day and can't be as present and patient as I want to be with her." Anya wiggles to be put down, and toddles over to the sandbox in their backyard. "If I don't get up at night, she's unhappy. If I do get up, neither of us is happy the next day."

Amelia sits down on the edge of the sandbox near Anya, who is scooping sand into a little tin pot. "I had to figure out what was best for the both of us. I decided that we were better off when I slept at night, even if she cries for me. So that's what we're working on right now. The first few nights, it was hard when she cried. But she's crying less each night, and I definitely feel better getting some sleep. Our days are more fun." Anya dumps the pot of sand, and looks up into Amelia's smiling face. The mutual love in their gaze is palpable.

At first glance, it may seem that the needs of mothers and daughters are in conflict. But if we look more carefully, we see that, ultimately, helping girls thrive is inseparable from helping mothers thrive—and that goes for girls of all ages. Mutuality means taking the needs of both mothers and daughters into consideration. These needs are not exactly the same; in fact, they can be quite different and require thought and negotiation to fulfill. Amelia realized that it was better for her *and* for Anya to help her baby learn to sleep through the night. Our teenage and younger daughters don't always have the maturity to determine what they need either. But as mothers, we can work toward achieving a balance. Through our work as therapists and with the Mother-Daughter Project, we have witnessed that mutuality is the key to the ongoing well-being of our daughters, ourselves, and our relationships.

Finding Mother-Daughter Mutuality

For the women and girls in our group, mother-daughter mutuality can look different at different times. For Phoebe and Amy, a day spent at the beach rollicking in the waves is a great example of mutual engagement—one form of mutuality. When Libby and Vanessa raise their voices, regroup, and figure out who gets to use the family car on the weekend, it exemplifies other facets of mutuality: mutual empathy, authenticity, and empowerment. In order to solve their problem, they have to recognize they each have desires that they want to fulfill (Vanessa wants the freedom to see her friends; Libby wants to go to a movie). Only when they have really shown themselves (authenticity) and listened to each other with empathy can they resolve the conflict in a way that suits them both (empowerment).

Mutual thriving takes all kinds of forms. Our colleague Susan has a stepdaughter, Sadie, fifteen, and a daughter, Dora, eight. Most Saturday afternoons, Sadie babysits Dora for a couple of hours, fulfilling her family's rule that everyone needs to pitch in with household chores and give her parents some free time. Dora loves to have her sister's undivided attention, and in return lets her sleep late on weekend mornings. After Dora's 8:30 bedtime, Susan or her husband, Peter, take turns taking Sadie to play air hockey at the local arcade or to a "grown-up" film or they all stay in playing Texas Hold 'Em or Scrabble. Mutuality might mean your daughter cooks a simple supper so you have time to hem the dress she wants to wear. It might mean you have a "pajama day" together and lie on the couch reading novels. Mutuality and having a good relationship are interdependent, but mutuality isn't necessarily about being together every moment.

Mutuality, in any relationship, is achieved through negotiating how to meet one's individual needs while also nurturing the relationship and the needs of the other person. In the words of Janet Surrey, from the Stone Center at Wellesley College, "It involves a willingness to continually adapt to change, and accept the frustration of not yet understanding or being understood."[1] For mothers and daughters in particular, mutuality can be thwarted by the expectation of mother-daughter disconnection. If conflicts are interpreted as a sign of separation, efforts toward genuine connection can stall. Needs go unmet and relationships flounder. Likewise, when outside circumstances make it impossible for girls and mothers to each have what they need to get by (for instance, a flexible, interesting, and affordable after-school situation for an eleven-year-old), mutuality is also thwarted, especially if mothers and daughters blame each other for what is lacking. This is precisely why the Mother-Daughter Project emphasizes simultaneously meeting the needs of mothers, daughters, and mother-daughter relationships in our mission to sustain girls through adolescence.

We can discover more about what makes mutual thriving possible with the following questions that, unlike those in the previous chapters, focus on times when you, your daughter, and your relationship were all flourishing *simultaneously*.

Bring to mind a time when both you and your daughter felt happy and well, then ask:

What felt good to each of us at that time? What felt good about how we were relating with each other?

What needs of hers were being met? What needs of mine were being met? What needs of our relationship were being met?

What made the mutual thriving we experienced possible? Who or what was supporting us?

It's bliss when everything clicks with our daughters, but what about when things are not so wonderful? In rough times, we can ask ourselves if it might make a difference to use the intention of taking care of our daughters, ourselves, and our relationship, all at the same time, as a guide. What happens if we strive for mutual well-being?

Dear Mom, I hate you.

"That's how Amy started a letter she wrote to me when she was thirteen," Phoebe, an anthropology professor, told us. Pulling a folded sheet of paper from between the pages of her journal, she read:

Dear Mom, I hate you.

You are so mean and annoying that I just can't stand you. You aren't supportive of some things and decisions that I make, and now you can't even talk to me without fighting. Do you remember when I used to have sleepovers with Heather? Well, even then I knew I liked dad better. I remember distinctly.

You can't stand it when people don't appreciate what you have done, but you still never appreciate the hard work I put into my homework. You should be willing to spend a few of your precious minutes to help me complete something or do something that I forgot. I also happen to notice that you don't like to drive me anywhere, and I really don't like this.

I used to think that you didn't try hard enough because you

were always so cranky, especially after you rested. Now I know that you do try hard, but for some strange reason after you do something nice to someone else or go on a short vacation, you're very cranky, and expect everyone to be nice to you.

Another thing I don't like is that you seem to think that you are a wonderful mother—well you're not. You also blame everything on someone else (like me).

There are two reasons that I'm writing this letter: 1) so that you are aware, 2) so that you will be more supportive when I go to the Harry Potter party.

—Amy

P.S. You are not all flaws, and you are not the worst mom in the world. I am waiting for your owl.

Phoebe tucked the letter back into her journal. "In *Harry Potter*, owls deliver the mail. It means she wanted me to write back." She continued, "I was devastated. I had no idea she felt this way. I had been trying my best and I thought we had a good relationship— then this. I cried and cried. I felt so helpless, like no matter what I did, it wasn't going to be enough. What made it all the more painful was that just the week before we had thrown her a huge party. A number of her friends were having bat mitzvahs, and she wanted her own coming-of-age event. She seemed to love it at the time. The party was a lot of work, and the next weekend I went away by myself to a friend's cabin in the mountains to regroup. A few days later I come home to find this letter.

"I *had* been cranky when I got back so I felt terrible. It was a rough reentry—from complete relaxation right back into the de- mands of everyday life. But now my worst fears were coming true. My daughter was miserable. I was a cranky, selfish, unlovable mother, and my daughter was rejecting me. It felt like the begin- ning of the end for us.

"After I cried, I picked up the phone and called Libby and

read her the letter. Speaking with her helped me so much. I knew she had hung in there through some challenging moments with Vanessa, and I knew how much they loved each other. Libby helped me look underneath the surface of the letter to see what Amy really wanted and needed. She told me, 'Yes, Amy was feeling hateful toward you when she wrote the letter, but it's because she loves you and misses you. This is a painful moment, but it doesn't mean that Amy doesn't want to be close to you.' "

Libby suggested that Phoebe reread the letter with the assumption that Amy wanted to be close but didn't know how to say it and that she had missed her mom over the weekend. She told Phoebe not to feel guilty about going away and said, "Now Amy is stressed out and that's why she is so angry at you. Because you're rested, you can be there for her."

Phoebe went back and rewrote Amy's letter,

Dear Mom,

I am so angry, hurt, and frustrated right now. I am stressed by how much homework I have. I want to do well in school, and have been working hard on my homework. I don't like that I have procrastinated as much as I have, and I feel even worse when you remind me of that. I want to make my own decisions about when to do homework, but it would be great to get emergency help from you when I miscalculate.

I missed you when you were gone. I want you to see and appreciate my abilities and values, and how hard I am working. I want you to see how hard I work on my homework in particular. I want you to be involved in what I care about, to give me support, and to just keep me company. I care about what you think of me, and I want you to think well of me.

It makes me feel so bad when you are cranky and yell at me and criticize me. I don't want our relationship to be mostly about fighting. I'm confused why you get extra cranky when you've done something nice for someone or after you've been away. I want to feel that you are glad to see me. I want to feel glad to see you. I want us to have a good relationship.

I am working on growing up.

Love, Amy

"It was scary for me to write that letter but it rang true and it allowed me to respond in a way that was helpful to Amy," Phoebe told us. "When I replied to her, I wrote her as if she had sent me this letter instead of the 'I hate you' one. I pledged my support for her homework, and apologized for my crankiness. I said that I loved her and missed her and wanted to be there for her as she faced final exams. I explained that my time away had been replenishing, and because of it I was more able to be there for her. And I asked her if there was anything in particular that I could do to be helpful to her that day.

"I went to her room with my response. She was sitting on her bed with books open all around her and I handed her the letter. About twenty minutes later, she brought me another note. I was nervous to open it, but this one said, 'Tea. And quiz me on the Civil War.' I made us both a cup of tea, with cream and sugar, how we both like it, and went to her room and quizzed her for a couple of hours.

"Later, when she felt calmer about her homework, I told her how painful it was to receive a letter that started with 'I hate you.' She said, 'I know, I thought about that afterward, and I'm sorry.' That was important to me.

"That evening I found another note on my desk. It was very short: *Dear Mom, I love you. Thanks for the note. Love, Amy.*

"She got it. She felt heard. It felt bold to assume that she loved me and wanted to be close when she was writing how much she hated me and what a bad mother I was, but that was the deeper truth." Difficult moments can be opportunities for growth. When Phoebe responded to Amy's letter by acknowledging honestly how they both felt and helping them find a common ground, their relationship moved toward greater intimacy and mutuality.

Emergency Guide for Fostering Mother-Daughter Mutuality

Having a "Dear mom, I hate you" moment with your daughter? Here's a guide to get you moving back toward mutuality.

1. Step back, get centered.

What do you need *right now* to help you find your equilibrium? Change the topic, breathe, lie down, call a friend, or take a walk. No matter what she says, assume your daughter loves you and wants to stay connected with you.

If you have written them down, read over the list of qualities you think make a thriving mother-daughter relationship (created in the previous chapter). Think about who shares your hopes for mother-daughter mutuality. Talk to her father if he is part of your support network, or a friend, or if that's not possible, imagine what they would say. Be gentle with yourself. Mothering is one of the hardest jobs in the world.

2. What does she need?

Now focus on your daughter. Think about, write, or draw responses to:

What is she feeling?

Hint: Emotions are contagious. Often what you are feeling strongly at difficult moments is also what *your daughter* is feeling. (In the earlier example, when Phoebe first read Amy's letter, she felt hurt, stressed, and bad about herself, which is how Amy was feeling.)

Why is she feeling that way?

What is she trying to communicate?

What might she need?

How can she get what she needs? (Remember, you might not be the one to fulfill her needs at this moment.)

Who else can help?

3. What do I need?
Now focus on yourself. Think about, write, or draw responses to:

How am I feeling?

Why am I feeling this way?

What do I need?

How can I get what I need? (Remember, your daughter doesn't have to be the one to fulfill your needs at this moment.)

Who can help?

4. What do we need?
Now focus on your relationship. Bring to mind how you and your daughter successfully got through a difficult time in the past. What helped you reconnect? How can you apply that skill and knowledge to the present situation?

5. Take a nurturing step.

From all your responses above, choose a first step to try in getting back on track with your daughter. It can be something very simple, like having a cup of tea together or putting on music you both like, or more complex, like writing her a letter, or having a conversation. It may also be appropriate to take a breather and suggest that you each do something you enjoy but separately. Perhaps treat her to take her buddies for a slice of pizza or have her dad take her on an outing while you e-mail a friend. Mutuality is a process. Your daughter may be too upset to respond gracefully to your first efforts, but she will register your intentions for mutuality and connection. Every step you take makes it more possible for her to extend herself as well.

6. Afterward, acknowledge anything hurtful.

In the heat of a disagreement, you or she may have said or done something painful or ugly. When the situation cools down, offer apologies to your daughter and/or tell her plainly and calmly if something she said was hurtful. Clearly explain how you would prefer to communicate.

Staying connected with our adolescent daughters in ways that are mutually satisfying and agreeable takes work, especially when she is fuming over one of the typical heartaches of being a teenager—breaking up with a boyfriend, being left out of a peer group, receiving a poor grade, perceiving that her parents are "clueless." Sometimes our daughters will feel like we are being intrusive when we try to communicate with them and other times, when we don't pick up on a slight shift in the weather of their mood, they see us as distant. Your daughter is growing and changing—faster than you may always be able to keep up with. Remaining open to her evolution and making an effort to evolve alongside her increases the odds of maintaining the type of authentic relationship that will nourish her as she comes into herself as a woman.

After ten years of observing the successes of women and girls involved with the Mother-Daughter Project, we have concluded that the easiest and most efficient way to have a mutual relationship—and thereby *have the opportunity* to aid our daughters as they pass through adolescence (and simultaneously have our own needs met as mothers)—is with the nurturance of a caring community that includes children, their parents, and other supportive adults who care about children. It also helps to start planting the seeds of good communication and positive self-esteem *before* your daughter hits puberty. Whether or not you decide (or desire) to become a part of a mother-daughter group, the next chapter will help you identify your own sources of support, including extended family, friends, teachers, coaches, and professionals, and orient you toward the task of preparing your daughter for adolescence. In Part II, we'll offer specific activities developed by the Mother-Daughter Project that address the difficult issues most girls face at each age as they grow up, and at the same time nourish mother-daughter relationships.

CHAPTER SIX

Creating a Community for Mothers and Daughters

"If women truly want to make a difference in their daughters' lives, then the most important thing they can do is create a community of women for daughters to grow into."

—Mother Daughter Revolution

One of our friends, Grace McKeene-Rodriguez, forty-five, a businesswoman from Wisconsin, gathers regularly with her large extended family. At the edge of a lake during a barbecue or in the kitchen after a family birthday, Grace, her sisters, her cousins, and her aunts relax and talk about their lives. As the women discuss marriages, careers, dreams, and regrets, one by one, daughters and nieces creep in close to listen. Grace remembers sitting at the feet of her aunts when she was a young girl, and now she loves being one of the aunts in the circle, a source of womanly wisdom for the next generation. Her sisters and cousins are happy that their daughters can confide in Grace, someone they trust completely. They all are grateful for their community of women.

Fostering a community that nurtures girls and mothers is the heart of the Mother-Daughter Project. Women have always sought the companionship and support of other women. Just as our grandmothers and great-grandmothers sat together around a quilting frame talking about their lives as they stitched, mothers today can draw sustenance from the company of other women. When our children are babies, it's completely natural for a few mothers to meet at a playground and instantly start sharing the most intimate tips on breast-feeding, diaper rash, how to soothe a colicky baby, or find time and energy for a romantic night out with one's honey. When children are toddlers and preschoolers, mothers trade war stories about separation anxiety, weaning from pacifiers, and handling tantrums and bedtimes.

Unfortunately, our parental support networks, if we have them, often begin to fade as our children grow up. When kids enter kindergarten, mothers tend to drift apart and become more isolated. Group playdates and outings are replaced by after-school programs or playdates supervised by a single parent or caregiver. Those mothers (or fathers) who have been working part-time or less may return to their full-time jobs. It's generally much easier to take care of a five- to ten-year-old than a baby, toddler, or preschooler, and parenting without much outside help has its bumps but feels doable for many parents. Common problems such as shyness or adjusting to a longer school day seem less intense, immediate, and scary than the problems typically associated with babies, toddlers, and preschoolers.

When Libby's daughter, Vanessa, was nine years old, she told her mother, "When I grow up, I want to be just like you—exactly the same." Like many girls her age, she felt, *mom's the best!* Yet, as you now know from Chapters One through Five, mothering can become much more demanding again when children reach the preteen and teen years, and we can feel confused about our relationships with our daughters and unsure of ourselves as mothers. Your beautiful, healthy girl of ten may suddenly insist she is ugly and fat, or your athletic eleven-year-old may be devastated when she gets her period. You notice that a fourteen-year-old boy keeps calling your twelve-year-old daughter and you worry about his intentions. The support and advice of other mothers can be a lifeline for addressing problems like these.

The benefits of connecting with other mothers are intuitively obvious to many, if not most, women. Likewise, we know that our daughters need the companionship and support of other girls. The Mother-Daughter Project promotes bringing these two circles of support together. Using the traditional bonds of the extended family as our inspiration, we've seen that intergenerational connection is the key to our goals of nurturing daughters, nurturing moms, and nurturing mother-daughter relationships.

Parents, siblings, and caregivers are the center of a child's universe until about age seven, but as a girl grows up, she seeks out information from sources beyond her immediate family in order to find her place in the world. Relationships with girls, mothers, and other caring adults help preteen and adolescent girls form healthy identities. At eight, as she wonders, "Who am I?" and "How do I fit in?" girls look to their close friends, extended families, teachers, parents' close friends, and the media these adults make available to them at home and school. If this inner circle of important people and influences in a girl's life share her parent's values, those values are confirmed. The earlier that others affirm such girl-positive ideas as "girls and boys are equally intelligent and capable" the more natural they will seem to her as she matures. At age ten to twelve, girls actively seek information from an even wider circle—kids she admires who aren't her friends and the media her friends are exposed to and talk about. Preteens also closely observe which friends seem happy and successful and who is being rewarded for what. At this age, supportive connections with other mothers and daughters increase a girl's resilience and her resistance to the often unwholesome or consumerist messages she is likely to encounter in her daily life. As a teen, a girl expands her gaze even further in order to determine where she will eventually belong outside of her family and immediate peers. According to *Raising Teens*, "There is no question that a growing circle of adults and peers influences teens' thinking and decisions during adolescence."[1] If a girl has caring connections with other adults, she can learn firsthand how different women build successful lives in accordance with their values and has many mentors and many examples of how she can make her way as she grows up.

Children learn from modeled behavior. As Jennifer Baumgardner and Amy Richards, authors of *Manifesta*, a book that gives voice to the emerging "Third Wave" of the Women's Movement, put it,

"Girls and women (and men, too) learn mostly by example, not lecture. If women are positive about their periods, their cellulite, and their strengths and talents, they will no doubt enhance girls' lives and self-esteem."[2] If a girl has little exposure to adults or peers who share her mother's pro-girl and other positive values, those values are likely to be called into question. In her book *A Tribe Apart: A Journey into the Heart of American Adolescence*, Patricia Hersch monitored a group of adolescents to gain an understanding of the realities of their world.[3] Hersch found that a significant problem facing adolescents is the lack of adult role models to help them. Additional studies by Girls Scouts of America, the 4-H, and Big Brothers/Big Sisters confirms that our kids, both girls and boys, need close, loving relationships with adults—and not just their parents—particularly adults of the same sex.[4] All it takes is one or two caring relationships with other women to provide girls with the kind of adult modeling that will be of huge benefit to them as they head out into the world more and more independently.

Moreover, it is easiest to parent within the context of community, be it extended family, a network of friends and neighbors, or a mother-daughter group. It is not always possible to meet all of our children's needs by ourselves. We need not only the support of friends, neighbors, and family, but also caregivers, teachers, tutors, coaches, doctors, and sometimes other professionals, such as speech therapists or school psychologists. None of us are mothering alone. This chapter will help you to identify and connect with others in your community who can support you and your daughter—and offer some initial guidance for starting your own mother-daughter group.

Identifying Your Network of Support

Some of us, like Grace, have large extended families that meet regularly for Sunday dinner and to celebrate birthdays and holidays. But nowadays it's more common to live far away from our clans and gather only on special occasions. How do we create a network of support? Humans are social animals. Many of us are already reaching out by forming playgroups, book clubs, gay parent support groups, adoption alliances, knitting circles, sports teams, and many other types of organized groups. More casually, we receive succor and inspiration from our friends, colleagues, and neighbors as we juggle the details of our busy lives. And we all have transitional times when our local circle of trustworthy friends is discouragingly thin, such as after we move or change jobs.

The Mother-Daughter Project encourages you to consciously acknowledge and take stock of your existing network of support to help you strengthen and adapt it as a resource for you and your daughter as you approach her adolescent years. Thinking about which people in your life will back up the values you cherish as a mother, and looking for ways to include other caring adults in your daughter's world will both sustain you as a mother and strengthen her resilience if she runs into a rough patch on the road to growing up. The following questions can help you identify and appreciate the forms of support you already have in place, and help you ascertain whether you want to find more support for you, your daughter, and your relationship.

Which relationships in my life have been most satisfying to me? What qualities characterize those connections?

Where do I see those qualities in my current network of friends, relatives, colleagues, and neighbors? Who do I turn to first in times of trouble or heartache?

What difference do these relationships make in my life? What do I do to nurture them?

Who in my life is most likely to share my values about girls and mother-daughter relationships? What kinds of connections do I have with other mothers of daughters? With other girls?

What opportunities does my daughter have to form friendships with other girls whose families share values that are important to me?

What relationships does my daughter have with caring adults who share my values? What does she get from those connections?

Is there someone in my network of support that I would like her to have a stronger connection with? What difference might that make for her?

What qualities or values that are important to me are lacking in my current circle of support? What kinds of connections are lacking in my daughter's life?

If I imagine an ideal community of support for my daughter and me, what would it be like? What difference would it make to us if we had it?

Creating a Mother-Daughter Group

As our daughters head toward adolescence, it is not unusual to feel that we could benefit from deeper and more focused connections with other people who are concerned about the welfare of teen girls. You may already enjoy a robust community that actively shares your hopes for you and your daughter, but if you don't (like many of us mothering today), you can create one yourself. Cocreating a mother-daughter group with other moms and their girls is one way to create a supportive intergenerational community. Any mother can start a mother-daughter group. In the appendix, we offer step-by-step instructions for starting a group and taking care of it over the long haul. While meeting regularly with a group does take time out of a mother's and daughter's (busy) schedules, we have found that mother-daughter groups are a tremendously efficient way to parent. In a few hours, once a month, moms get support and wisdom from other moms, daughters learn pro-girl values, girls form healthy peer and intergenerational relationships, critical teen issues are discussed, mother-daughter bonds are strengthened, everyone laughs a lot, and, if you want, a potluck meal is included. In our experience, gatherings of both mothers-only and of mothers and daughters together are something everyone looks forward to and are a highlight of each month.

Mother-daughter groups that follow the Mother-Daughter Project model offer specific advantages to women who are raising girls today. First, they create a context in which mother-daughter connection is the norm. Communication lies at the heart of any positive relationship, and a mother-daughter group fosters communication and intimacy. As mothers and daughters speak about the most personal and important aspects of their lives or witness the other having fun on an outing or adventure, each mother-daughter pair deepens their understanding of each other as individuals. A mother-daughter group also provides an oasis during times of tension. At a moment when your daughter wouldn't choose to spend time with you alone, she'll accompany you to the group so she can see her friends and *their* moms. Even if you are in a phase of barely speaking with each other, calmly being together for a couple of hours will help sustain your relationship. The group's explicit support of mother-daughter connection also means that everyone there is rooting for you and your daughter to find your way through the present difficulty, and their faith in your bond will inspire you and your daughter to keep trying.

Mothers have as much to learn from daughters as daughters do from mothers. As teens, many of us felt our mothers turned away from the difficult realities of our adolescent lives. When exchanging knowledge becomes a one-way street, relationships break down. While there are many overlaps, our mothers' lives, our lives, and our daughters' lives differ in significant ways. By creating a community in which mothers and daughters can safely share the truths of their lives both joyous and painful, we close the gap that has separated generations of women.

Having other mothers to lean on eases daunting parenting tasks. It may feel relatively easy if your daughter is in that sweet period of childhood when none of the big issues have yet to surface, but around the corner will be new challenges. *Time for the sex talk?* you gulp as your eleven-year-old daughter starts IM'ing a boy in her class. Time to teach her how to counter sexual harassment. Stay safe on the streets. Love her body. Identify an appropriate partner. Have a satisfying job. These challenging tasks are made more difficult by the common expectation that parents should accomplish them alone. Joining with other mothers makes teaching your girls these life lessons more comfortable, pleasant, and effective as you tackle them collectively.

Amy (of the famed "I hate you" letter), now seventeen, is the most private and shy girl in our mother-daughter group. Throughout her childhood and adolescence, when her mother Phoebe, a professor, tried to address important personal issues with her, like how she could stay safe while walking alone to school, Amy would immediately say, "Can we please change the topic?" In the mother-daughter group, however, Amy was happy to listen in as other girls and mothers discussed street smarts, menstruation, sexuality, and a myriad of other intense topics.

The challenges girls face while they are growing up can be excruciatingly personal. Most find it easier to learn about evocative or frank topics such as the physical changes of puberty or body image in the company of other girls. They are less put on the spot, and if they feel awkward, they can just sit back, eyes glued to a doodle pad of anime characters or their latest knitting project, but ears open. Girls can compare their own responses with others' and let someone else bring up the questions about which they are intensely curious but are too embarrassed to ask, such as how to insert a tampon or can you get pregnant using the withdrawal method of birth control. For younger girls, it is far more comfortable to acknowledge that the "French kissing" they see adults and teenagers doing looks disgusting—and *why would anyone ever do that?!*—with a group of pals. The same goes for eleven- to thirteen-year-olds admitting they might actually want to do just that one day (*but will you get a disease?!*).

Ultimately, other girls are what keep a girl enjoying and coming to a mother-daughter group. Every girl craves good friends. A mother-daughter group can provide them with a stable, encouraging circle of peers who have learned with their mothers' encouragement to appreciate each other as individuals. If a girl ever feels lonely or ostracized at school, at a mother-daughter group, she won't be forced into a devil's bargain between fitting in with peers and being true to herself. This is a place she can both belong and be genuine.

While some of us are by nature more quiet and private and less likely to join a formal mother-daughter group, others can't wait to get started. If you are the mother of a seven- to ten-year-old, a great time to get started is now. It may be tempting to relax into the relative ease of early elementary school years, but the solid, loving bonds most mothers have with their seven- and eight-year-old daughters and girls' intellectual curiosity and emotional openness at this age make it an effective moment to begin preparing them to withstand the pressures of adolescence that may be just around the bend. If you are less inclined to be part of an organized group, hanging out regularly with just one other mom friend and her daughter and trying some of the activities we suggest in Part II is an easy way to reap the benefits of intergenerational connection.

The Difference a Mother-Daughter Group Can Make

In our mom-daughter group, over the course of years, we developed trust in one another's parenting skills and practical wisdom to help one another when we were suddenly faced with new and unfamiliar challenges. For Libby, Vanessa's mom, the mothers-only group and the mother-daughter group proved invaluable both to her individually and for her relationship with her daughter.

From the time Vanessa started seventh grade through her sophomore year of high school, Vanessa's relationship with her mom, Libby, was tempestuous. As a little girl, Vanessa and her mom had a close, easy relationship. They loved to spend time together, doing things like putting together a jigsaw puzzle on a snowy weekend afternoon, or reading together snuggled in bed. Vanessa was happy at school and often told Libby stories about her friends and schooldays and proudly showed mom her completed homework assignments. Both Vanessa and Libby expressed their emotions openly and arguments were rare.

When Vanessa entered seventh grade, however, anything to do with school was now off-limits to Libby. What had started in sixth grade as an occasional disagreement over the level of independence appropriate for Vanessa now turned into frequent, intense fights, where one or both of them would lose her temper, yell, and storm off in a huff. Libby, ashamed and embarrassed that she didn't have better self-control, often blamed herself for their difficulties. Sometimes she found herself blaming Vanessa for being "an impossible teenager." Often she felt sad that their warm, close relationship had become so difficult and problematic.

"I'd always wanted to have a daughter. I hoped I could have a close relationship with her—something I never had with my own mother. When Vanessa suddenly acted like she couldn't stand me, I couldn't help feeling like I was failing."

Libby brought up her concerns about Vanessa at a mothers' meeting. While a stated central goal of the group was to promote mother-daughter connection, she had started to doubt whether she and Vanessa were meant to stay close. Libby felt like every other mother and daughter got along better than Vanessa and she did. "Maybe Vanessa needs to separate," Libby said to the mothers one day. "Maybe I'm too controlling. Maybe I'm not patient enough."

When Sarah, Kay and Maggie's mom, shared how challenging life had been for her and Kay during a similar period in Kay's adolescence, Libby felt reassured. (As you may remember from Chapter Four, Sarah often found that the most effective way to work through tiffs and reconnect with Kay was through dance.)

Kay, like Vanessa, was an intense kid, which at times made her journey through adolescence more turbulent than it usually is for a girl who is relatively laid-back and easygoing. This emotional intensity often made it difficult for Vanessa to brush off the everyday snags in the life of a teenager, from the slight of a friend to witnessing bullying to a breakout of pimples. Having the input of other mothers going through similar challenges helped Libby not to misinterpret Vanessa's anger as a need for distance. Rather, they allowed her to see that the volatility of the relationship had as much to do with Libby's intensity as Vanessa's and was something they could learn how to negotiate. "Come on, Libby," Sarah would joke, "who ever called you 'laid-back'?"

Listening to the other mothers describe ways they managed to spend time with their daughters inspired Libby. Maybe she and Vanessa couldn't easily have a heart-to-heart talk at this stage, but they could still enjoy going to the movies together or in the summer strive toward swimming longer and longer distances at the lake near their home. When Phoebe described giving Amy foot rubs or Sarah described looking for opportunities to drive Kay so they'd have that time together to talk, sing, or listen to music while riding in the car, Libby felt determined to continue to work at finding ways to have positive connections with Vanessa.

Libby noticed that when she and Vanessa had a difficult ride going to a mom-daughter meeting, marked by tension and disagreement, the ride home was often smoother. The couple of hours spent with the other mothers and daughters worked as a balm for their relationship. Listening to each other in the accepting company of others helped ease the intensity of their interactions. It also helped both of them remember that they loved and cared deeply about each other and both shared the desire to have a good relationship.

When Vanessa was seventeen, she reflected on the question *What impact has the mom-daughter group had on you?* "When I look back, I realize there was a period when I wasn't too gung ho on the idea of going to the mom-daughter group, but my mom always made me go. I'd be like, 'No way! I'm not going!'—that was around middle school. But as I got older, I started feeling glad that my mom had made me continue. I have good friends there, plus it's been good for me and my mom. It's kind of like we listen better when we're at mom-daughter. I really appreciate how helpful it's been to have all these people who I care about help me and tell me they love me. If every kid could have a group of people telling them that all the time, then middle school might end up being a little more bearable for everyone!"

What Libby needed most during that time she got from the other mothers: compassion for how hard it was to face an angry teen day after day, encouragement to not take Vanessa's anger personally, ideas for speaking with her daughter to try to find out what was wrong, reassurance that she was a good mother, and invitations to take breaks from mothering and join one of her adult friends to do something relaxing and fun.

Vanessa and Libby's story illustrates the powerful benefits of a mother-daughter group that is specifically dedicated to helping mothers, daughters, and their relationships thrive. Had Libby responded to Vanessa's anger by assuming Vanessa only wanted distance, not only would their relationship have suffered, Libby might have withdrawn and lost the chance to help her daughter navigate adolescence.

Helping you, your daughter, and your relationship thrive by banding together with other mothers and daughters are the four cornerstones of the Mother-Daughter Project. Building from this foundation in the chapters to follow in Part II, we share detailed developmental information unique to girls and offer educational and esteem-building activities and ideas for you and your daughter as she grows up from age seven to seventeen.

PART II

Mothers and Daughters
Banding Together

• • • • • • • • • • • •

Each of the following chapters addresses one year in the life of
your daughter and one hot topic that she will face just around
the bend, helping to guide you as your girl grows up from age seven
to seventeen. We begin each chapter by explaining where girls are
at developmentally in a particular year and what potential challenges to look for on the horizon, such as body image, sexuality, and
safety.

We then offer playful, age-appropriate ways to address critical issues *before* your daughter is in the midst of them, starting with
grounding her in girl-positive perspectives, then taking on negative
messages she may encounter as she moves out into the world. Our
mother-daughter activities are designed to be appealing and fun for
girls and moms while strengthening girls' resistance to the dangers
of teen culture. They also nourish healthy mother-daughter connection. Along the way, we bring you into our own community, sharing
more real-life stories of the mothers and daughters in our group in
all our clumsiness and grace.

To support you as a mother, we provide dynamic questions related to the issues covered in each chapter, which you can consider
in your journal or discuss with other mothers. These questions are

framed to help you understand your own experiences as a girl, and your daughter's experiences today as you clarify your hopes for her and for your relationship. Reflecting on your own passage through adolescence is a significant component of the Mother-Daughter Project. We have found that hearing the stories of other mothers is profoundly helpful in expanding our appreciation for our mothers and ourselves.

Every girl is an individual. Our descriptions of girls' ages and stages are *not* intended to be comprehensive (that would take a much bigger book), but rather to focus on the crucial issues specifically affecting girls and mothers in contemporary culture. Since rates of child development vary widely, the ages given are approximate. Likewise, the touchpoints of adolescence cycle through our daughters' lives again and again. A topic may be pertinent at an earlier or later time in your girl's life than the age at which we present it—your eight-year-old may suddenly be body conscious, or your fifteen-year-old may be just getting her period. Not to worry, you can use the information on that topic to guide you in mothering girls of any age.

Our descriptions of girls and mothers and the activities and interventions we suggest are based on our observations in the Mother-Daughter Project, our psychotherapy practices, consultation with adolescent experts, and related research, but much more research and resources are needed to help us know how to best parent our teens. Not intended to be definitive, the Mother-Daughter Project is a work in progress, a living model that we hope mothers will change and improve to suit their own situations.

We designed this section for easy handling. Read it straight through, flip to the age or topic that interests you most, refer to it as your girl grows up, start a mother-daughter group based on our curriculum, or use it one-on-one with your daughter—whatever meets your needs at the moment or in the future. We know you are busy doing the hard work of mothering.

CHAPTER SEVEN

Celebrating Girls

Seven Years Old—In Love with Mom and the World

Seven-year-olds are as happy playing Queen of the Tigers in a makeshift fort beneath a sheet as they are with any expensive toy from the mall. They thrive on the magic of everyday life. With her imagination firing, a girl this age imbues herself and her environment with every possibility—one minute she's piloting a spacecraft from the top of the monkey bars and the next she's prowling through the "jungle" in the backyard. Playing is how seven-year-olds make sense of life's gifts and hardships and locate themselves in the world. A girl who hears a relative is sick will set up a hospital for all her stuffed animals; after watching the Olympics on TV, she will transform herself into a snowboarder sliding across the kitchen floor in stocking feet.

Seven-year-olds listen to their parents' and teachers' lessons without much skepticism. They are proud of their academic accomplishments, and make a big show of learning to read and do math calculations. While they soak up knowledge like sponges, their minds are highly fluid and associative. They are just starting to develop the cognitive skills to sort out truth from fiction, and will still choose to paint a picture with purple grass and an orange sky if they're partial to those colors.

At this age, girls feel free to love their mothers unabashedly.

Time with mom? What could be better? A seven-year-old daughter is thrilled when she gets us all to herself. She has at least a few years to go before believing mom isn't cool. Her feelings for us are based on her own direct experiences. She knows that mom is the one who hugs and kisses her and puts a Band-Aid on her knee when she falls off her bike while pretending to be a flying horse.

Girls in a secure family situation also love *themselves* unabashedly at this age. Their high self-regard and refreshing honesty is untainted by preteen anxieties. When we started the Mother-Daughter Project back in 1997, when our daughters were seven, one of our goals was to nurture each girl's sense of self as much as we could *before* she even came close to adolescence. Our aim was and is to help girls hold on to the parts of themselves that are spontaneous, strong, outspoken, and wonderful at this age, because this girl-self is the bedrock upon which she will develop her adolescent and adult identity.

Adolescence may feel like a long way off when your girl is seven, but now with the marketing of makeup, fashion clothing, and other teen accoutrements to the eight- to eleven-year-old set, girls are beset with teenage anxieties at younger and younger ages.[1] We worry that girls' self-regard will start to fade at younger ages, too, and for this reason encourage you to start thinking about ways to bolster your daughter's resilience early.

Seven is also a watershed moment because at eight, the magical thinking of early childhood begins to fall away and girls want to know the facts, even painful facts, like who the tooth fairy really is. Eight-year-old girls care about rules and the ways things "really are"—in their paintings the sky is blue and the grass is green. At eight, girls are developing the cognitive abilities to differentiate things into groups with similar characteristics. Since they tend to love the neatness of categories, they are vulnerable to adopting stereotyped ideas of what it means to be female.

In today's world, girls see fantastic opportunities and encouragement for women all around them, contributing to their sense that girls are valuable and smart and loved. But, unfortunately, subtle and some not-so-subtle vestiges of sexism still lurk in corners of many girls' lives. Across the United States, girls are playing extracurricular sports, but at recess, a game of kickball or soccer, played almost exclusively by boys, dominates the center of the playground at many schools, or the boys play basketball while the girls mainly hover around the edges of the court. Girls hear boys sneer *you're a girl* as a cutting insult to another boy. The racks at Old Navy, the Gap, and Wal-Mart are filled with highly gendered clothing for children, sending the message that boys and girls occupy completely different spheres. Moreover, the boys' items tend to be rugged and sporty while the girls' clothing is flimsy and impractical—and increasingly tight and scanty—even at a very young age.

As girls eight years and older strive to figure out what it means to be a girl, they draw conclusions from all of their experiences of how females are portrayed and treated, both positive and negative. There are many ways mothers of seven-year-olds can help daughters conclude it's great to be a girl in order to strengthen their positive self-regard as they grow up. As mothers, we can use the playfulness of this age and our daughters' connection to us as our point of departure.

"The art of playing with girls sustains both women's and girls' courage," Harvard professor of human development and psychology Annie Rogers wrote in 1993.[2] Our general philosophy of how to teach girls the life lessons they need is to embed them in the activities they like to do most. At the Mother-Daughter Project, we call what girls like to do *girl culture*. Girl culture is extremely diverse and for each individual girl or small group of girls, preferences change as they grow up. At seven, a girl may best enjoy drawing; at eleven, taking pictures with a digital camera and manipulating them into funny images on the computer;

at thirteen, using a video recorder; and at sixteen, writing a scene for a short screenplay. For Maisie's daughter Gabriella, an intense love of playing make-believe was encouraged by her mother and ultimately led to theater camps, attending a performing arts high school, and an interest in pursuing an acting career. When we engage with our girls and participate in the activities *they* love, we are honoring girl culture and each girl's unique interests. Celebrating *their* culture *with* them offers our daughters a full sensory experience of the story that girls are important.

For seven-year-olds, playing with mom is not only developmentally appropriate, it eases you and your daughter into getting started on regular, thoughtful bonding and educational activities. If you are creating a mother-daughter group, simply playing together is a fun, easy way to get to know all the girls and moms during the first year.

··············

Play is fun and easy, but will it really help our daughters? That's the question Libby, Vanessa's mom, raised when our mothers' group was planning our first mother-daughter meeting. After we had been meeting together for nine months, the women decided it was time to introduce the girls.

"The first get-together should be fun for them," said Maisie, Gabriella and April's mom, thirty-two at the time.

"The whole year should be fun," said Sarah, Maggie's mom, then thirty-eight.

"Fun in a girl-empowering way," added Phoebe, Amy's mom, thirty-six.

"Mothers and daughters having fun *together*," contributed Libby.

"Okay," said Sarah. "What does that entail?"

Maisie came up with the suggestion that over the course of the year each girl could bring a game and teach it to the others. It could be the kind of spontaneous games that girls play together, such as capture the flag or hide-and-seek, or they could choose an activity such as going swimming or ice skating.

"Playing games sounds great," said Libby tentatively, "but is it enough? Is playing games all year going to be getting them ready for being teenagers? Shouldn't we be doing more?"

"Something more girl-empowering?" asked Phoebe.

Katy, Marisol's mom, spoke up for the first time. "In the next few years, the girls are going to be hearing the message to separate from us. What could be a better investment of our time and energy than having a good time with them now?"

"That's right," said Maisie. "Mothers *playing* with daughters *is* girl-empowering."

"It's telling them to take up space in the world," added Phoebe.

"I remember playing jump rope at recess squished off to the side of the boys' football game that filled the whole schoolyard," said Katy. "That's still the way Marisol's playground is."

Maisie said, "Well, I was playing that football game with the boys. Girls don't just jump rope and play with dolls."

"No, but some do," said Sarah. "The point is, we'll invite our girls to choose the games *they* like to play, whether it's jump rope or football or whatever."

"Okay, I'm convinced," said Libby. And we marked our calendars with the date of our first mother-daughter meeting.

Mothers Reconnecting with Their Girlhood Selves

Remembering the freedom and joy of seven is rejuvenating for moms. In 1994, Carol Gilligan, in collaboration with eminent voice teacher Kristine Linklater, gathered women and girls to speak, write, play, and move together in theater workshops designed to help girls hang on to their true voices and women recover the strong sense of self they enjoyed as girls. As a participant, SuEllen learned firsthand how energizing it is to remember one's feisty girlhood.

In journals or in conversations with other mothers, you can dip into your own childhood by remembering yourself at whatever age your daughter currently is. Doing so gives you new perspective on your daughter and on yourself as a mother. Age seven can be particularly delightful to remember as you ask yourself:

What did I love to do when I was about seven?

When did I feel the best? Whom did I love to be with?

Remembering your mother when you were young also gives you new perspective:

What are my favorite memories with my mother when I was a young girl?

What did I love to do with her?

While early childhood is often a marvelous time, it can hold heartache, especially if you were dealing with family difficulty, such as serious illness or divorce. You can honor your girlhood self despite the challenges by asking:

What value or hope that is precious to me was I able to hold on to through that difficulty?

What helped me hold on to that value or hope and get through that difficult time?

Who was most helpful to me?

At any age, you can deepen your understanding of your daughter by thoughtfully reflecting on her present stage of development. When she is seven, you can ask:

How would I describe my daughter now?

What does she love to do?

What do we love to do together?

If seven (or any age) is a time of difficulty for your daughter, you can strengthen what is positive in her life by asking:

What hope and love is my daughter able to experience despite present difficulties?

How is she able to hold on to that hope and love? Who or what helps her?

What difference does it make to her and to me that she can experience this hope and love despite present challenges?

Mothers and Daughters Learning to Play Together

Often the biggest impediment to playing with our daughters is our unavoidable exhaustion from a triple shift of homemaking, wage-earning, and parenting. Your daughter may pester you to play with her while you are scrambling to get dinner together or when you finally get to collapse onto the couch after doing the dishes, but for it to contribute to her sense that being a girl is great, you *both* need to feel like playing. Planning in advance when that will be lets you say to her, "This isn't a good time for me to play because I need to rest, but Saturday morning I'd love to help you make a blanket fort. Right now is a good time for you to play on your own (or with a sibling or friend)." Respecting your own needs models for her how women take care of themselves and helps her develop the lifelong skill of entertaining herself.

While one-on-one time with daughters is important, we suggest inviting another mother-daughter pair or more to join you in some of the activities we describe. It's actually more efficient (not to mention more fun) to get some adult companionship at the same time that you are bonding with your daughter and contributing to her sound sense of self. If you are part of a new mother-daughter group with girls aged six to nine, devising and playing games can cover a whole year of get-togethers.

What Does Your Girl Love to Do?

Notice how your daughter plays. Ask her about pretend games, playground games, or playdate games she likes. Some of our daughters' favorite group games included kick the can, capture the flag, spud, Ultimate Frisbee, clapping games, and jump rope. We recommend focusing on games that children "author" and teach themselves instead of store-bought activities. Make-believe games that girls love include playing house, dress-up of all sorts, playing with stuffed animals or dolls, pretending to be animals or explorers—there's no limit to girls' imaginations. Some girls love organized games like hopscotch or whiffle ball while others enjoy going to a playground or riding bikes.

As you play with your daughter, notice: Which games make her happy and content? Which often lead to tears, tantrums, or moodiness? Which games are in line with your hopes for her, and which draw her away from your vision of what it means for girls to thrive? You can gently guide her toward what works for her. She may have a game she just loves called *crush the ants*, in which she is a giant stomping on villagers living in the cracks of your walk, but if it goes against the lessons you want to teach, calmly discourage her ("Our family cares about the natural world, so we're not in favor of killing ants as a game") and find another way for her to be powerful and invincible ("Oh, no! Can you save the ants from the invasion of these twig monsters?"). Watch particularly closely when her play centers around TV shows or advertised toys to see if they reflect your hopes for her as a girl. Is being a "Bratz" part of your vision for her, or voting to cut people out of a group like on *Survivor*-style reality shows? If not, offer alternatives: "In our family, we work together. Let's pretend we're stranded on a desert island, and our job is to be sure *everyone* survives. Do you want to be the captain?" We can honor what our girls love while simultaneously sharing our values with them.

Playing Girls' Games with a Group

Set a date and invite other mothers and daughters for an afternoon of playing the girls' favorite games together. Everyone can contribute an idea, and if you don't get to them all, schedule another get-together—rest assured the girls will be clamoring for another mom-daughter game day soon. Here are a few favorites of our mom-daughter group to get you started.

Name games. For a first get-together or anytime there's someone new, it's good to start with a name game. An easy one is to stand in a circle and have each person say her name while making a movement with her body—spinning around, clapping hands, marching, and so on. Everyone repeats her name and movement and the next person in the circle takes a turn. Everyone repeats the second person's name and movement, and then everyone repeats the first person's name and movement again. Continue around the circle, repeating all the names and movements. Guaranteed to result in everyone knowing everyone else's name in ten minutes. Variations include name and favorite color, name and favorite food, favorite animal, and so on.

Our initial gathering of daughters and mothers started with a name game. As we stood in a circle outside of Sarah and Maggie's home, Maisie demonstrated how each person could say her name while making a movement with her body. "Maisie!" she said, as she planted her feet like an archer and pulled back on an imaginary bow.

"Maisie!" we repeated, drawing back on our bows and letting pretend arrows fly. Maisie looked to her right, but Amy, seven, was studying the ground with great intensity.

Maisie turned to Maggie, seven, on her left, who jumped into the middle of the circle and spun around. "Maggie!"

We all jumped and spun. "Maggie!"

"And repeat Maisie's name, too," said Sarah.

"Maisie!" Arrows flew. As we continued around the circle, the shy girls, like Amy, gathered courage by watching, repeating the names, and laughing together as we all got to know one another for the first time.

Group games. Invite the girls to figure out a fair way to choose who gets to share her game first, such as eenie meenie minie mo or drawing straws. Let them be the experts on the parameters of their games, and just help as needed with the process of taking turns and listening. Don't be surprised if figuring out the rules or deciding who gets to be the baby cheetah takes longer than the actual game; communicating and negotiating are essential social skills that girls learn by playing in groups.

In our group, Maggie got to choose the first game after learning one another's names. "My favorite game is . . ." she paused for effect. "Kick the can! The person who's IT kicks the can, and then counts to a hundred while everyone hides." Her mom, Sarah, set an empty soup can on the asphalt walk.

"When we play, someone *else* kicks the can," said eight-year-old Gabriella.

"Yeah, that's right," agreed Maggie. "So then, um, the person who is IT goes and finds everyone, and has to beat them back to kick the can."

"And if she catches them, they have to stay in jail," added April, age six, "but they can get out if someone comes and tags them."

"Yeah. Ready?" finished Maggie. "Not it!"

"Not it!"

"Not it!"

"Not it!"

"Not it!"

"That's not fair!" said Vanessa, age seven, "I don't want to be IT."

"That's how we usually do it," said Gabriella with a shrug. Vanessa looked ready to cry and started to turn toward the house.

"It sounds like Vanessa would prefer a different way of choosing who's IT," said Sarah. "Any ideas?"

"How about eenie meenie minie mo?" asked Maggie. "Is that okay, Vanessa?"

"Yes," she said, blinking rapidly and rejoining the group. April was IT.

The game started and mothers and daughters scattered. ". . . Ninety-nine, one hundred. Ready or not, here I come!"

Maisie peeked out from the bushes.

"I see Mommy!" April screeched triumphantly as she sprinted toward the can. Maisie raced her, but April kicked the can first. "I got Mommy! I got Mommy!" she sang, jumping up and down. "Now you're in jail."

"Okay," said her mother, panting. "Where's jail?"

"On the steps. Now I have to find everyone else." In a whisper she added, "You can help me if you want." Her mother nodded. "Give me a sign if you see anyone." Her mother gave her the thumbs-up. "I love you, Mommy," she said, still in a whisper, then yelled at the top of her lungs, "I see Marisol behind the fence!" before racing to kick the can.

You may be surprised how delighted your daughter will be that you (and other moms) are playing hide-and-seek or spud with them, and you may be surprised by how much fun you have, too. Singing and clapping *Miss Mary Mack Mack Mack, all dressed in black, black, black,* racing sleds down icy slopes, dressing up as pirates, playing touch football—it's exhilarating to vividly remember your own girlhood by playing like a kid. You might get muddy or sweaty or cold, but then you will all get to come inside for lemonade or hot chocolate with apples and cookies as your daughter snuggles on your lap.

Endings. In fact, playing together is so exhilarating that most girls won't want to go home. At the end of the afternoon, our daughters didn't want to leave, so we agreed to one last very short game. Maisie gathered us in a circle and taught us how to make rain. She rubbed her palms together, then Vanessa, next to her, did the same, and so on around the circle, the swish-swish-swish growing louder as we each joined in. Maisie began to snap her fingers, and as we each followed, the sound of raindrops spattering to the sidewalk moved around the circle. Next it started to pour, as first Maisie and then the rest of us clapped our hands, then slapped our thighs. When we also stamped our feet, the rainstorm surged into its full power, then subsided as the stamping ceased and the slapping became clapping, which turned into snapping, sounding like raindrops dripping from trees, then swish-swish-swish like the wind in wet leaves, then one by one, we were quiet as we raised our arms above our heads to welcome back the sun. We all loved making the rain come and go and the sun come out so much that we decided to end every meeting this way—and ten years later, we still love to.

Playing with our daughters implicitly conveys respect for their preferences and supports their job of growing up, encouraging communication, negotiation, and the use of their voices at a time when their sense of self is still so strong. Play is kids' work. When a mother joins her daughter's favorite game with her, a girl learns she is worthwhile. When a group of mothers and girls play the girls' favorite games, they learn that they in particular and girls in general are worthwhile. It tells them that whatever they love to do—whether that is freeze tag, throwing a dollhouse tea party, or double Dutch—is important. It's a profound lesson for girls to carry into their futures.

CHAPTER EIGHT

Fostering True Friendship

Eight Years Old—Branching Out

The primary job of an eight-year-old girl is to figure out how the world works. Eight-year-olds are curious about everything— nature, relationships, current events, family histories—and seek out the truth with passion. At this age, girls strive to create a coherent picture of reality. They are drawn to rules and to what they see as authoritative sources of information: parents, teachers, and, increasingly, books. Typically, they feel close to their mothers, and want to learn from them.

At eight, girls' friendships are easy and fluid. They enjoy being with playmates, and they will accept most newcomers. Self-consciousness is not yet a big issue. But looking ahead, by age ten, friendship becomes a hot issue and will continue to be for many years. From the preteen years on, the meaning of friendship expands beyond companionship to include the search for identity.

As we anticipate the years to come, we see that at ten, girls start scrutinizing themselves and others in new ways. As they define their own abilities and preferences, they begin to notice and compare what is rewarded at home, at school, among their peers, and in the wider culture. If what they see "outside" (for example, rudeness being rewarded with social status) does not jibe with what they have learned at home (treat everyone with kindness and respect), this is the time they may begin to question their parents' authority and values on friendship, among other issues.

Ten-year-old girls' knowledge of the world is superficial. Each new cultural sound bite they encounter can significantly shift the dynamics of what they consider "in" or "out." Girls must constantly make decisions about where they stand on the issues of the day: Is it fun to play soccer with the boys at recess, or is it disgusting? Do I care about fashion or not? Preteens are also increasingly aware of social status.

A girl's impulse to fit in with her peers is often at odds with her desire to be genuine to herself. Many girls feel compelled to give up their true voices in order to belong, because, to be themselves, what they need are friends who value and positively reflect back who they really are. Such friends are not always easy to find.

Today, we are in the midst of an anti-girl backlash against the pro-girl ideas that were promoted in the 1990s by writers like Mary Pipher and Carol Gilligan. Its focus is girls' relationships with other girls, setting up girls and mothers to expect and accept the disintegration of girls' friendships during their preteen and teen years. A generation ago, girls were called "catty"; now the sweeping insult is "mean." Popular movies such as *Mean Girls* depict "queen bees" and "alpha girls" stomping their way to the top of the social heap in miniskirts and stiletto heels. In fact, the paradigm has become so entrenched it is used to define girls' relationships in other time periods, as in Libba Bray's Victorian-era young adult novel *A Great and Terrible Beauty*[1] and other cultures, such as in the film *Memoirs of a Geisha*. The February 24, 2002, *New York Times Magazine* cover showed a girl in her early teens held in a giant fist like a voodoo doll, with huge pins stabbing her arms, shoulders, abdomen, breasts, and heart. While the article purported to be sympathetic to the plight of "beta" girls (also depicted as "wannabes"), a more girl-hostile image is hard to imagine.

Girls are not unfailingly generous in their relationships, but we know from our work as psychotherapists and in the Project that the vast majority have the potential to be caring and kind. In our experience, the more love and support a girl receives both at home *and* from her peers, the more loving and supportive her actions are likely to be. A mother-daughter group offers a girl a steady source of respect, inclusion, care, and kindness where she can both belong and be genuine, strengthening her sense of self-worth and her ability to negotiate her larger social scene with greater integrity and grace.

When girls are experiencing exclusion, ostracism, or bullying, or are in a school setting where that kind of behavior is the norm, they are much more likely to be similarly unkind to others. Girls trying to meet the impossible standards of the Perfect Girl may end up forfeiting their voices, their bodies, their intelligence, and their money. They may resent and act unfriendly to other girls who, on the surface, appear to be getting social privileges—to be well liked by other girls and boys—without making the same sacrifices.

In 2002, at a lecture for psychotherapists in Lenox, Massachusetts, Carol Gilligan described the actions of girls excluding other girls as a reenactment of their own inner experience of the need to exclude precious parts of themselves in order to exist in a world that denigrates them. As such, girls develop strategies to survive as best they can. While our culture is busy scrutinizing the "mean" behavior of today's girls, boys' behavior can go unchecked. One striking example is that school authorities too frequently allow boys to publicly harass girls without repercussions, rather than create a secure academic environment in which girls and boys alike can thrive. Instead of directing their anger at a boy who might call them a "dog" or a "whore" in the corridor between classes, girls may choose a safer and more vulnerable target for their rage and embarrassment: other girls.

Every girl is at some time left out of a desired social group, hurt by a friend, or teased by peers, but if she knows what true friendship means to her and if she has a group of peers where she is always welcome, she will be able to withstand the pain of other relationship mishaps without losing her sense of self or feeling she needs to betray her values to survive. Encouraging girls to maintain connections with the friends they meet through summer camp, sports teams, a mother-daughter group, or other activities outside of their daily routine can provide a positive alternative if they get pigeonholed in an undesirable role (get a "reputation") or stuck in a negative social dynamic with another kid at school. At age ten, when Amy, Phoebe's daughter, was in fifth grade, she was more interested in playing soccer than in flirting with the boys and gushing over Britney Spears like many of the other girls in her grade, and she felt isolated and out of place in school, especially since her best friend since kindergarten had stopped inviting her over and barely spoke to her during the day. While her friends from her mother-daughter group didn't erase the sadness of being left out, they did give her the love and sense of belonging she needed to feel good about herself, allowing her to hold on to her own identity as a smart, athletic girl with a goofy sense of humor who thought math was "way cool" and kissing boys was still gross.

The group also supported Phoebe through her daughter's difficult time. During mothers-only meetings, the other mothers calmed Phoebe's fears that her shy, unconventional daughter was on a path to loneliness or would be permanently scarred by her social isolation. They assured her that Amy was being genuine to herself, that there was nothing wrong with her for not embracing teen culture at age ten or eleven (or ever), and that with the love of her family and the group, Amy would be *fine* and would have a fresh start soon and new friends when the pool of girls was bigger in middle school. Maisie arranged for her daughter April, who was a year younger and went to a different school, to have a weekly playdate with Amy when the girls could play "horse" out at the basketball hoop and scooter around the neighborhood. In middle school, Amy did find a whole new crew of friends, and now at sixteen, she is a cherished member of a group of girls who love and appreciate her for who she is.

The skills required to gracefully negotiate the social complexity of friendship, to be a true friend and also to navigate compromised relationships, take a lifetime to master; girls at eight are taking baby steps. They may suddenly cancel a playdate when they get a better offer or deliberately mention a birthday party in front of someone who wasn't invited. They may use the promise of friendship as a bargaining chip. At ten and up, the stakes are higher and the slights are more pointed and wounding. How can we support our daughters with the difficult task of learning true friendship? The receptivity of eight gives mothers a chance to offer lessons and experiences that will enhance girls' relationships in the years to come.

Mothers Provide a Powerful Model of Female Friendship

Women's friendships with other women, like girls' friendships, are often portrayed negatively in the media. When the term "Mommy Wars" was coined, journalists wrote that the biggest problem facing mothers today was one another. In fact, mothers and other women count on one another all the time and have for generations—for emotional support, to babysit or pick up a child after school, for companionship. Our friendships with other women are a powerful example to our daughters.

As we do our best to be a good friend or neighbor, our daughters are watching. We don't need to be perfect—when our girls see how we try to put our relationship values into action or work to repair things if they go awry, they are learning what we want them to know. In a mother-daughter group, daughters regularly get to see women working together. The examples of friendship mothers offer help to make sitcom catfights and other negative representations of female relationships look ridiculous.

It is useful to understand our own attitudes about friendship in communicating with our daughters. Reflecting on our experiences with other girls when we were young can give us insight and perspective. In a journal or among other mothers we can ask questions like:

Which girlhood friendships were most satisfying, and why?

What did I value in a friend? Do I value the same things now?

What messages was I receiving about girls' relationships from the media or my peers?

Did my friendships change as a teen?

When did friendships become hard or elusive?

How did/does my social setting work for or against friendship?

What kinds of friendships did my mother have when I was a girl?

From there we can clarify our hopes for our daughters' friendships:

What qualities do I hope characterize my daughter's friendships?

How do peers and the wider culture influence relationships among girls today?

Supporting True Friendship Through Mother-Daughter Activities

Finding friends. There may be times in your girl's life when it feels as if she hasn't got a friend, whether you've recently moved to a new city, or she's just on the "outs" with her group at school. The pain of loneliness is compounded when girls are shunned or even worse, harassed, for not conforming to local standards of social desirability, whether by virtue of race, body size, religion, lack of interest in conforming to the Perfect Girl ideal, their love of academics, and so on. Peer abuse can be overt, like tripping a girl as she gets off the school bus, or insidious, like spreading out at the lunchroom table and claiming all seats are taken so there isn't room for a former friend who no longer fits in to the crowd because she has to wear a back brace for scoliosis.

At these difficult times, one way mothers can support their daughters is by showing them that they are lovable, and reminding them of some of the people who have cared about them before. Find an old photo album or go through old cards or letters and reminisce about favorite times with friends in years past. Ask yourselves, *How did we first meet our favorite buddies? What did we love about them? What did they love about us?* Create a wish list for the kinds of friends you and your daughter would both like in your lives now. Ask, *What is a first step in making new friends?*

Girls' night in. If you have a close grown-up friend or two, invite them and your daughter and a pal or two of hers for a "girls' night." Any activity you all enjoy, such as going out to dinner, playing cards, or watching a movie, can provide the starting point for sharing the joy of true friendship with your daughter. At eight, she'll be honored to join the grown-ups as she benefits from developing her own relationship with your friends. When mothers and daughters find themselves in a confrontational phase during adolescence, it can be invaluable for a teenage girl to have another trusted female adult to confide in and seek advice from. Your friends share your values. Bring them into your girl's life.

In a mother-daughter group, you can promote similar connection with other mothers by having each daughter plan a meeting with a mother—but not her own. In our experience, eight-year-olds love this, and take it very seriously. Mothers get to know another daughter more personally, finding out what they have in common. A girl and woman who discover they both love to sing can organize an afternoon of karaoke. Dancers can teach dances they loved as girls (anything from the Virginia Reel to the Hustle is a hit with most eight-year-olds). Storytellers can invite everyone to bring an object from home that has meaning for them and share the meaning behind it. As girls and women share what is important to them, different cultural backgrounds and interests are explored as connections are built.

Friendship rules. With girls this age, friendship can be explicitly addressed in many ways. In a mother-daughter group or at home, girls can be invited to create guidelines to promote mutual respect and harmony. Eight-year-olds love creating rules, such as "No laughing *at* someone" or "Come on time, and call if you're not coming." After these guidelines are established, you can ask the girls, *What do you value most in a friendship?*

Mural making. Cocreating a single work of art is a great way to bring girls together. Mural making is fun and easy with a bunch of your daughter's pals or in a mother-daughter group. All it takes is a big piece of poster board or paper and lots of crayons, markers, or paint. A way to get started is to choose a symbol for the group (some ideas we had: a bird, a boat, a wolf pack, and so on) that could be the official symbol for the group going forward. One person draws a large outline and the rest decorate it together. The emphasis might be on process, but the outcome will undoubtedly be beautiful and the girls can take turns bringing it home.

When Katy, a window display artist and painter, and her younger daughter, Kaili, did this activity with their mother-daughter group when Kaili was eight, the girls chose a butterfly as the group symbol and Katy drew the outline. Everyone brought markers and crowded around the kitchen table, coloring away. At first the girls and moms made designs like rainbows, hearts, and stars, but then, taking their cue from Kaili, each girl drew a portrait of herself and her mother somewhere on the wings, and wrote "Mothers and Daughters Together" in their best handwriting around the edge of the mural, the second-graders printing, the third-graders writing carefully in cursive.

Where do you stand? A school game our daughters taught *us* called "Where do you stand?" is lively and evocative. Imagine a line on the floor. One end is *Strongly Agree*, which follows a continuum through *Undecided* in the middle to *Strongly Disagree* on the other end. One girl reads a series of statements about friendships that have been prepared ahead of time. When she reads, "What I value most in a friend is trust" or "It's okay to tell secrets in front of other girls," each girl and woman moves to the place on the continuum that represents her views. Girls tend to run and jostle for the exact spot they want, while also keeping an eye on the others. For each statement, one or two people might explain why they chose to stand where they did.

....

The activities described above strengthen mother-daughter bonds while teaching the lessons of friendship in a fun way. In groups, they bring girls closer to other girls, moms closer to their daughters, and moms closer to other moms, all the while creating a secure peer environment for girls *and* teaching friendship values for now and the years to come. A mother-daughter group is a tremendously efficient way to multitask mothering.

Making Friends with Barbie

Teaching girls to respect *all* other girls and women is key to having positive, mutual friendships as they grow up. One day, at mother-daughter group, Phoebe did a little show-and-tell, and all of us, mothers and daughters alike, learned a lesson from—can you believe it?—Barbie.

After the mother-daughter activities, the girls went outside and climbed on a big pine tree, leaving the mothers inside to relax and talk.

"I have something to show you," Phoebe said. She continued, "Last week, Paul and I hired a babysitter and actually had a date."

"Woo-hoo!"

Phoebe smiled. "I really like the babysitter. She's in eighth grade, and good with the kids. This time, she and Amy pulled out the Barbie dolls."

Maisie grimaced.

"Exactly," said Phoebe. "I don't buy Barbies, but Amy has received a few as gifts."

"Amy knows you don't like Barbies," said Sarah, "so she played with them with her babysitter. Is that a big deal to you?"

"Actually, her babysitter *doesn't* like Barbies. She *hates* them. The next morning, Amy reported to me that the babysitter had told her Barbies were bad because they make girls think they should be skinny with big boobs and wear high heels all the time. And she didn't just say that Barbie sends the wrong message. Look. . . ." Phoebe pulled out a shoebox full of dismembered Barbie parts, their faces and torsos scrawled with red marker. "I mean, she should have asked me first, but good riddance."

While the other mothers huddled over the box, Sarah stayed in her chair, somber. "We shouldn't disrespect other women, even Barbie."

"What?" Phoebe looked up, surprised. "She's just a doll."

"But she represents real women," said Sarah. "That's why you don't think Barbie is a good example for your daughters, right? But what kind of an example is this?" She picked up a Barbie body minus head and arms, with red marks across her breasts.

Phoebe was very still for a moment, her cheeks a bit flushed. "You're right. I agree with you. I believe all women should respect one another."

Together we decided to explain to the daughters that one should never put down another woman because she looks different or has made different choices from our own.

"Sarah, I want Amy to hear how we need to respect all girls, even Barbie," said Phoebe. "If you say it, it'll have more clout."

"Okay, but I don't want Amy to feel on the spot."

"We'll take care. That's part of being respectful to *her*."

After we figured out what it was we wanted to say, we coaxed our daughters down from their game in the tree with popsicles.

Maisie, the school teacher, led the way. "Everyone, hold out your popsicle." Red, green, orange, and purple ice pops pointed toward the center of our circle.

"You each like different flavors, right?"

"Right!" the girls chorused.

"Does that make the other girls' choices wrong?"

"No-o-o."

Maisie put her arm around Sarah's daughter Maggie, who was sitting next to her. "So, would it be okay to be disrespectful to Maggie just because she likes lime and you like grape?"

"No-o-o," the girls said.

"What if Maggie wasn't your friend, would it be okay to disrespect her then?"

"No-o-o."

"Why not?"

"Because it's not okay to disrespect anybody."

"What if a girl likes spinach popsicles?"

The girls made faces on cue. "But you still shouldn't be mean," said Vanessa.

"What if a girl dresses differently than you? Could you be mean to her then?"

"No-o-o." Slurp.

"What if a girl is trying to look like Barbie?"

"I like Barbie," piped up Vanessa.

"But if you didn't, could you dis' her then?"

"No-o-o." Slurp.

"Why not?"

"Because you shouldn't dis' anybody."

"Not even Barbie?"

"She's a doll, Mom," said Gabriella.

"Well, the kind of girl Barbie represents?"

Then Amy spoke up. "My babysitter says Barbie hurts girls because she wants them all to be superthin like her."

"Is that what *Barbie* wants?" asked Sarah. "Or is that what the people who make Barbie want?"

"It's not really *Barbie*'s fault," said Vanessa.

"Barbie probably hates having high-heel feet," said Gabriella.

Maggie chimed in, "Even when she goes barefooted she has to walk on tippy-toe."

Later, Amy and Phoebe examined the box of Barbie parts together. "I think we should bury them," Amy said. She looked up at her mother. "In a nice way."

Teaching your daughter compassion and opening her eyes to the potential companionship of all other girls will help her resist cliques and find the peers who will truly nurture her as an individual. As she hits the teenage years, her friends will become the center of her world. The lessons you offer now on friendship will help ensure that the world is one that sustains her.

CHAPTER NINE

Welcoming Cycles

Nine Years Old—Big Changes Ahead

Nine is often a girl's last year of unfettered girlhood. Most girls this age haven't entered puberty, or if they have, neither they nor their peers are paying much attention or passing judgment on the physical changes they may exhibit. Nine-year-olds relish the freedom and pleasures of childhood as they take increasing pride in being more capable, responsible, and independent. They might ride their bikes all the way to the park, execute a cookie recipe with minimal assistance, read a long chapter book, master their times tables, or help choose a sleepaway camp for the next summer. Each milestone encourages them to move through their days with even greater confidence. As you savor this moment when your daughter is still truly a kid, keep in mind that dramatic changes lie just around the bend.

Puberty can enter our daughters' lives with breathtaking suddenness. One day your daughter is hanging upside down from the swing set trapeze bar freely baring her girlish chest, and it seems like the very next day she's telling you she has underarm hair and could you please get her some deodorant? The range for when puberty begins is wide, but generally, girls will experience some changes by around ten or eleven years old. If puberty begins earlier, younger girls might even find their growing breasts, bottoms, or sprouts of body hair somewhat amusing, but an eleven-year-old's increasing awareness allows her to realize, often with some shock, that her unencumbered physical self is transforming into the body of a woman.

Puberty couldn't feel more personal, although starting with breast buds, it is a public event in the life of a girl. While girls, like boys, experience the arrival of underarm and pubic hair in private, the presence or absence of breasts is obvious to everyone. A girl may feel like a walking billboard advertising her exact state of development. Depending on her disposition and the response of her peers and the adults in her life, your daughter may be proud and happy for others to notice, she may be indifferent, or she may be self-conscious. Any of these responses is healthy and normal and mothers can support their daughters by respecting their preferences. You can ask your daughter if she is more comfortable wearing a camisole, bra, or no bra. If she starts wearing baggy T-shirts or layered clothing, that is fine. You can also honor her request to change clothes in private.

One of the biggest events of a girl's puberty is getting her period. While most girls get their first period between ages ten and fourteen, some girls reach menarche (the onset of menstruation) as young as nine or as old as sixteen. Girls eleven and younger are often chagrined when menarche arrives, desiring neither the physical ability to ovulate (nor become pregnant) nor the practical responsibilities that having their period bestows. A girl of twelve will often have friends who are starting to menstruate and will wonder about when she is going to get her period, too. If menarche has not arrived by age thirteen, a girl may be watching for it and thinking about it every single day, but typically she rarely speaks about it, even with her closest friends or her mother. Sometimes letting her have a quick private chat with a trusted pediatrician or volunteering to ask on her behalf, if that is more comfortable for her, can alleviate some anxiety. Simply reminding her that some girls don't get their periods until age sixteen may be reassuring.

Girls of all ages experience complicated feelings when they

get their periods: pride, anger, sadness, embarrassment, resignation, relief, worry—among others. They can feel like honored bearers of important and mysterious grown-up secrets, but they can also feel acutely at risk of public ridicule and humiliation. What if the boys find out? What if they leak in public? Even a young woman of sixteen or older who has been menstruating for a number of years may feel mortified if she stains her bed sheets or underwear in the privacy of her own home. Girls fret that getting their periods will mean an end to some of their favorite activities. As any grown woman knows, menstruation is not without its discomforts and inconveniences, which you can explain to your daughter after you have laid a foundation of positive knowledge about female cycles. However, it is also important to tell your daughter that women run marathons, scale the Himalayas, and travel to space while menstruating, so she will be able to swim, bike, do gymnastics, ride horseback, or do whatever it is she likes to do, too.

Menarche is fraught with contested meanings. Starting to menstruate is a singularly important event in a girl's life, bestowing undeniable evidence of her maturity, health, and her ability to create new life, but these positive meanings are often obscured by girls' feelings of embarrassment and by anxiety over what menarche signifies, and undermined by the historical negative associations that linger today and find their way into our psyches. Anthropologist Judy Grahn and others suggest that a girl's or woman's inner perspective on menstruation arises from the attitudes she learns from her culture.[1] Just reading the word *menstruate* on this page can cause a twinge of embarrassment. This is the case, in part, because, in many ways, getting your period is still considered taboo and infused with age-old connotations of impurity and shame. Euphemisms abound. The terms *sanitary products* and *feminine hygiene* used to refer to pads and tampons imply that menstruation, and by extension the female sexual organs (and femaleness in general), are unclean. In fact, the human mouth contains far more germs than the vagina, and requires brushing and flossing, whereas the vagina is a miraculous self-cleaning organ. While some girls bond through events such as buying their first box of tampons from a male sales clerk, it's a blow to a girl's sense of self when the most dramatic sign of becoming a woman is construed not as a blessing, but as a curse.

While we need to teach our girls the basic physiology of the female reproductive cycle, the physiological story of getting your period commonly told in health class is insufficient to alleviate the negative attitudes about menstruation most girls will encounter. As mothers, we want to help our daughters feel strong and healthy about growing up and becoming women. Getting your period is a significant rite of passage for which we can create new stories and celebrations. You can teach your daughter that menstruation means knowledge, power, and belonging (even if you feel uncomfortable with the subject and aren't completely convinced yourself). Menarche brings her the *knowledge* that she is maturing: She is healthy, and she is fertile, but she is not pregnant. Her period lets her know that she has the *power* to get pregnant or not get pregnant when she ovulates in about two weeks. Having her period also means *belonging* to the community of women.

At nine, Marisol's younger sister, Kaili, who is part of a second mother-daughter group of younger girls, was already showing signs of puberty. Kaili gave the changes scant attention as she continued to create fantasy games at the top of the monkey bars and play indoor soccer with as much exuberance as ever, but her mom, Katy, knew that menarche was likely to arrive within a year or two. She wanted to help Kaili feel comfortable, proud, and prepared when it did. Katy was fourteen when she got her period and Marisol thirteen, so she didn't have any personal experience to draw upon about reaching puberty so young. She turned to the women in her mother-daughter group and asked if they would consider collectively teaching their girls about getting their periods as part of their group activities for the year.

Drawing on the most successful activities developed for our group of older girls a few years before, Katy and the other moms and daughters embarked on a yearlong adventure of activities (all described below) geared toward investigating the monthly cycle of the moon, which gradually introduced the girls to the topic of menstruation. They concluded with a ceremony honoring the girls' readiness to get their periods. Each mother planned and led one or two meetings over the course of the year.

When Kaili did begin to menstruate in fifth grade at age eleven she sobbed into Katy's shoulder that she didn't want to have to grow up. Katy gave her time to cry and grieve, and then presented her with the letter and bag of gifts she had received from their mother-daughter group two years earlier, to be opened when each girl first got her period. Sitting on her mother's lap, Kaili dried her tears and opened the pretty lavender bag. She pulled out a red silk scarf and draped it around her shoulders as she read the letter of congratulations written to her by all the other mothers and girls. Katy watched Kaili's demeanor shift from dismay to growing pride. Kaili then called up her closest friend from the mother-daughter group, who came over to congratulate her before they disappeared into her room to chat and listen to music.

When our daughter crosses the bridge to womanhood, some of us feel a twinge of sadness about the fact our little girl is growing up, as well as concern that she will soon be facing the challenges of being a young woman. Anticipating the mutuality of a more mature relationship can be a source of comfort and joy, however, as can recognizing that she will also soon be enjoying the many wonderful aspects of being a young woman. Knowing that we can have a positive impact on her journey fortifies us. For our girls, finding positive ways to communicate about menstruation makes this sometimes-difficult transition much easier. It also sets the stage for critical conversations about intensely intimate topics such as body image and sexuality that you will want to have with your girl as she matures. Through fun, multisensory activities, you can use the curious, playful window of nine years old to vividly convey that becoming a woman is a joyful experience and teach her the facts about menstruation before they become an issue.

Remembering Puberty

For most women, a daughter's impending development evokes feelings and memories of our own puberty, both sweet and painful. As with every topic, understanding our experiences helps us be positive and clear when we communicate with our girls. Questions that invite useful reflection or discussion include:

How did I first learn about puberty and menstruation?

What was my experience of developing breasts and the other changes of puberty?

What was it like anticipating and then getting my first period?

What kind of conversations did I have with my mother about it? What did I like about our communication? What would I have liked to be different?

What do I know of my mother's experience of puberty and menstruation as a girl?

What were my family's and my community's attitudes and practices around menstruation when I was a girl? What effect did they have on me? What, if anything, would have better met my needs at that time?

Understanding our communities' current attitudes lets us examine how they do or don't fit with and support our own values. We can ask:

What views of puberty and menstruation are prevalent nowadays?

In my community (and my daughter's community), in what ways, if any, is shame, weakness, or separation associated with menstruation?

In what ways, if any, is power, knowledge, or belonging associated?

What connotations do I want becoming a woman and women's cycles to have for my daughter?

A great by-product of spending a year teaching our daughters a more affirming story of becoming a woman than the one we learned as early adolescents is that moms come to believe it more deeply ourselves. Telling first period stories in our mothers' group was poignant.

"Here's how I learned about menstruation," said Maisie. "When I was twelve, the week before I went away to summer camp, my dad got out this book of frog anatomy, you know the kind with the transparent pages? And he showed me a picture of a frog's reproductive system."

"Your dad?" asked Phoebe.

"Yep."

"Are you sure it was a frog's reproductive system?"

"Yes, *frog*," said Maisie. "And he was like, 'So, when you're at camp, this might happen to you.' I didn't have a *clue* what he was talking about. The way I learned about periods was that another girl at camp got hers. She was all upset and crying. The counselors told her that she would have to shower more so she wouldn't smell and wear pads so she wouldn't get blood all over. When I got my own period, there weren't any pads in our house. I tried to use a tampon, but it hurt like hell, so I just made my own pads by rolling toilet paper around my hand and putting it in my underwear."

Katy was the last to share. "Well, despite having *three* older sisters, there was absolutely no sign that anyone in my family was ever menstruating. When I was nine I saw this book on my big sister's shelf, *The Facts of Life.* So that's how I found out." She paused. "Then in junior high, all my friends got their periods before me. Bathroom time was everyone showing off their blood to each other on pads."

"That's intense," said Sarah.

"It was this big important way to belong," Katy continued, "and I didn't have mine yet. So, when I was thirteen, I brought in a little bottle of red food coloring and put some on a pad to show my friends. That's how I resolved the dilemma."

"Very creative," said Sarah.

"You know, I've never thought about it that way—I've always kind of felt like a cheat. But it was pretty creative!" Katy laughed.

Bit by bit, sharing the stories of our own puberties while developing honest and empowering activities for our girls dissolved the shame that we had all felt in our youth.

Celebrating Natural Cycles

Tides ebbing and flowing, days growing shorter and longer, sap rising in the spring—the rhythmic cycles of nature are all around us, and any of them can be used to symbolize the cycles of women's bodies. The connection of the moon's monthly waxing and waning to women's monthly cycles is particularly fertile ground for instilling girls with the knowledge that women's cycles are also beautiful and completely natural, and inspired our mother-daughter group's year of fun and easy-to-do activities for nine-year-olds. (The moon's twenty-nine-day cycle of nighttime light and darkness actually contributed to the biological evolution of the human twenty-eight-day fertility cycle of ovulation and menstruation.)

You can start by investigating and celebrating the moon and its cycles without ever mentioning puberty. Gradually, focus more directly on women's bodies and rhythms and then discuss the practical aspects of menstruation. Finally, it is uplifting to conclude the year with a ceremony celebrating a girl's readiness to become a woman whenever her time comes.

Reclaiming moon wisdom. Most nine-year-olds are interested in the stars in the sky, and they also like solving riddles. Since a basic awareness of the lunar cycle fell out of common knowledge with the advent of electric lights, rediscovering the patterns of the moon feels like magical wisdom to girls. To start your explorations of the lunar cycle, figure out the riddles in the following poem together with your daughter. She'll love it if she's quicker than you. You can take a book on the moon or the solar system out of the library to aid you. Mother-daughter groups can do this activity at the first meeting of the year. After solving the riddles, have a find-the-moon picnic.

HOW TO FIND THE MOON

From east to west I make my way,
Just like the sun I rise,
But I delay an hour a day
My dance across the skies.

To find the youngest crescent moon,
Look west when day is done.
The baby moon sleeps in her spoon
And follows home the sun.

To find the waxing quarter moon,
At dusk look overhead.
The maiden moon gets up at noon,
At midnight goes to bed.

To find the moon that's full and bright,
At sunset watch the east.

The mother's light will shine all night,
And set when dark has ceased.

But never look in evening skies
To find the waning moon.
The moon that's wise will midnight rise
And go to bed at noon.[2]

Answers to each stanza:

1. The moon rises in the east about an hour (fifty-one minutes) later each night, travels across the sky, and sets in the west.

2. The young crescent moon rises in the morning about two hours after the sun and trails the sun across the sky all day, but can only be seen after the sun sets, looking like a spoon in the west for about an hour until it, too, sets.

3. The waxing first quarter or maiden moon rises in the east at about noon, and can often be seen in the eastern afternoon sky. It is overhead at sunset and sets in the west around midnight.

4. The full moon is easy: It rises in the east at sunset, crosses the sky all night, and sets in the west at dawn.

5. The waning quarter moon, or wise moon, rises at about midnight (which is why it can't be seen in the evening), is overhead at dawn, and can be seen in the western sky in the morning.

Find-the-moon picnics. It is a big adventure for girls to be outside at night and they love going on find-the-moon picnics, especially if other girls are invited. Most neighborhoods offer a view of at least one phase of the moon at sunset over the course of a month. (Check the newspaper or Internet for the exact time the moon rises in your local area and plan accordingly.) As you embark on your picnic, invite your daughter or the girls in the group to figure out where to look for the moon in the sky. You can then spread out a blanket and eat dinner by moonlight in your backyard or park or head back inside, lower the lights, and have an indoor picnic. Girls love coming up with types of food to bring that remind them of the moon, perhaps baguette rounds with cheese, round and crescent-shaped cookies, apple slices, quesadillas, and croissants.

Moon goddesses and heroines. Every culture has their own: Artemis from Ancient Greece, Chang'e from China, Ix Chel from the Mayan people of Mexico, Kaguya-hime from Japan, Mama Quilla from Peru, Rhiannon from Wales, Yolkai Estan from the Diné (Navajo) people of North America. Most libraries house collections of myths and stories from around the world, which you can use to research moon goddesses with your daughter. It's particularly fun to read or retell them gathered around a fire or by candlelight, and girls also enjoy making up their own moon stories.

Creating Beautiful Knowledge "In Every Sense"

Girls learn in many ways, and nine-year-olds respond to lessons that are rich and sensory. As we begin to teach our daughters more specific lessons about female cycles, we use taste, touch, smell, sight, and movement in order to deeply instill pro-girl and pro-woman knowledge about female cycles. We have learned from our work with girls of all ages involved with the Mother-Daughter Project that the more vividly information can be presented the better chance it has to counter the negative portrayals of women's bodies and cycles to which girls will eventually be exposed.

Bountiful anatomy. Making a figure of a woman or Mother Earth of fruits, vegetables, and flowers is a tasty and colorful way to convey female anatomy. This is a lovely activity to do when local farms or gardens are in full harvest. Start the day with an outing to a farm stand or urban greenmarket if there is one nearby, but a trip to the supermarket is just fine. In a mother-daughter group, have everyone bring a small bag of their favorite fruit, vegetables, or flowers to the meeting. Moms can help daughters cut the produce into interesting shapes, and using fingers and toothpicks, cocreate a female figure on a large platter or cutting board. Anything goes! We have made a face of peeled cantaloupe with blueberry eyes, green grape hair, and red pepper lips. Mothers can lead an anatomy lesson by cutting an orange in half for breasts, and nine-year-old girls will spontaneously pop on raspberry nipples. You can, if you choose, use various pieces of fruit to introduce female reproductive organs, including the uterus, fallopian tubes, vagina, vulva, and clitoris. This positive and playful spin on the female body will consciously or subconsciously stay with your daughter for a lifetime. After you're done, be sure to take pictures, then enjoy a healthy feast.

The Moon Dance of the Body. Creating a dance where mothers and daughters each assume the role of a different hormone or aspect of the female body and then move through the monthly cycle is a sure way for daughters to learn the specifics of the reproductive cycle. (If you are in a mother-daughter group, this might be an activity to assign to one or two of the more theatrical moms in the group.)

Designate the center of the room as the uterus. Two girls or moms stand on either side, representing the ovaries, each holding a package of flower seeds (or carton of eggs—if you dare), while two others stand face-to-face and make a "gateway" with their arms to represent the cervix. One girl plays the Moon, another plays the hormones, and everyone else sits quietly on the floor, holding red and pink scarves, representing the lining of the uterus (the blood). Begin by singing a soft song you all know or play quiet music. The Moon and hormones dance around the ovaries for a minute or two and then choose one to release an egg (take a seed out of the package) and give it to them. Then they tell the girls and moms on the floor to wave their scarves gently, gradually stand up, and carefully pass the seed among them. Now switch to a lively song or music, and encourage the girls to dance around more exuberantly and wave their scarves—nine-year-olds love this—until the Moon says, "Fly out into the world!" and all the dancers run out through the cervix, one of them carrying the seed.

When our mother-daughter group did this activity, the nine-year-olds and their mothers were enthusiastic participants, dancing, singing, and waving silk scarves. After the first run-through the girls immediately asked to do it again. April, who had been an ovary the first time, begged to be the Moon, Vanessa wanted to be the "gateway-thingy" ("Cervix," corrected Sarah, the nurse), Gabriella wanted to be hormones, and Maggie called out, "Who wants to be blood? It's fun being blood!" prompting Amy and Marisol to take the red and pink scarves from her as she picked up the package of seeds. We shared another cycle of the Moon waxing to full, the hormones dancing, the ovary releasing an egg into the care of the uterus, the Moon waning, the blood in the uterus dancing more and more wildly, then flying out into the world through the cervix. (A script for the Moon Dance of the Body can be found in the appendix.)

Talking About Menstruation

After about half a year spent learning about and celebrating nature's cycles and the female body, girls will be ready for practical information. It's time to break out some pads and tampons for your daughter to examine and listen to first period stories from grown-up women. We suggest alternating more explicit lessons about menstruation during this year with outings and activities that nine-year-olds adore, such as a trip to a zoo or nature center, or a make-your-own ice cream sundae party.

Addressing the topic of menstruation in the company of other mothers (or women friends or relatives) enriches the experience. Daughters benefit from hearing first period and how-to-deal-with-menstrual-emergencies stories from their own mothers, but other women add valuable perspectives. While you might breeze through your period cramp free, another mother may wish she could take a day off of work every month to cuddle a hot water bottle in bed—and so may your daughter.

You can certainly introduce your daughter to menstrual paraphernalia on your own, but having a group of girls checking out tampons and pads together can lighten the event considerably. In our group, Maisie first taught the girls how to make her emergency pad out of toilet paper. Phoebe then unwrapped a tampon to show the girls and described how to use the applicator to insert it. The girls weren't the slightest bit inhibited and immediately began firing tampon rockets all over Sarah's living room, seeing whose could go the farthest. Once the adults had corralled them around the kitchen table, Sarah provided glasses of water with a few drops of red food coloring for them to experiment with. The girls looked like little mad scientists testing the tampons' absorbency by dipping them into the solution and watching them swell. Whispering and giggling, they then went en masse into the bathroom to try on the pads, emerging with smug smiles and sideways glances. In teaching a subject most of our mothers barely spoke of with us, we were all glad to have the support of other mothers, although at age nine, your daughter will probably be quite matter-of-fact about discussing the practicalities of menstruation one-on-one.

Creating a Ceremony to Celebrate Menarche—Ahead of Time

We imagined that our mother-daughter group would celebrate each girls' first period with a ceremony, but we discovered that when the time arrived a few years later, our newly self-conscious preteens and teenagers wanted absolute privacy. Amy, for instance, wrote a formal letter to her mother when she got her period at age thirteen, and wouldn't allow either of her parents to explicitly refer to periods or pads until she was sixteen. A ceremony to honor getting their periods? What could be worse?! Unless a girl is part of a culture with long-established menarche ceremonies (which is quite rare today), it is unlikely that she will want any kind of community celebration when she gets her first period, even with just close friends or her mother-daughter group. Instead, we recommend that after your year of studying cycles, you hold a ceremony *then*, as Phoebe and Katy did for their younger daughters' group, to honor their knowledge, maturity, and readiness for menarche. (If your daughter happens to be open to a celebration when she actually gets her period, then by all means, have one.)

The girls' ceremony was held on a perfect sunny June morning in a private backyard surrounded by trees. Dressed in self-chosen celebratory clothes of red and pink and purple, the girls brought strawberries, cherries, watermelon balls, jars of cranberry-raspberry juice, deviled eggs, cookies, and cream puffs for the feast afterward. Under the shade of a large willow tree, the mothers and daughters wove flowers together to make crowns. When they were all ready to begin, someone took a formal photo of them together with their mothers—"like a wedding . . ." the girls proudly whispered to one another.

To begin, one of the mothers said, "We gather today to honor our daughters and their year of studying cycles. We know that girls often want to celebrate their first periods in private, so today we honor you all together to celebrate that each of you knows everything you need to know to be ready whenever your period arrives." After toasting one another and singing "River," one of the group's favorite songs, it was time to name and thank their ancestors.

"I wish to honor my mother, Amelia, and my grandmother Elizabeth," said Katy. Her daughter Kaili, now ten, said, "I wish to honor my mother, Katy, my grandma Amelia, my abuela Rosa, and my great-grandmother Elizabeth." One at a time, shyly, but with increasing confidence, women and girls named their maternal relatives.

The mothers distributed lovely purple bags for the girls to bring home and open when they got first periods. Then each mother-daughter pair brought out a symbolic gift to add. Kaili and Katy gave tiny origami cranes that flew on a thread above twenty-eight translucent pink beads, with a large faux pearl that looked like the moon hanging at the bottom. Kaili gave one to each girl, who received it solemnly. Phoebe and Eliza went last. "We have two things. First, this," Eliza said, holding up a small gold mesh bag filled with round white seeds. "These are seeds of the moonflower, so you can plant a moonflower when you get your period if you want. And here is this," she said, holding up a small red bag. She opened the drawstring and pulled out a red silk scarf. She then gave each of the girls their seeds and scarf. The mothers sighed and beamed as they watched their young daughters, with long gangly legs and big feet, no hips or breasts yet, and flowers in their hair, running about with their red silk scarves that caught the breeze, fluttering, waving.

....

You can plan a ceremony yourself with female friends or relatives or a mother-daughter group. Nine- and ten-year-olds thrive on adults' and peers' attention, and they generally love being crowned with flowers, honored in special rituals, and plied with gifts for whatever reason. Mothers and daughters can spend a whole afternoon planning an event that suits them.

The more "serious" the ceremony, the more powerfully it will give your daughter a sense of pride about growing up and becoming a woman. Your group can decide on what to call the ceremony, what to wear, where to meet, who will come (just the group, or family and friends, too?) and what kinds of foods to bring. In the planning stages, you can write a collective letter of congratulations and place it in fancy envelopes. On the day of the ceremony, be sure to have cameras and tissues handy—has your girl ever looked more beautiful?

Does this mean our daughters will now all feel perfectly comfortable getting their periods? Absolutely not. Some of them, maybe your girl, will feel embarrassed and hide the evidence, despite your best attempts to introduce her to the changes in her body in the most positive way you can. However, the girl-friendly knowledge you impart will be a resource she can always draw upon. In only a couple of hours a month, moms and daughters can recast the story of women's biological cycles. Intergenerational bonds are strengthened, and snacks are included.

The conversations you have with your preteen daughter about menstruation not only prepare her for puberty, but also lay a solid foundation for good communication about the challenging topics of body image and sexuality in the years just ahead.

CHAPTER TEN

Learning to Love Our Bodies

Ten Years Old—Capable and Outspoken

Most ten-year-old girls live *in* their bodies. They know what their bodies can do and are proud of it. Their gross motor skills are well developed, and girls this age eagerly show the adults in their life if they can do a handstand or perform a sequence of the latest dance moves. Although ten-year-olds will beg to spend much of their free time with friends, they are generally content hanging out with their families at home.

At school, boy-girl dynamics are in a transitional phase, moving from the tendency to socialize with the same gender at eight or nine to the genuine interest and crushes of eleven or twelve. Although they may start mimicking older kids and talk about who is "going out," it's rare that a boy and girl of ten would do much more than fast dance together or hold hands. In the classroom, ten-year-old girls, as a group, are uninhibited intellectually and outspoken about their views. They make curious, energetic companions on road trips or museum outings, and often have a lot to share with parents about geography and history. At the same time, they are open to learning from their mothers (and fathers). Because their fine motor skills are also well tuned, if mom enjoys cooking, sewing, crafts, carpentry, or gardening, this is a time when domestic arts can flourish.

By eleven, girls' gaze begins to turn inward and they start

looking *at* their bodies, often critically. They wonder, *What is my body* supposed *to look like?* It's an especially tough question for a girl of this age, because the physical changes of puberty are unpredictable. At eleven or so, some girls shoot up and become temporarily tall and thin relative to their peers, while others gain weight before they gain height. Both body types can make a girl feel out of sync and self-conscious. Breasts may be completely absent or voluptuously present, seemingly overnight. The suddenness of these changes can make her feel physically awkward and cause her to see her normal, growing body as "fat." Moreover, she is beginning to take stock of her strengths and weaknesses, comparing them with what her parents, teachers, friends, and the wider world prizes. One thing she commonly discovers by this age is that popular culture prizes one particular female body type.

Being skinny is *the* most important attribute of today's Perfect Girl. A girl may be athletic, kind, and intelligent; she may even have gorgeous hair, teeth, and skin, but if she's not thin, she will likely feel she's not measuring up. While thin has been "in" since the 1960s era of Twiggy, the glamorization of the skeletal body type has reached a new height in the 2000s. While some celebrity rags and fashion magazines cry occasional crocodile tears over the parade of anorexic or near-anorexic actresses, models, singers, and heiresses that slink across their pages, much more editorial space is devoted to extolling their beauty and chic. When the vast majority of female icons are underweight and every log-on to e-mail flashes a picture of the latest überthin female celeb, it's virtually impossible to avoid the message that being ultraskinny equals success and recognition. In the United States today, it is rare to find a young woman (or adult woman) who is completely at ease with her weight.

At eleven and twelve, girls are combining self-scrutiny with their ongoing desire for mastery—making them especially susceptible to believing that their bodies should conform to prevailing standards of thinness. Like using correct spelling in a book report, executing a perfect *tour jeté,* or maintaining composure in front of their friends when they fall off their bikes, they want to get things "right"—including their physical appearance. They are still immature and their expectations for themselves are often unrealistic and extreme. A girl may think she's terrible at math because she got 75 percent on a quiz instead of her usual 94 percent or believe she's World Cup material after scoring a goal in soccer. When her favorite uncle says she's "pretty," she may fantasize about becoming a model. If the flesh on her thighs spreads out when she sits on a chair, she thinks she's overweight. It is critical to support our daughters' body image and teach them healthy eating habits before they become teens when self scrutiny becomes even more intense, and they become highly conscious of how others look at or "rate" them. (It's worth noting that even sophisticated college women who are able to deconstruct and analyze the anorexic ideal in theory can still be victims of eating disorders. Imagine what this means for girls as young as eleven or twelve.)

The good news is that at ten years old, most girls are still questioning intensely, speaking their minds, and open to rejecting the dictates of the Perfect Girl if they are proven to be false (or as a ten-year-old girl might say, "stupid"). Even if they act the part of an adolescent on occasion, most have not yet been seriously drawn into teen culture. Ten years old is a great time to encourage them to love themselves and appreciate the beauty of every body type, and also to convey that the message "thinness equals goodness" is indeed stupid.

Diet Traps

Be aware that reduced calorie diets are dangerous for growing girls and young women. Restricting calories not only leads to fatigue, irritability, depression, impaired brain development, learning problems in school, and brittle bones, it has been long established to be completely ineffective in leading to long-term weight loss, and, in fact, may actually contribute to overeating and obesity.[1] The greatest danger of calorie-restricted diets, however, is that they can lead to debilitating and life-threatening eating disorders that girls are most at risk for developing between the ages of twelve and twenty. While not every diet turns into a full-fledged eating disorder, eating too little affects girls' minds as well as their bodies, leading them to obsess even more about their supposed imperfections. At the same time, girls who are visibly losing weight almost always receive a great deal of positive attention spurring them to diet more. It is very difficult to diet excessively, so girls who manage to keep going become completely preoccupied with resisting cravings or burning calories, and food becomes their dominant waking thought. The idea of eating/not eating takes on huge significance: Food is evil, fat is evil, I'm bad because I ate something.

When Katy's daughter Marisol was thirteen, her best friend, Jasmine, developed anorexia. Previously robust, curvy, and of average weight like Marisol, over the course of six months, Jasmine shrank to her prepubescent weight and stopped menstruating as she increasingly limited what and how much she ate. When she had dinner at Marisol's house, everyone else at the table ate their fresh sweet corn from the cob, while Jasmine sliced hers off with a knife, pushed the kernels around her plate, and only nibbled at a few leaves of romaine lettuce and a sliver of roasted chicken. Katy was worried both for Jasmine and for Marisol, who was a similarly studious, cooperative girl. Marisol had always loved to eat her mother's home-cooked meals of fresh vegetables, lean meats, whole grains, and occasional apple pies, but Katy knew that anorexia could trap any girl, especially if her best friend was already in its clutches. As Jasmine's weight continued to drop, Katy noticed that Marisol seemed increasingly stressed when Jasmine was around, and had started making disparaging remarks about her own body. One day, Marisol came to Katy, asking what she could do to help Jasmine. Katy wasn't completely sure herself and suggested that they bring it up at the next mom-daughter meeting.

The group listened to Marisol's concerns about Jasmine and brainstormed solutions. They concurred that the most important job of a friend was to be loving and caring, and that the most helpful thing Marisol could do was to be an example to Jasmine that it's possible to be happy while eating well, free of anorexia's rules and requirements. Marisol brightened immediately and said, "I'm already doing that!" Characterizing healthy eating as the generous act of a good friend offers a girl a powerful alternative to misguidedly thinking she should join her friend in undereating. They also supported Katy's decision to call Jasmine's parents and let them know that she and Marisol were worried about Jasmine.

At moms-only time, Katy said she had noticed that Marisol was making critical remarks about herself. She also told the group that Marisol had said that when she looked in the mirror she looked out of shape compared to Jasmine and she wanted to get rid of the mirrors in the house. At the time, Katy had been taken aback by the magnitude of her daughter's suggestion, but talking with the other moms made her realize that Marisol was getting drawn into the self-judging mind-set of anorexia and that she needed to take dramatic action. The next morning, she and Marisol took down all the full-length mirrors in the house. Marisol found it much less stressful to step out of the shower without having to look at every detail of her naked body revealed in a full-length mirror, and so did Katy.

Katy called Jasmine's parents and was relieved to find that she was already under a doctor's care. It's not easy informing another child's parents about a potential eating disorder or other problem like smoking, drinking, or doing drugs, and it's hard to predict whether the information will be met with gratitude or anger. Using I-statements such as "Marisol and I have been noticing that Jasmine has been undereating at our house and felt morally obligated to inform you in case she had managed to hide this from you. We would be reassured if we knew that her pediatrician was aware of her dramatic weight loss. . . ." frames the call as one of concern instead of judgment.

After learning that Jasmine did have an eating disorder, Marisol committed herself to eating and exercising healthfully and spent time with her friend almost every day. It took three years for Jasmine to fully recover, but now, at seventeen, she and Marisol are still close friends who can enjoy eating an ice-cream cone together on a hot day.

Anorexia and bulimia steal girls' spirits. When mothers and daughters are able to be close in adolescence, they can help their daughters fight eating disorders. Girls with eating disorders become lost in the wilderness of their condition. The same holds for girls who are depressed, become addicted to drugs or alcohol, or who enter an abusive relationship. Mothers know their daughters' many wonderful qualities perhaps better than anyone else. They can offer encouragement when their daughter feels like a failure, and they can hold on to a vision of their daughter's true self and keep it intact while they take steps to help her resist and return.[2] We strongly recommend speaking with your daughter's pediatrician if you suspect your daughter might be suffering from an eating disorder.

As mothers, we want to protect our daughters from problems related to eating disorders and having a distorted body image. However, research reveals that, ironically, teaching girls directly about anorexia and bulimia makes them more likely to engage in those behaviors.[3] While researchers are still unsure of exactly why this is, anorexia experts speculate that discussing the details of eating disorders with girls actually provides them with ideas for how to purge, restrict calories, or overexercise. It is common for anorexia and bulimia to spread like fire through a group of girls or women. In this context, it is particularly chilling that there are a number of pro-anorexia Web sites today where girls and women swap diet and purging tips, share extreme weight loss goals, and trade images of skeletal movie

stars. Luckily, there are also *anti*-anorexia Web sites, such as www
.narrativeapproaches.com, that inspire resistance to the lies of
anorexia and bulimia.

As if our work weren't hard enough, childhood obesity is epi-
demic in the United States, and an unprecedented number of
girls today are also at risk of becoming overweight from seden-
tary lifestyles and too much junk food. Many girls get little or no
exercise, spending their free time IM'ing their friends or sitting
in front of the TV. Fast food franchises in our neighborhoods
and local convenience stores stuffed with sugary, fatty snacks
mean that the foods most readily available to our families are often low in nutritional value and high in calories. The unrealistic
ideal of the stick-thin Perfect Girl can make normal girls feel like
failures, and sometimes they overeat junk food to comfort themselves, then consequently gain weight in a vicious cycle. Lack of
exercise makes it that much harder to maintain a healthy weight.

So how do we successfully promote body health for girls despite all the complications? At the Mother-Daughter Project, we
start by teaching our young daughters that good health comes
from how a girl or woman feels in her body and how she takes
care of it, not what her body looks like. Our different genes mean
that different body types are healthy for each of us, short or tall,
voluptuous or lean. Just like taking good care of our feet does not
mean trying to shove them into shoes that are far too small, taking good care of our bodies does not mean trying to make them
all match the same superthin ideal.

However, it can be extremely difficult for a larger girl to feel
good about herself. Discrimination is real and hurtful. We can
support girls who are facing stigmatization because they are
heavy, not by telling them to change their bodies, but by
teaching them that "Every Body Is Beautiful." The campaign
starts at home. Replace fashion magazines with subscriptions to
New Moon: The Magazine for Girls and Their Dreams. Put up art
that features voluptuous female bodies. Watch movies or television programs featuring the actresses Kathy Bates, Katherine

Mansfield, Queen Latifah, or other fabulous full-figured women.

To promote a healthful lifestyle and eating habits, turn off the TV and go out and exercise with your daughter. Get rid of junk food snacks, fill the fridge with healthier food (like whole wheat bread and crackers, low-fat milk, cheese, and yogurt, precut veggies, sliced lean deli meats, dried fruit and nuts), put a bowl of fruit on the counter, and let your daughter eat as much as she wants. Children and teenagers may complain for a couple of days when they can't find their favorite chips, cookies, or soda on the shelf, but they will soon adjust and at home, at least, will eat reasonable portions of the nourishing food that is available to them.

Most girls and women who are full-figured and live healthy lifestyles are manifesting a body type that has a specific ancestral source usually from a culture that revered larger women. Scouting out one's heritage and finding others with similar body types can make a huge difference in promoting self-esteem. In *Women Who Run with the Wolves*, Jungian psychologist and storyteller Clarissa Pinkola Estés, herself a large woman, described how empowering it was to find her ancestral kin in Tehuantepec, Mexico: "Who lo! were a tribe of giant women who were strong, flirtatious, and commanding in their size. They patted me and plucked at me, boldly remarking that I was not quite fat enough. Did I eat enough? Had I been ill? I must try harder, they explained, for women are La Tierra, made round like the earth herself."[4]

Mothers Provide a Powerful Model of Body Love

Is there any topic more loaded for us women than our appearance? In order to help our daughters as they encounter unrealistic expectations of female beauty and make it into adulthood as strong, healthy women, it is vitally important for us to understand our feelings about our own bodies. There are no shortcuts on this one! Girls learn from the behavior and attitudes we adults model. How many of us complain about our weight? Many women are stuck on the diet wagon. Maybe getting physical exercise means a quick trot through the grocery store. We also worry about having a "bad hair day," whether our breasts are too large or too small, whether it's time for botox or liposuction. The list goes on and on. Sometimes it can be really hard to think of something positive to say about our own bodies, but you can start by remembering that it was your body that allowed you to be your daughter's mother. As Katy once said, "I appreciate that my body gave me Marisol and Kaili . . . and it feels good that my girls can come to me for a warm, soft hug when they need to."

Some useful questions to get you thinking about body image and body health issues include:

Can I think of and describe a time when I felt good in my body as a young girl? As a teenager?

In what way did I experience my body negatively?

How did attitudes about girls' bodies of the people and culture around me affect my experiences of my body?

Understanding our mothers helps us understand ourselves. We can ask:

How did my mother experience her body as a girl? As a woman?

What expectations about bodies was she trying to live up to or resist?

How did she feel about my body when I was a girl? When I hit puberty?

How did her experiences and feelings affect me?

Likewise, how we feel about our bodies today doesn't just affect us, it affects our daughters, too. Our girls are always watching and learning from us—the positives and the negatives. As women and as mothers we can ask:

Nowadays, when do I feel best in my body?

Who or what supports me in experiencing my body in a positive way?

Which body expectations do I put the most energy into trying to live up to or to resist?

What challenges do I face in loving my body? What helps me overcome those challenges?

What do I appreciate about my body?

What kind of support do I need to not criticize my body, or other women's bodies, in front of my daughter?

Clarifying our hopes and concerns for our daughters guides us in guiding them. To be able to support our daughter's body image and health, it helps to know what we want for her and what she is up against. We can ask ourselves:

When does my daughter seem to feel best in her body?

What are my hopes for her body health? For how she feels about her body?

What worries me about her body health? About how she feels about her body?

What expectations of what her body "should" be like are influencing her? Are influencing me?

Supporting Body Love and Health
Through Mother-Daughter Activities

A sensory, positive approach is needed to teach girls to love and care for their bodies and to feel beautiful and lovable. In our year of Mother-Daughter Project activities, we celebrate everything good about girls' and women's bodies: feeling good physically, being strong and capable, enjoying delicious food, feeling comfortable and beautiful in our bodies, and creating diverse images of female beauty. Once we have a thorough grounding in positive body experiences, we then critically investigate the ways in which commercial media try to lead girls and women to feel bad about their bodies—and think about what we can do about it.

Feeling good in our bodies. Together, you and your daughter can share activities that make you feel good in your bodies. The possibilities are endless: exchanging foot rubs, swimming, yoga, swinging in a hammock, playing Frisbee, climbing monkey bars, snuggling together under a blanket with books, soaking in a hot tub, doing an at-home facial or pedicure. Nothing beats feeling comfortable and relaxed in our bodies for promoting body love. Trade off doing something she loves with introducing her to something you love. Ten-year-olds are happy to try new things. Together you can find a feel-good activity you both enjoy and make it a regular practice in your lives, promoting body love and mother-daughter connection at the same time. It's twice as fun if you have a friend of yours and a pal of hers join you. In a mother-daughter group, each girl and mom can take turns sharing a favorite feel-good activity with the group.

Being strong in our bodies. Feeling strong and capable in her body lets your girl focus on and appreciate what her body can *do*, not just what it looks like. We all know exercise and athletics are good for girls. It has been well documented that girls who engage in sports during adolescence have higher self-esteem, lower pregnancy rates, and lower levels of drug and alcohol use. But your daughter doesn't need to be part of an organized team to reap the benefits of having a fit, healthy body. Tennis, hiking, canoeing, karate, swimming, biking, dancing, walking—what makes her feel strong in her body? What makes you feel strong? Share these activities with her. A group of mothers and daughters can take turns introducing the group to their favorites, or try out new things together. For example, our group hired the sensei at a woman-run karate dojo to spend a few hours teaching them all the basics of self-defense. Another mother taught the group yoga, while another organized a hike.

Feeding our bodies. Once in a while, plan some mother-daughter time to savor a delicious, well-balanced meal. Decide what you both love to eat, and how that fits into a healthy diet. If you like to cook or bake, most ten-year-olds will be thrilled to cook or bake with you; otherwise, find a restaurant with delectable food and pleasant surroundings, and your daughter will be honored to join you for a special night out. It doesn't have to be fancy or expensive. Mother-daughter groups can cook or bake together, eat out at a yummy, casual restaurant, or create a scrumptious meal by potluck.

Seeing and celebrating real bodies. As you relax together on the beach or at the public pool, your daughter gets a chance to see real women's bodies up close. Reality is a potent antidote to the airbrushed, digitally slenderized images of models and actresses she sees on the computer and TV screens in your home and at the movies. At ten, your daughter is still learning what's real and what's fiction, and it helps her have an accurate perspective about her own body to know that healthy bodies come in all shapes and sizes, not just a skeletal one-size-fits-all. In a mom-daughter group, girls look up to the grown women, and when they see you putting on a bathing suit and living comfortably in your bodies, it helps them to be comfortable in their bodies, too. Don't worry, you don't have to *feel* 100 percent positive about your body to do this—the important thing is to be willing to put on a swimsuit or shorts and join your daughter in some fun, physical activity *without criticizing your body or the bodies of other girls or women.* Even if you feel ill at ease and want to say, "I hate how fat my thighs look," it is important to restrain yourself. Instead, remark to your daughter how good it feels to lie in the sun or soak in a hot tub. Later, with other women, you can get support for how hard it is not to complain about your body. It bears repeating: Make a practice of *never* criticizing your body in front of your daughter (in speech or in action), and guide her not to criticize others' bodies. If she says to you, as happened to Phoebe one day at the beach, "Why does your belly stick out like that?" you can say to her, "Honey, this is what a woman's body is like." Find opportunities to tell your daughter and her friends (and *your* friends) that they are beautiful. Far from leading to overfocus on appearance, your regular, low-key compliments will give them confidence and help them resist critical self-scrutiny.

In addition, point out to her positive representations of women in the media, such as the advertisements for Dove soap that feature real women with gorgeously real bodies. Take her to watch strong women playing sports (she'll probably have as much fun watching a high school volleyball match as going to a professional event) or flip through Jane Goltesman's tremendously inspiring book *Game Face: What Does a Female Athlete Look Like?*[5]

Creating your own images of beautiful bodies. Engage your girl in drawing, painting, or sculpting your own versions of female beauty. This helps you both move from being passive recipients of images created by others to being active creators with the authority to decide for yourselves what is beautiful. One way to expand your notions of feminine beauty (and avoid replicating high-fashion thinness) is to depict goddesses and other mythical women, those particular to your cultural heritage or favorite storybooks, or entirely new ones you make up. The more vivid and unusual the media, the more powerful your creations will be in replacing weak, pouting, emaciated images with strong, happy, beautiful girls and women. When Sarah and Maggie led this activity, they invited the other mothers and daughters for an afternoon at a lakeside beach. After some swimming and lounging around in the sun, Sarah and Maggie started making a mermaid sand sculpture, inviting everyone to help. The mothers and daughters all joined in scooping and patting the sand into place, giving their mermaid a gorgeous, voluptuous body. Girls scampered about gathering stones, flowers, and leaves, which they carefully arranged as eyes, earrings, necklace, and navel. When it came time to go home, mothers and daughters lingered to admire their creation as the late afternoon light fell across her generous belly and broad shoulders, deeply imprinting a nourishing image of female beauty in their memories.

Teaching Daughters to Take Apart Media Messages

After sharing experiences that make you feel good in your bodies, it's time to take on the ways that some images in the media can lead girls and women to feel bad about themselves. Ten-year-olds are able to engage in the critical thinking necessary to understand the following ideas, which are contained in the activities below:

1. Media messages aren't necessarily true, right, or good.

2. All media images are created by specific people for specific purposes, and you can decipher and decide if they fit with what you think is right and wrong.

3. You don't need to tolerate images or messages that make you feel bad.

Becoming skeptical and active participants in the creation of pop culture images and messages will help our daughters become savvier media consumers over the long run.

Exposing the intentions of advertisers. This lively role-playing game exposes the strategies and lies of the diet and fashion industry so that girls can better resist them. Ten-year-old girls are great truth-seekers and generally throw themselves into their parts with enthusiasm and aplomb. This activity works best with at least two moms and two girls, and it's even more fun with a bigger group. Start by dividing into two groups—investigative reporters, and executives marketing a new diet product. Girls can use props to help them get into character, like notebooks and pencils for the journalists and briefcases, legal pads, and pens for the corporate team.

Moms can help the reporters come up with questions like: What are your intentions? What are your hopes and goals for girls and women? How do those hopes match with girls' actual goals for themselves? What are your strategies to get women and girls interested in dieting? What other companies do you own, and how do you use those companies to support dieting? What worries you? What weakens you? Isn't it actually true that all bodies are beautiful? Isn't dieting dangerous for girls? Isn't it true that the only way to have a healthy body is to eat well and exercise? Isn't it true that happiness, success, and love have nothing to do with body size? Isn't it actually just as bad as racism or sexism to try to make girls and women feel bad if they are larger than average? Isn't it true that in cultures that admire voluptuous bodies, heavier people live just as long and are just as healthy as people who are thin?

Meanwhile, the executives design a marketing campaign for their diet product to maximize profits. (Ten-year-olds are great at thinking up ways to convince others that their "products" are fabulous.) To get started, you can outline to the girls the influence that corporations can have on creating opinions in the realms of medicine (for example, funding obesity studies but not studies that demonstrate the negative consequences of dieting), film (does the company own a movie studio?), beauty, public policy (who decides what's a healthy weight?), television (they may also own a TV network), and so on, as well as by regular advertising. You can also talk about ways that marketing campaigns are vulnerable: Fad and calorie-restrictive diets don't work in the long run, all bodies are beautiful, the only way to have a healthy body is to eat well and exercise, being thin will not make girls happy, and so on.

After some brainstorming, bring the groups together. Corporate executives then drink a pretend truth serum (neon blue sports drink poured from a cruet looks suitably ominous), the reporters pose their questions, and the fun begins! Afterward, talk about any new understandings of the tactics of the diet industry, and share a meal of some delicious food.

Changing media images to make girls feel good. Gather a range of the typical magazines that your girl might see at the supermarket or the dentist's office, and invite her to page through them, looking for images that make her feel happy and good about herself, and ones that she doesn't like. As you work, chat about who makes ads or publishes magazines and what their intentions are; for example nonprofits like New Moon or the Girl Scouts usually have an idea or value they are trying to promote, while for-profit publishers and companies, like *Teen Vogue* and the Gap want to sell things and make money.

Have your daughter create a wall of honor with the images that make her feel good. Then suggest she select an ad or image that makes her feel bad or seems disrespectful to girls or women. With scissors, glue, construction paper, and markers, she can change the image to one that makes her feel good. Alternatively, create a lively girl-positive jingle or make up a TV commercial that celebrates girls. This activity is fun to do with friends or in a mother-daughter group, working in pairs or individually. Everyone can share their creations, explaining why she does or doesn't like certain images, and how she changed them to be respectful and give her a positive feeling about being a girl or woman.

When Maisie led this activity, as moms and daughters paged through all kinds of magazines, the girls expressed their opinions with typical ten-year-old loudness. "Look at this!" shouted her daughter April, holding up an action shot of a teen surfer who returned to the sport with only one arm after being attacked by a shark. "That's inspiring!"

"Ugh!" Squeals and snorts came from the other end of the room. Three girls were looking at a picture of a scantily clad woman draped in a sexual pose over the hood of a car. "That's disgusting!"

"Why do you think there are images like that in ads?" Maisie asked.

"To catch our eyes," said Amy.

"Why does the person making the ad want to catch our eyes?" asked Sarah.

"So we'll notice what they want to sell," said Maggie.

"So they can make money," said Gabi.

"What do you think of using those kinds of images of women to make money?" said Maisie.

"I don't like it," said Maggie.

"Yeah," said Amy. "It doesn't have anything to do with cars."

We continued looking through the magazines for another five minutes and then split into groups to find pictures that made us feel good and change images or ads that were disrespectful or made us feel bad.

At sharing time, Gabi and Katy showed how they changed the image of the woman draped over the car. Gabi pointed to their new two-page spread as she explained, "Well, first we changed her head" (actually pasting another face right over the original) "because she didn't look happy, and then we gave her a new top, because she had on this really ugly cheetah bra. We decided we didn't like how skinny and weak she looked, so I drew a skirt and pasted it over her, and then we put rollerblades on her because we love to rollerblade." The original ad now was entirely covered with gluesticked replacement pictures that made us all feel happy.

The next image was even more difficult. Amy and Marisol showed an ad featuring six women in Playboy Bunny–like outfits crouched in metal rabbit cages, against one of which leaned a skateboard—the item the ad was selling. One woman looked like she was trying to bite the metal wire of her cage, while the others had docile expressions. Later, at mothers-only time we would share how shocked we were that our girls had found such an outrageous picture. However, at the time, we bit our tongues to see what they would say.

Marisol began, "We thought this was totally disgusting."

Amy added, "It's stupid, too, because what does this have to do with skateboarding? So here is what we did." And they launched into the commercial they had created, pretending to rocket into view on skateboards, two strong wild girls doing tricks and flips at the skateboard park, ending with a big hug and high five. We all cheered. It was a relief that the girls could hold their own against some of the nastiest pictures that the popular media could throw at them.

The time spent supporting a girl's body image at ten pays off when she becomes an adolescent. Although she would often rib her mom for being a die-hard feminist who criticized every ad she saw, when she was thirteen, Gabriella learned that it was eating disorders awareness week and sent her mom, Maisie, a card that said, "Thanks for being such a good role model against eating disorders." Among local teens, the girls from our group are notably comfortable in and with their bodies, participating in a large range of physical activities unconstrained by conventional body-type expectations. The summer they were seventeen, Maggie and Vanessa both stepped into swimsuits every day to work as lifeguards, and not once did their mothers hear them complain about how they looked, just how long their shifts were. Maggie performs African dance and Amy performs salsa, Gabi is an aspiring professional actress. Marisol swims three times a week, Vanessa works out at the Y, and April is a three-season athlete. As young women, the six are all strong and spirited, have never dieted, eat healthfully, enjoy their food, get a lot of exercise, and reflect the beauty of every body type, ranging from tall and curvy to gorgeously voluptuous to lean and athletic.

Strengthening your daughter's intrinsic girlhood appreciation of what makes her body feel good and how it is strong, capable, and uniquely beautiful supports her in resisting the glitzy million-dollar advertising campaigns that aim to make her insecure about her looks so she will buy more products. Teaching her to love and take care of her body and to be a critical media consumer will help her stay healthy and avoid sacrificing her dreams and desires on the altar of thinness as she makes her way into teen culture. Moreover, supporting her self-esteem, enjoying fun, healthy activities together, and showing respect for her growing analytical sophistication at age ten all set the stage for maintaining a sound mother-daughter connection during the turning point year of eleven.

CHAPTER ELEVEN

Hanging Out and Having Fun (Shhh!) with Mom

Eleven Years Old—In Transition

Eleven-year-old girls have a foot in two worlds. One minute the little girl snuggles next to us, chatty and happy. The next a surly teen appears, rolling her eyes and slamming doors. Some eleven-year-olds still play on the swings at recess, while others posture for the boys in the schoolyard. As the glitter of adolescence begins to call, the outside world enters their lives as never before. Many eleven-year-old girls avidly discuss clothes and fashion, the latest hit songs, and television shows with their friends. The voice of their peer group assumes more and more power.

In their relationship to parents and especially mom, girls this age still feel like children. With peers, they can test their self-confidence and budding maturity. They often feel a great allegiance to a group that they've chosen. According to the Girl Scouts Research Institute, the major issues of eleven- and twelve-year-olds are "wanting to be liked" and worries "about fitting in."[1] As we've discussed in the previous chapters, they're also in the midst of puberty *or* hyperaware that they're not—both states can exacerbate concerns about their place in the social scene and in the world at large.

Emotional vulnerability and the importance of membership are so critical that girls (and boys) need lots of reassurance that their friends still like them and want to be with them. They don't want to, in any way, appear uncool or immature, since that might jeopardize their social standing. It is useful to remember this when your eleven-year-old daughter freaks out over apparently inconsequential details like the color of her shoelaces or being asked to wear a hat at the beach. Be patient. Just as girls learned the skill of crossing a busy road when they were younger, they're now learning skills of group membership—how to get along with others, with less parental guidance than when they were younger. By the end of this period (eleven to twelve), they typically display more social poise and less frustration.

Girls are learning more about themselves as well: their likes and dislikes, their values and concerns, how they are similar to their mothers, and how they are different. They may be intensely critical of mom's appearance in a clumsy effort to distinguish themselves. At eleven, girls are figuring out whether being smart and competent is acceptable, or how athletic it's okay to be. Though this is a time when they may drop an activity that they loved doing the year before in an effort to assert their independence, if you can encourage them to stick with it, they will gain confidence as they increase their mastery of skills they've been acquiring for the past few years: perhaps athletic competence, playing a musical instrument, or excelling in academics.

Many girls will enter middle school at the end of this year, often leaving behind the safety of elementary school for an unknown, exciting, and sometimes frightening environment. If your daughter is one of the lucky ones whose elementary school continues through eighth grade, you may just have a bit more breathing room before adolescence arrives with a vengeance.

In two short years, our eleven-year-olds will be teens themselves—and don't think they don't know it! As they aspire toward that more grown-up world, what are they learning? The popular media commonly portray teens as rude, difficult, and dangerous. According to the Harvard School of Public Health's report *Raising Teens*, they're shown as "frightening . . . hostile, violent, delinquent, alienated from parents and families, and resistant to any assistance. Teenagers are depicted as perpetrators or victims of crime and violence, problem ridden, and disruptive, even more so for young people of color."[2] Eleven-year-olds pick up on this—and as teen culture is marketed to younger and younger children, we see even seven- and eight-year-olds swaggering rudely or posturing like sexy models.[3] You can send the message that real teenagers are perfectly capable of being kind, helpful, and caring.

Another widespread but false notion is that teens' relationships with their parents are inevitably troubled and stormy. Many movie and sitcom moms make mother-loathing seem appropriate, since they portray mothers as diabolical (*Desperate Housewives*), clueless (the mom in the otherwise mostly girl-positive movie *She's the Man*), or (incredibly often) dead (*Whale Rider, Stripes, Fly Away Home,* and a plethora of Disney cartoons from *Snow White* to *Bambi* to *Finding Nemo*). There are relatively few media portrayals of overtly positive mother-daughter relationships and smart, loving moms, though thankfully some do exist, such as in the movie (and book) *Cheaper by the Dozen*. With little experience for comparison, your daughter may take in the media presentation of teens as back-talking mother-haters as the model to aspire to, and if her similarly influenced circle of friends disparage their mothers among themselves or rudely talk back, your daughter is drawn further toward the idea that she is supposed to pull away and treat you with disdain, too.

But remember: She really doesn't want to pull away from or be mean to one of the people she loves most in the world (you); if she acts that way in a family that generally treats one another with love and courtesy, it's because she thinks that's what growing up means. In her attempts to act grown up you may see her try out the personae of both media-inspired teen-from-hell who throws you out of her room and family-inspired thoughtful teen who does the dinner dishes—alternating with little-girl behaviors, like playing with her favorite dolls and stuffed animals or asking you to tuck her into bed and read her a story.

Distance is not what eleven-year-olds need. They want to create a more grown-up identity that lets them find their own place in the world, but they don't need to disconnect from their mothers to do this. They often look outside their families for confirmation on how the world works, but they don't necessarily look far; the example of just one mother who is close to her daughter is enough to let your daughter know it is okay to love her mom. That's why this year we emphasize fostering mother-daughter connection through negotiation and mindful togetherness.

Staying Close While Increasing Freedom

It's good for moms and daughters to think about this period as a time of renegotiation. These days, eleven-year-olds tend to spend more time alone, often because parents are working and after-school activities aren't available.[4] They are also more reflective than when they were younger, and many enjoy writing in their journals in the privacy of their rooms. In addition, the big changes of puberty can make them feel tired and want to spend more time in bed napping or reading. Many girls and their parents believe they have the maturity to handle a couple of hours by themselves at home, but it's important to pair new rights with additional responsibilities. You can show your daughter that you respect that she is starting to grow up by negotiating these with her. New rights might be staying home by herself for a few hours, using the stove while you're in the house, working as a mother's helper for your neighbor or getting a paper route. Or maybe she can go by herself to a nearby shop, walk the dog, ride her bike or walk over to a friend's, get her own library card. She's also likely to want to have more overnights at friends' houses.

What privileges and responsibilities you allow her depends on many factors: the kind of neighborhood you live in, whether there are adult friends and neighbors looking out for your kids, how much risk you can personally tolerate for your daughter, and myriad others. Linking new rights, like choosing her own weekend bedtime, with new responsibilities, like waking herself up in the morning with an alarm clock, honors both these aspects of maturity and makes negotiations clearer and easier.

But how to ensure that her new privileges are safe, positive experiences? When eleven-year-olds are asked, *What makes you feel safe?* the vast majority define safety in terms of relationships: They feel safe when they trust the people they're around. "Family members are integral to feelings of safety, with mothers (76 percent) and fathers (60 percent) topping the list of relatives girls were with when they felt most safe."[5]

All children need to know their limits and will often test you to find out. You may begin hearing the proverbial *But Cleo's mom lets her go to the mall, hang out with friends, wear sexy clothes to school,* and so on. Whether they acquiesce easily or put up a fight, kids are (sometimes secretly) relieved to learn where the boundaries are—and that's as true at eleven as it is at seventeen. Remember that despite her posture of coolness, in reality, your daughter knows next to nothing about the wider world or even about teen culture, although she may think she does. She may believe you don't understand her because you don't know what it's like to be an aspiring teen, but when your daughter is eleven, the truth is, you know *more* about teen culture than she does. One valuable tactic is talking with other mothers about the choices they make. Calling the mother of your daughter's best friend and saying, "I'm concerned about Instant Messaging. What do you think?" opens up discussion about how to handle this new territory and verifies to our daughters that we aren't the *only* moms who set limits.

We want to help our girls retain the childlike parts of themselves while also encouraging their new growth. We want to give them enough freedom to develop their own identities, but not so much as to leave them feeling ungrounded or unsafe. While your daughter may already be pushing hard against you, trying to establish herself as her own individual, she also still wants to feel secure and loved. At times you may lose touch with the fact that you enjoy being together because so many interactions at this age involve setting safe boundaries, and the tension that inevitably comes with this push/pull. Consciously making some time focused on the two of you apart from the outside world strengthens your relationship and allows both of you to appreciate your continuing bond.

Play is children's work, a major vehicle for learning about the world and how they fit into it. Hanging out is an adolescent's form of play. Spending time with our daughters—"hanging out"—during this period sends a message that they can grow up and become more independent while still retaining the love and connection that sustain all of us. Supporting both independence and connection for your girl often means listening carefully to what's important to her and joining with her in activities. Simply hanging out together then becomes a way to foster her emotional safety.

Often, eleven-year-old girls take less initiative in wanting to do things with mom. You don't want to crowd your daughter's new desire for independence, but you can look for small opportunities to foster connection.

"I look for ways to join Maggie, since she's less interested in joining me. She enjoys physical activities, like Frisbee, so I'll ask her if she wants to play a game with me. Or this year when she was doing a school geography project, we looked at pictures of her trip to Europe with her dad and talked about the things she learned," Sarah reported at a moms' get-together when Maggie was eleven. At the same time, she supported Maggie's growing independence. "She likes to have more time by herself in the house. We live in a safe area, and she feels more confident being alone, so I've figured out ways to support that. After school, I might drop her off at home to make herself a snack and start her homework while I get to take a walk around the neighborhood."

In our most difficult moments with our daughters, we can temporarily forget that they still long for connection with us. When your daughter seems to be turning away from you, ask yourself:

How can I support my daughter's ability to feel she has some independence from me while maintaining a closeness that enables us to communicate?

What stresses may my daughter be experiencing that she's venting at me?

What supports do I need to help me negotiate this changing relationship with my daughter?

The following questions invite you to remember how your relationship with your own mother changed when you were a teen and to rearticulate your hopes for your relationship with your daughter now.

Can you remember a moment when you felt a close, loving connection to your mother at this age? Describe moments you most enjoyed with her.

What kinds of things did you like to do with your mom?

Was there a change in your relationship with your mother as you entered puberty?

What do you think your mother appreciated about you at this age?

What do you think your mother didn't understand about you at this age?

While it can be hard to take, an eleven-year-old's volatility is normal and a part of the process of her growing up. According to adolescent expert A. Rae Simpson, "A teenager or preteen who suddenly becomes more antagonistic is sometimes showing signs of important developmental changes. As with a toddler, high levels of conflicts in teens tend to be temporary."[6] In responding, we can be most helpful as mothers by expecting changeable moods and behaviors while articulating consistent values and expectations for our girls and letting them know they are loved. Simpson recommends that parents "take the emotional high ground by providing opportunities for closeness that teens can sometimes accept and sometimes reject."[7] What does "taking the high ground" look like in real life? When your eleven-year-old daughter throws her social studies book across the room and calls you the "stupidest mom in the world" you might try to respond by saying, "It's hard to write a whole report. However, I expect you to express your frustration in a way that doesn't involve throwing things or calling anyone stupid." Then leave the room. She may continue to act rudely, but you don't need to respond again; she heard your expectations for her behavior, and she wants to live up to them, even if she can't manage to at the moment.

Once you're alone, congratulate yourself on your efforts and intentions to interact with her in a helpful way—because doing so is hard and exhausting. It's much easier to get drawn into a fight or respond in a passive-aggressive way or simply withdraw. Ask yourself:

What do I need right now to be able to respond to my daughter in a calm and helpful way while she is upset and being rude?

The answers are different for each of us. Sometimes it's enough to simply remember the big picture of what is going on: She is hitting a developmental challenge that's hard for her and she feels overwhelmed or bad about herself and is taking it out on the person she feels safest with. Other times it helps to talk to a friend or do something personally restorative, like listen to music or go out for a walk somewhere pleasant.

Once you've filled your own well a bit, think about what would help your daughter remember that she is lovable and capable. Often it's helpful to make her something good to eat or drink (most eleven-year-olds are growing like crazy and are often hungry) and take it in to her without comment. With the snack, she gets the implicit message that you love and care about her, and she will feel enormously relieved. Then later, at a time when she is not upset and you are both more relaxed, talk about what has helped her deal with that kind of difficulty in the past. Ask her (in so many words):

Have you ever overcome that kind of difficulty before? (For example: Have you ever managed to do a really hard writing assignment before?)

How did you do it? Was anyone helpful to you then? Might something like that help now? In what way?

What kind of a plan makes sense to you? What can we do now to start putting that plan in place?

What can I do to be helpful?

Eleven-year-old girls like questions like these because they honor their growing problem-solving abilities and are respectful. Finally, at this calmer moment (or another), talk about what kind of relationship you want with each other now that she is growing up and ask her what she thinks makes a good mother-daughter relationship. This conversation may only last three minutes, but it's a powerful touchstone you can refer back to. When it's smooth and easy, like when she walks the dog while you run out for a video for you both to watch, you can say, "It's nice to see how we have the kind of cooperation and fun that we both want in our relationship!" When it's turbulent, like when she yells that she hates you for making her wash the dishes, you can say, "It's not okay to say you hate me. I'd like us to treat each other with the kindness we both want." Likewise, when *you* have a bad moment after a long day and harshly snap at her to put away her backpack, you can say, "I'm really sorry I snapped at you. That's not how I want to be with you. I know we both want to treat each other with kindness." Not only do you take the sting out of your snapping at her, you are also modeling how to apologize.

Maintaining Connection Through a Mother-Daughter Group

Staying connected to your daughter does take more effort these days, and if you already have a mom-daughter group, it will help a great deal. Perhaps you've been sailing along, enjoying the last few years of ease with your daughter, but now you sense a shift in the wind. Mothers of toddlers or preschoolers have regular opportunities for connection with other mothers as they arrange playdates or pick kids up from preschool, for example. By elementary school those opportunities are diminishing. By middle school, a time when we can use support every bit as much as when they were babies, the opportunities to connect with other parents are completely evaporating. One mother we know, Joan, reports that her fourteen-year-old daughter's best friend's parents call their girl on the cell phone from their car in the driveway when they pick her up from Joan's house instead of walking up to the house, ringing the bell, and saying hello. In the past, when girls grew up within a large extended family—grandmothers, aunts, older cousins, older siblings—it helped them learn about the world and becoming a woman in it *and* supported moms. One function of our mothers' group is to replace that traditional extended family of women.

Mother-daughter groups can also discourage the myth of separation. Since the notion that our daughters need to disconnect from us during this transition is so prevalent, we've all bought into this idea, even without realizing it. But individuation is not about separation. It's about developing healthy boundaries between self and others while maintaining intimacy, as we learn to recognize our needs as valid and how to gracefully make them known. Many psychologists believe that emotional autonomy develops best under conditions that encourage both individuation and emotional closeness.[8] So our goal is to encourage and allow our daughters to express their own ideas, even when their ideas and feelings differ from ours, *and* to encourage connection by fostering an open dialogue that respects the ideas and opinions of both mother and daughter. The problem is, your daughter probably lacks the sophistication to communicate or even know why she is feeling or acting unpleasantly. She may at times be as prickly as a porcupine, and you may want to get as far away from her as possible. Having another mom friend or friends to go to for encouragement can help you stick by her through the rough spots.

Shortly after Amy started sixth grade she began to pull away from her mother, Phoebe. She had always been a loving and cuddly kid, but she now said, "Go away!" whenever Phoebe offered a hug—even at home, when none of her friends were around. No more kisses at bedtime. Amy put in earphones and listened to music when they were in the same room, and no longer spoke to Phoebe about her day at school. She started doing homework in her room instead of at the kitchen table. Without asking, she took the electric drill and installed a chain lock on her bedroom door. Phoebe wanted to respect her privacy, but she worried—what did this behavior mean?

One day she asked Amy if everything was all right, if there was anything she was worried or upset about.

"No, everything is fine," she snapped at her mother.

"Is anyone bothering you?"

"No one but you."

Phoebe told her, "Sorry. I know you're growing up, but I'm hoping we can still stay close."

"Well, I don't. I want as much distance as possible. Now get out."

On the edge of losing her composure, Phoebe left. Amy slammed the door and locked it. The soundtrack for *Rent* blared from her boom box. They started having this kind of interaction almost every day.

Amy was expressing the "get away from me" attitude that is common for preteen girls. It was painful for Phoebe, and she didn't know what her approach should be. Should she simply respect her privacy? Remove the lock? Punish her for her rudeness? She was used to having fun with her daughter. The year before, when Amy was ten and always hungry arriving home after school, she would chat nonstop between mouthfuls of macaroni and cheese about her classroom pond water terrarium or confide that her friend had watched *Titanic* twenty-seven times and had a crush on Leonardo. Over the summer, they had started designing a tree house, swam all the way across a local pond, eaten homemade chocolate-chip cookies while reading at either end of the couch, their legs intertwined in the middle. Hang out now? Forget it. They could barely be in the same room together.

Phoebe arrived at the mothers' group upset and confused by her interactions with Amy. She was scared that the connection she hoped for was impossible and that she was losing her daughter. She was worried that Amy's behavior would only get worse. The other mothers reminded her that they had experienced similar confrontations and empathized about how hard it was. They helped Phoebe bring to mind moments of closeness they still shared, in between the strife, such as reading *Little Women* together at bedtime, one chapter a night. When Amy hunkered down in bed with her stuffed animals and listened to the exploits of Jo and Amy and Beth and Meg and Marmee, both mother and daughter were at ease. Phoebe said, "Bedtime is the one time I can count on being close to Amy. She lets go of being 'cool' and just wants her mom to tuck her in."

Often the hardest obstacle to overcome to stay close to our daughters is believing that it's possible and that it is good for them. With the help of the mother-daughter group, Phoebe hung on and focused on keeping their bedtime routine intact even if their interactions during the day were heated. She carefully planned out her evenings so she wouldn't be too tired by the time Amy was ready to go to bed at nine o'clock. Once

Phoebe reestablished in her own mind that her relationship with Amy could include both closeness and increasing freedom and independence, she started to think about what else might be happening in her daughter's life to make her act so rude and withdrawn. When girls act out at this age it is commonly a plea to be heard. Underneath the bluster, they may be feeling *"Life is changing, and I'm scared. I don't know how to handle my feelings and all these changes. Isn't it your job to keep me safe and happy, Mom?"*

Phoebe could now see that Amy was trying to grow her wings, and they were still awkward and tender. One way that Amy was branching out at that time was by playing the lead role in her class play. It wasn't until after it was all over and she visibly relaxed that Phoebe became fully aware of what a stretch it had been for her. Amy was glad she did the play, and glad that it was over. Phoebe realized that without the other moms urging her to stay connected, she might have pulled back herself and never have known what her daughter was going through.

"Now when she says mean or distancing things to me, I listen carefully to hear whether she is actually feeling worried or stressed about something," Phoebe said later. "At her age, she does need more privacy, but she wants to be close, too. She is hugging me again. At bedtime, she sometimes says, 'Mom, let's have a conversation,' and we'll talk about her plans to build a porch for her tree house or she'll share a song she has written. When I say, 'I love you,' she says, 'I love you, too.'"

Mothers and Daughters Together: Let's Have Fun!

Too often, girls can start to think that moms are a drag, that they keep you from doing cool things. So, this year, perhaps more than any, it's important that moms and daughters (whether individually or in a group) find ways to have fun together.

Movies. Watching them—and making them. Watching movies with your daughter, just the two of you or with a group of mothers and daughters, is a great way to hang out and share an experience. Choosing a movie with a girl-empowering theme, like *Bend It Like Beckham*, or one that raises difficult subjects, like *Antonia's Line*, is a good way to start conversations. Hearing the differing opinions of other mothers and girls helps individual girls hone their own ideas. Pro-girl possibilities include *Crouching Tiger, Hidden Dragon*; *Whale Rider*; *Rabbit-Proof Fence*; *Fly Away Home*; *She's the Man*; and *Little Women*.

Even better, if you can get hold of a video camera, girls love directing and producing their own movies. Brainstorm a few characters, invite some friends over, come up with a simple plot, and then put the girls to work as producer, actors, and videographer. Moms can join in as stage crew and secondary actors.

Alternatively, use the curriculum guide in *Heroic Girlz* (see the bibliography) to write and perform (and/or film) your own play. When our girls were eleven, they created a remake of the martial arts fantasy film *Crouching Tiger, Hidden Dragon*, using a backyard and local rocky stream as the set. While Vanessa felt shy about acting, she was quick to lead the girls into the woods to find sticks for the fight scene (the trick to safe but realistic stage swordplay is to hit just the other person's sword, not her body). Movie remakes meet eleven-year-olds right where they live: doing something grown-up (making a movie) in a familiar and comfortable way (playing pretend with other girls and moms). When the movies include strong female roles, girls get to practice speaking and acting with power.

Sharing the world. Eleven-year-olds are curious about the world, but apprehensive. They want to appear knowledgeable and grown up (even though they aren't), and they welcome opportunities to expand their range of experience with backup from their mothers. What new thing does your daughter want to do or see? With her or a group, go see women's or girls' sports, basketball, soccer, tennis. Take her to a Sweet Honey in the Rock or Dixie Chicks concert, attend free Shakespeare in the Park performances, make a road trip to the Women's Rights National Park in Seneca Falls, New York. It can be fun to go with other mothers and daughters.

Mother-daughter slumber parties. Eleven is a good age to start a tradition of mother-daughter slumber parties. With just your daughter, some of her friends, and yours or your mother-daughter group, plan a sleepover party. Best is to have the house or apartment (or at least part of it) to yourselves, banishing other siblings and parents to stay with friends or relatives for the night. Girls also love to go camping or sleep out in the backyard if moms are up for it. Have a potluck or take-out dinner, then get into your PJs and play games, exchange foot rubs, go outside and look at the stars, or whatever else you like. Prioritize mothers and daughters spending time together, but also allow some time for girls to be with girls and moms with moms.

Beforehand, assign the girls responsibility for making breakfast (you provide the food, they prepare it), something you feel confident they can handle on their own. While moms are off for an early walk or sleeping late, the girls aren't merely buttering toast; they're stepping up to increased responsibility and recognition. They will be proud and honored to welcome you to the table they set up. Slumber parties are easy to do and offer rich rewards, promoting mother-daughter intimacy (seeing is believing, and girls get to see other girls enjoying time with their moms), community bonding and tradition building, fun and relaxation, and opportunities for girls to demonstrate their increased maturity.

Simple pleasures. Elaborate activities may be exciting, but in fact, when we ask the girls what they'd like to do with us, they usually come up with simple things like playing cards, sledding, apple picking, or going for a picnic. Other possibilities: Take museum trips, get ice cream in the park, go to the zoo, ride bikes. Have a game night—play charades, Pictionary, Apples to Apples, or any other favorite board games. Check the bibliography for books offering novel ideas for games that build trust, foster creativity, and are fun.

The point is less *what* you do than the fact that you earmark time just for you and your daughter. For us, it's the consistency that's been powerful over the years: Once every month, or every six weeks if we're all really stretched for time, we have those few hours set aside for our daughters. (Day-to-day, we do a lot *for* our daughters, often far more than we do *with* them.) The intention during these times is to be *with* your daughter, sharing activities that you both like.

Bear in mind, there are times when planning a special outing with your daughter at this age may backfire. Remember, she's looking to her peer group these days—and you're not it. Let's say you decide to see a new movie, but as you enter the theater, your daughter notices a couple of her girlfriends going to the same movie. The outing that a moment ago felt special, just the two of you, now poses the threat that someone might judge her as a loser for going to the movies with her mom. Even when she feels completely comfortable, if she suddenly can't stand the shoes you're wearing, or the way you smile too much, you can bet she's feeling intensely self-conscious. Shopping is probably the most acceptable way for mothers and daughters to spend time together, but even then, choosing clothes can be a source of contention. For this reason, it's helpful to plan special outings with at least one other mom and her daughter. The idea is to reinforce that this is what mothers and daughters do—they actually have a good time together.

If you harbor expectations of some kind of perfect mother-daughter bonding with your eleven-year-old, you'll likely feel disappointed when conflict erupts. What can you do instead? First, tell yourself that conflict is part of discovering how to have healthy, mature relationships. You and your daughter are learning how to negotiate conflict, and you'll get better at it. It's *not* a sign that your daughter needs to separate or that somewhere along the way, you failed as a mother. It means she requires more experience at identifying her needs and learning to ask specifically for those needs to be met. For both moms and daughters, learning how to get needs met, how to resolve a conflict, maybe even have a fight, without losing control, or how to express an opinion in a calm and clear voice, are powerful lessons. Actively employing negotiation and togetherness with your eleven-year-old daughter lays the groundwork for maintaining a positive relationship and keeping channels of communication open as she enters adolescence and needs your guidance on important issues such as desire, sexuality, and safety.

CHAPTER TWELVE

Cultivating Desire

Twelve Years Old—Curious

At twelve, sex is looming on the horizon like a blazing red sun at dawn. Girls at this age are generally in the full tilt of puberty, feeling or anticipating the stirrings of sexual desire, and some of them are beginning to explore. They may be having their first crush. They may be "practice kissing" with a friend, playing "chase and kiss" games with the boys on the schoolyard, or playing structured kissing games like Spin the Bottle.[1] Or more. Our daughters often feel shy and secretive (and sometimes guilty) about kissing or engaging in sexual games, but sexual exploration is a normal, healthy aspect of development. The truth of the matter is, girls at twelve are often starting to discover themselves as sexual beings.

Many mothers hope their daughters won't become sexually active for years and want to bury their heads in the sand. While some girls will have a slow, tender start, holding hands and kissing, it doesn't always happen that way. If moms don't talk about sex with their daughters, they will simply absorb the sexual values they see on late-night TV and in PG-13 movies, and glean from the talk they hear in the hallways at school or from boy-girl parties and school dances. That means we need to open up the complex issue of sexuality and desire with her now, before passions are running high and access to the complicated messages of sex in our culture has increased even more.

In a few short years, many girls will be exploring their sexuality with a partner. Although our mothers' group specifically encouraged our daughters to hold off having sexual intercourse until they were at least eighteen, these days, it's common for girls to become sexually active at an earlier age. According to the National Center for Health Statistics, 46 percent of girls between the ages of fifteen and nineteen have had sexual intercourse,[2] and many more are exploring sexual touch in relationships with boys or girls. Research on teenage sexuality shows that the younger a teen girl is when she first has intercourse, the more likely she is to regret it. At eighteen, most teens report having positive initial experiences and are more capable of handling the responsibility of safe, protected intercourse.[3]

As our girls awaken sexually, the lure of love and romance intertwined with sex is filling their view—in magazines and movies, on television and the Internet. What are they learning about sexuality and desire from the outside world? To them, it looks like everybody is doing *it*. Younger and younger girls are dressing in a sexually provocative manner. Nubile young girls' bodies are being used to sell pretty much everything, from cars to milk. Take a walk through the magazine aisle of your local store and what are you likely to see? The message repeated endlessly is buy these clothes, this makeup, that sound system and you'll not only look sexy, but you'll get the guy (and he wants sex). Rarely do we see that sex is also about love and commitment, emotional vulnerability and responsibility. Nowhere do we see that sexuality is also about listening to our heart's deepest desires.

At the same time as girls are being bombarded with sexy images and sexual innuendo, the current government-supported programs of abstinence-only sex education send a different message. "Good" girls and boys are not supposed to be sexually active. While abstinence may be an appropriate component of sex education, there continues to be a great need for girls (and boys) to receive comprehensive sex education that includes information on sexual orientation and gender identity, contraception,

STDs, and responsible consensual sexual activity. Far too often they aren't getting the information they require to make informed decisions.[4] Researchers at SIECUS, the Sexuality Information and Education Council of the United States, have found that sex education that teaches teens about both abstinence (celibacy) and contraception/disease provides the most effective strategy to help teenagers delay initiation of sexual intercourse.[5]

Most twelve-year-olds are more curious and fascinated by the subject of sex than they are embarrassed by it. They want to hear the inside scoop. Just as, a few years ago, learning about cycles was fun and interesting for nine-year-olds, girls are less self-conscious in learning and asking questions about sex at age twelve than when they are older and already sexually active (or thinking they should be). If you have laid a gradual foundation over the years through teaching about reproductive cycles and body health, then conversations about sex should be fairly easy and natural. If this is the first time you are bringing up intimate and challenging topics with your daughter, you may feel nervous, but your daughter will likely be grateful and pleased. Don't worry if it feels like unfamiliar territory to you—just plunge in. Now is a critical time to open up lines of communication before she's in the thick of her teens.

As an alternative to the messages bombarding them from the media or coming from the often inadequate sex education they may be receiving at school, we want our daughters to learn about safe sex *and also* hear that sexual feelings are a normal, healthy aspect of being a woman. We want to teach them that women are entitled to our sexual desires. It's important that they know that *looking sexy* may have little to do with *feeling sexual* and that sexual experiences with a loved one involve intense emotions along with physical sensations. As author Sharon Lamb writes in *The Secret Lives of Girls: What Good Girls Really Do—Sex Play, Aggression, and Their Guilt*, ". . . we want girls to know their bodies, to understand pleasure, to gradually grow into their development so that puberty does not attack them with a vengeance, and to love themselves as sexual beings."[6]

When mothers talk to their daughters about sex, it is usually within the context of making safe choices—which is crucial, but rarely do they address sexual desire in a specific way. In her interviews with teenage girls, Sharon Thompson, author of *Going All the Way: Teenage Girls' Tales of Sex, Romance, and Pregnancy*, found that adolescent girls whose mothers had shared information with them about sexual desire and pleasure had the most positive sexual experiences, and they did not engage in sexual activity earlier than their peers.[7] And that bodes well for their futures. A common sexual problem for many adult women is a lack of sexual desire, which some researchers believe may begin in adolescence when girls' sexual desires often go unrecognized and unacknowledged.[8] Encouraging your girl to voice her needs and wants can also support her in many other arenas as a counterbalance to the intense pressures that young adolescents feel to "fit in." So, along with explaining the nitty gritty of physiology, contraception, and STDs, this year we will explore the concept of desire with our daughters.

Your Own Story of Desire and Sexuality

Before we can expect to talk openly, honestly, and comfortably with our daughters about sex and desire, it's important to take a compassionate look at our own desires and our sexual pasts and think about how they were influenced by the circumstances of our lives. It can be illuminating to write your sexual story, including what and how you first learned about sex; sexual experimentation including masturbation and childhood sex play; your first serious sexual relationship; and your feelings about sex when you were a teenager versus now. To get started, either alone or with your group, take out your journal and write responses to the following:

What have my experiences of desire in a general sense been like? What do I desire nowadays?

As I think of my most emotionally satisfying and physically pleasurable sexual experiences, what values that I cherish were present?

What kind of sexual experiences have I had? As a child? Teenager? Adult?

What messages did I get from my peers, my mother, my father, and the world around me about my sexuality? How did that affect me?

Now take a moment to compassionately reflect on the sexual experiences you wish you'd never had.

What qualities that are important to me for a positive sexual experience were lacking (such as mutuality, safety, respect, intimacy, gentleness)?

Are there ways I feel as though I have compromised myself sexually? What effect did that have on me?

Talking with a friend or a small group of mothers we have come to trust increases our compassion for ourselves as we hear that others have encountered the same messages and shared similar experiences. Many of us have had wonderful sexual experiences that inform our definition of good sex. We have also had negative experiences, ranging from unsatisfying to brutally traumatic, that exemplify what we don't want for ourselves or our daughters. If in the course of answering these questions, you uncover past sexual exploitation that you were previously unaware or unconscious of or if you generally think it would be helpful to you, we encourage you to speak with a professional.

....

Questions can also help us clarify our stance on our daughter's budding sexuality, and prepare us to talk to her about sex. On our own or with friends, we can also ask:

What hopes and fears might be present when I contemplate my daughter becoming sexually active?

What values do I hope guide her sexual choices?

What messages is she getting from her peers, from her parents, and from the world around her about her sexuality? How does that influence her?

As she faces sexual choices as a teen, what information do I want her to have about sex? Relationships? Having an orgasm? Protection against STDs? Birth control? What to do about an unwanted pregnancy?

At the Mother-Daughter Project, it is our deeply held belief that mothers have to do our own work before we are able to comfortably talk with our daughters. Many of us have never spoken about sex—it's intensely private and personal, and yet we want to have vital discussions with our daughters. Even if the conversation among the mothers is primarily an exploration of why this is a difficult subject to contemplate talking about with one's daughter, that alone has value. Openly acknowledging our fears and discomforts will help dispel them so that we send our girls a positive message about being an adult sexual woman.

When mothers meet specifically to talk about their sexual pasts, it's important to start with a reminder: This is tender territory. Handle with care. Hearing the voices of the mothers from our group offers a sense of what these conversations might be like.

"I wasn't particularly sexual when I was in high school. I'm not sure why. I guess I wasn't that into boys at that point." Sarah, then forty-three, began our discussion of our sexual histories.

"I was," Phoebe, forty, joined in. "I always had a boyfriend. I'd have these terrible fights with my mother. She was a good Christian woman and believed sex was reserved for marriage. I'm sure she thought I was having intercourse because I'd argue with her about it, but I was actually a virgin when I graduated from high school."

"My mother's line was, 'Just remember, a guy can walk away and zip up his pants.' There was no way I was going to take a chance and end up pregnant," Libby, forty-seven at the time, said.

Fear of pregnancy was of significant concern for each of us as young women—as it was for many of our generation, and still is today for some. An unplanned pregnancy can make you feel as though all your choices in life have abruptly come to an end. We recollected what it meant to have sex when there were few alternatives: no morning-after pill, less acceptance for unwed mothers, no access to abortion.

"No wonder my mom was so freaked out by my sexuality," Katy, then forty-two, said. "She probably thought I was sleeping with every Tom, Dick, and Harry because I was walking around dressed so provocatively."

"Me, I looked like such a goody two-shoes, but I was experimenting like crazy," Libby smiled as she remembers. "Just no intercourse!"

"My mama said"—Maisie, then thirty-seven, played up her Southern drawl—" 'Why, honey, you don't need to know about *that*! That's for when you're married.' But I was just such a big honkin' jock, I wasn't thinking too much about boys and sex and any of that."

When we explored the question *What did I learn as an adolescent about women's sexuality?* Libby summed up what she learned as a teenager: "It was about pleasing the guy." Looking at current depictions of female sexuality in popular magazines such as *Cosmopolitan*, the same message prevails. It often takes years for women to recognize that their own needs and sexual desires are as important as pleasing a partner. Other women in the group noted that the upsurge of feminist ideas in the 1970s helped them to feel entitled to mutually satisfying sex. We hope all our daughters will at some point in the future experience their sexuality in ways that fulfill them in the context of loving relationships, and telling them that directly sends a powerful message.

What Do You Like?

From the simplest question, "What kind of ice cream do you like?" to articulating the ways in which we like to be touched, knowing how to give and receive pleasure is critical to a good sexual relationship. How do we teach our daughters to identify (and not be ashamed of) what they desire and what gives them pleasure? Abstinence-only sex education primarily teaches girls to say no. As important as it is to have the power to say no to any unwanted sexual activity, it's also important to be able to say yes to one's sexual desires at the appropriate time.

In our year of exploring the theme of Desire, as with our curricula on Cycles and Bodies, we begin by creating a foundation of fun, positive, pro-girl experiences. Our activities offer girls lots of opportunities to ask themselves "what do I like?" We start by helping our daughters imagine what kind of day they would love (as described in Chapter One). We then focus on physical experience—what the perfect foot massage would feel like and how to communicate so they can get it. These simple activities implicitly convey that every girl is entitled to her unique desires. From that basis, we talk about intimate relationships and sexual desire, offering specific, concrete information on sexual anatomy, sexual decision-making (including celibacy), birth control, and protection against STDs. Not only does approaching this material gradually make it easier for the girls to digest, it's easier for moms to go slowly, too! And in between every content-oriented discussion or gathering, it's a good idea just to do something fun.

Exploring the Idea of Desire with Your Daughter

A day you would love. This activity teaches girls (and reminds mothers) that our own preferences are worthwhile. Acknowledging desire in the broadest sense provides a touchstone for later conversations about sexual desire. In Chapter One, we described mothers and daughters sharing their ideas for a day they would love. To do this activity yourself, generate a list of words from different categories such as the weather, recreational activities, social situations, food, music, and so on and write each one on a small slip of paper. Make multiple copies to ensure that everyone will be able to find the words she wants to describe a day she would love and include several blank slips of paper so words can be added spontaneously.

We purposely eliminate certain choices—for instance, there is no "shopping" as a category. While some women enjoy shopping with their daughters, it can also be a source of conflict. Instead we aim for words that strengthen the muscle of desire based on pleasurable experiences that nourish us in some way. Dinner by candlelight? A long soak in a warm tub? Playing with a puppy? Rolling down a grassy hill in springtime?

Spread out the slips of paper. One by one, each person can choose words to richly describe an ideal day. After choosing all the words you want, write for ten minutes. Then read your descriptions of a day you would love. The discussion afterward can be guided by the following questions:

How does it feel to imagine a day you would love?

What are the feelings that let you know what you want?

How did others' choices influence your choices?

As you were making choices, did one kind of great day stand out, or did you think of lots of different kinds of days to choose between?

In early adolescence, girls are prone to answer questions that begin "what do you want . . ." with "I don't know," as they begin to worry about what other people might think. This activity provides an avenue for articulating their wants and needs. As adult women, it is common for us to prioritize others' needs and preferences over our own, to the extent that it can feel downright unfamiliar to ask ourselves what we actually want. For both moms and daughters, it's liberating to imagine a great day and share our own likes and dislikes. Talking about our preferences gives us practice in actively *creating* our own experiences, as opposed to being passive recipients, which is the way female sexuality is often framed.

One-on-one or in a group, hearing about a day our daughter would love, and letting her know our pleasures, helps us see each other as unique individuals, while at the same time fosters intimacy—there is no pressure here to be "just like mom," and likewise, no reason to rebel. Acknowledging similarities and differences between us is reassuring in this context. You can plant seeds that honor your daughter's desires in many ways. Something as basic as asking her to plan a Saturday breakfast including her favorite foods provides a lesson. Learning to communicate preferences is a skill that can be developed.

Sensual Preferences: How Do You Like Being Touched?

When a girl reaches puberty and no longer has the body of a child, she can often exhibit a sudden lack of physical affection toward her parents. She may squirm out of your arms because she thinks only little kids hug their moms, and you (or her father) may wonder how to respond. Now that she is developing a more grown-up body, is it still okay to hug her? Tickle her? Carry her up to bed? The answer to these questions is yes—*if* she wants you to. Girls understand safe, respectful, loving, nonsexual touch when they experience it. The truth is that your daughter, like all humans at every age, needs physical affection at twelve as much as she did at three—but what feels comfortable to her and (to you) may be different. Ask her what she likes, and respect her wishes. Offering a foot or back massage can be one way you can give your girl comfortable physical touch, or inviting her to give you a massage if she likes. (See more on this below.) Make space for her to lean against you on the couch to watch TV or read a book. Invite her onto your lap if she'll let you, offer her a piggyback ride to bed or across the park, or ask if she'd like you to brush and braid her hair. Some girls prefer to keep a physical distance from their parents during this transition. Having a dog or cat to cuddle with or sharing nonsexual affection with her friends can give her the loving touch she needs. If your twelve-year-old or teenager is in a phase of not wanting touch from mom, respect her wishes, but periodically remind her, *Everyone needs hugs, even teenagers.* (This may be news to her.) Watch for signs that she may welcome a hug or massage from you again. Even the formerly affectionate, lap-sitting girl who won't come within ten feet of you now will probably find her way back to an occasional hug if you wait patiently and try to remain open. Helping our daughters get snuggles safely, from us or others we trust, helps protect them from seeking the physical affection they need in unsafe ways.

Getting the massage you want. This activity lets girls (and moms) practice discovering, asking for, and getting the exact kind of physical contact they want through giving and receiving a foot, shoulder, or head massage. The self-knowledge and communication skills girls learn are directly applicable to knowing and having their preferences honored in general, including sexually.

In a group, girls pair up with another girl, moms with moms, and we invite each person to spend a few minutes imagining what she would like if someone gave her a great foot, shoulder, or head massage. You can start with the question *What kind of a massage do you want?* After you've taken a moment to reflect, tell your partner in as much detail as possible what you would like. While you are receiving a massage, give your partner as much or as little feedback as you wish. Of course, if any touch makes you feel uncomfortable, it is important to stop and redirect your partner to a kind of touch that feels pleasurable.

Give specific permission to choose another activity if anyone prefers not to give or receive a massage. Suggest a quiet activity so that no one else will be disturbed. In our mother-daughter group, Vanessa and Gabi chose to chat quietly while Vanessa French-braided Gabi's hair.

Afterward, describe what you liked. Ask *Was it easy or difficult to express your desires?*

End by having one mother acknowledge that the kind of communication we use to get what we want in receiving a massage is the same kind of communication women can use to get what we want when they're in a sexual situation with a partner. In one sentence, you can let your daughter know that sex shared with a partner encompasses communication and mutual pleasure.

Just for Fun at Twelve

By twelve, except for special occasions, girls are often less interested in doing things with mom alone, but would love to have a barbecue or ride along a bike path or some other activity with another girl and her mother, or with a whole group. At this age, they are usually spending a lot of energy on mastering teen knowledge and skills with their peers, which can be stressful. So, while they might enjoy it if you went to a teen movie or listened to their favorite pop songs with them, it's more likely they would welcome (sometimes secretly) a chance to return to old favorites, such as playing Monopoly, baking cookies, or reviving a movie that you both loved when she was younger. You can also keep doing your girl's preferred "hanging out" activities we suggested for eleven years old, such as mother-daughter slumber parties.

Is What You're Wearing Getting You What You Want?

By age twelve, many girls are interested in wearing the latest teen trends, which change from year to year, but have tended in the last decade toward sexy, highly gendered clothing, even for girls younger than twelve. As women, we have learned from experience that sometimes such clothing can be wrongly perceived as communicating sexual availability and can lead to unwanted sexual attention. But girls often resist being told what to wear, and appropriate clothing can be a heated topic between moms and teenage daughters. It is productive to address clothing concerns with girls twelve and older by engaging them in evaluating what kind of response their clothing elicits, and deciding whether or not they like that response, and why.

One way to do this is with an at-home fashion show—with a surprise twist. (As with most activities with girls eleven and older, it's usually easiest if you invite at least one other girl and mom to join you.) Ahead of time, have a girl and mom write down on different slips of paper ten or twenty different situations in which a twelve-year-old in your community might find herself, such as in the school cafeteria, giving a presentation in front of her history class, sitting alone at a bus stop with a creepy adult male, walking two miles home from school, riding the subway, at a small party with good friends, at a big party with older teens, playing touch football, at a sleepover with their girlfriends, in the witness stand in juvenile court, at their grandparents' house, and so on. Fold the papers so the locations can't be seen and put them in a hat or container. Ask the girls and moms all to bring two or three different outfits—anything goes. The more variety, the better: slinky dresses, athletic wear, business suits, crop tops, grungy jeans. At the gathering, have everyone put on an outfit, then—without peeking!—choose a location out of the hat. That's where she is, wearing what she's wearing! Once everyone has a picked a location, ask:

> *How does it feel to be wearing those clothes at that location? What kind of a response are you likely to get from the different people who are there—boys, girls, men, women? What would that be like for you?*

> *What would you like about their responses? What wouldn't you like? Why?*

> *Which location would be most comfortable wearing what you are wearing?*

> *What would you be most comfortable wearing at the location you picked?*

Take a minute to write responses to these questions, then share responses with the group. If there is interest, everyone can take another turn. In this activity, both from their own responses and from hearing how other girls and moms feel, girls develop their own ability to discern what effects their clothing choices have in different situations, and make good decisions based on what they think is appropriate and how it makes them feel.

The "Big Talk"

Often we mothers can feel panicked when we contemplate our daughters becoming sexually active. We want to say just the right thing. We want to guide and protect them. Some of us wish our girls would limit their sexual explorations to hand-holding and kissing until they get married or are older teens, but we know that many teenagers make other choices. It can be difficult to know exactly when to have a direct conversation about sexual decision-making, contraception, and STDs, but we have found age twelve to be an ideal time. All year, by consciously building lessons on articulating desire without ever saying much about sex per se, we're preparing them for more practical information about sex. Your journal writing and mothers-only conversations are all part of the process, along with your previous conversations with your daughter about girls' and women's anatomy, puberty, and getting her period, as well as the conversations you will have in the future about safety, relationships, and rights and responsibilities.

Through our research, and through observations at the Mother-Daughter Project, we have found that at the end of the year, it is effective to have one or two focused conversations with your daughter that touch on values, relationships, sexual anatomy and physiology, and birth control. While this may seem like a lot to cover, once you've hit all your talking points, you will feel reassured that your daughter has been introduced to the most important information you can provide on sex and sexuality, and you will have set the stage for more discussions in the years ahead. But each mother should decide what she thinks will work best, and what feels most manageable to her.

The best way to prepare yourself for this conversation is to address the mothers-only questions we offered earlier in the chapter. These questions are designed to help you recall how you felt about sex as a teen, clarify your sexual values, and determine what kind of information you feel your daughter needs to make sound sexual choices. Then plan your talk and gather books (see the bibliography for ideas) and, if you choose, various types of birth control to show as examples. If you are doing the talk with your mother-daughter group, create a game plan and decide who wants to cover which topics. (It's a relief when another mom can address a topic that is less comfortable for you.) Barbara Huberman and

Sue Alford of Advocates for Youth, a group that champions efforts to help young people make informed and responsible decisions about their reproductive and sexual health, suggest that, when speaking to girls (or boys) about sex, we should listen carefully to what they are saying and asking. Huberman and Alford put it this way: "Remember that teens want mutually respectful conversations. Don't assume that a teen is sexually experienced or inexperienced, knowledgeable or naïve. Don't underestimate your teen's ability to weigh the advantages and disadvantages of various options. Give them the needed facts and help them explore their values."[9]

Whether speaking one-on-one with your daughter or in a group of mothers and daughters, find a completely private space where you won't be interrupted and have your books and other materials at hand. Remember, it means a lot to your daughter that you are bringing up such an intimate and important topic and there is no "perfect" way to do it. There will be many opportunities in the future to cover issues that beg repeating or clarifying. (After our talk with the girls in our group, several of our daughters said to us, "It's really nice to learn this stuff from our moms.")

It's helpful to begin by sharing that you hope your daughter will one day have a loving and satisfying sexual life, and that's why you want to talk to her about sex, love, and relationships and answer any of her questions. You can then speak about what values you hold about sex and what qualities you think make for good, healthy intimate relationships. (Some girls may be uncomfortable with the notion that their mothers have sex, but it's important to at least acknowledge that women and mothers are sexual beings, gearing how much you say to what your daughter is comfortable hearing.) Next you can explain that the whole body is a sexual organ, but that certain parts of the anatomy are especially sensitive. The book *It's Perfectly Normal* by Robie Harris is an excellent resource, as is *The Underground Guide to Teenage Sexuality* by Michael Basso.

You can let your daughter know that sexuality is about plea-sure, and that it's different for everybody. You can acknowledge that masturbation is normal and healthy; that many kinds of touch feel good in a sexual way, and one especially pleasurable part of sex is having an orgasm. Explain that from sexual thoughts and touch, sexual feelings and excitement build up and can peak in a climax or orgasm. In women, an orgasm is a release of sexual tension with pleasurable muscular contractions in the uterus and the muscles around the vagina.

Sex with a partner is the next topic. Set the stage by describing the qualities you believe are essential for a sexual relationship, such as love, mutual respect, and trust. It is easy to confuse physi-cal intimacy with emotional intimacy, and it benefits girls to en-courage them to hold off on having sexual relations unless they are in a committed relationship—especially if the scene at their future high school is one in which casual sex is the norm. Hear-ing a mom say, as Libby in our group did, "I had boyfriends in high school and I did fool around, but I was really glad I waited to have intercourse until I was eighteen" sends a positive message that they can, as older teenagers, be intimate while also waiting for the right time to have sexual intercourse. Delaying inter-course until they are mature enough to handle the accompany-ing responsibilities will help protect them from STDs and unplanned pregnancy as well as support their emotional well-being. At age twelve, it is also appropriate to let your daughter know that one girl in ten is primarily attracted to other girls, oth-ers are attracted to both girls and boys, and others are primarily attracted to boys.

It's critical for girls to be aware that if they do choose to have sexual intercourse at some point, they need protection against both unwanted pregnancy and STDs. Here is where the sex talk moves from a focus on pleasure, relationships, and choices to a focus on safety. Explain to your daughter that the only safe sex involves no exchange of body fluids. Ask her what she knows about safety and risks of sexual activity, and fill in the gaps in her knowledge to the best of your ability. Refer to your books as needed—this is good modeling for how she can find information she needs. Bring out condoms, diaphragms, cervical caps and rings, birth control pills, and any other protection you or the other mothers feel it is important to show your daughters. Twelve-year-olds are openly curious about these things in ways that self-conscious thirteen- and fourteen-year-olds are often not, since sex has become more of a "hot topic" for them at that point. You can also distribute condoms and show every girl how to put a condom on a banana. (If you've never used a condom, ask your health care provider to teach you how at your annual gynecological exam before having this conversation.) In this era of HIV and AIDS, proper use of a condom may save your daughter's life.

One important piece of birth control news is that in the United States, the Plan B "morning-after" pill (which works by inhibiting ovulation) is now available over the counter for emergency contraception after unprotected intercourse (such as when a condom breaks or when sex was unplanned or coerced), but only to women over eighteen, so mothers are in a position to offer help to teen daughters in obtaining it, if they can talk openly about sex together.

Whew! You are doing great—and you're almost there! Now it's time to answer any questions. Some girls may feel shy about asking questions aloud, and you can use a "question hat" placed strategically for anybody, girls or mothers, to put written questions in. A good way to end the conversation is by distributing a copy of *Changing Bodies, Changing Lives*, a book that provides accurate information and a comprehensive discussion of sexual and emotional health for teenagers, to every girl, as a resource she can use as she grows up.

．．．．．．．．．．．．．

You may be breaking out in a cold sweat just contemplating having this kind of conversation with your daughter, but when we had our nitty-gritty sex talk with our daughters, the atmosphere was relaxed and the girls took it very seriously; they felt like the conversation was a "grown-up" thing to be doing. As a group, they were relieved to hear that it was a good idea to wait until they were at least eighteen to have sexual intercourse. Here's how the conversation proceeded for us:

"We know that in the next few years, you girls may start having sexual experiences, you know, making out, touching, that kind of stuff," Libby began, once all the girls and their mothers were comfortably settled on the carpeted floor of Libby's private study.

"Maybe some of you have already tried kissing or looking or 'you show me yours, I'll show you mine,'" Maisie added.

"One day, when you are ready, we want you to be safe, so we're going to talk about birth control and protection, but first we want to tell you . . ." Sarah paused. The girls, all sitting in a row, stared intently at her. "Sex is for your pleasure, and it's especially wonderful as part of a loving relationship."

"There are lots of different ways to have sexual pleasure," Phoebe told them.

"Kissing, touching . . . you don't have to have intercourse to be close to someone," Libby added.

"Some girls feel pressured by their friends or their boyfriend to have sex before they feel ready. The point of being sexual is to feel good, both emotionally and physically," Katy said. "So you need to listen to your own body and your feelings and ultimately decide what's really best for you."

"Okay, we've talked about sex without intercourse, now let's talk about sex with intercourse and birth control," said Sarah, shifting gears.

"Do you remember how we showed you tampons and pads and talked about getting your periods?" Libby asked.

The girls nodded.

"This time we've got samples of all different kinds of birth control to show you so that when you are eventually ready to have intercourse you'll know how to protect yourself," Libby began.

First, we explained the basic physiological facts of how pregnancy occurs and what STDs are—even if girls have gone over this in health class or sex education, they may still be (often secretly) confused or unclear. We then pulled out the contraceptives.

"What's that?" April asked when Phoebe showed a diaphragm.

"A diaphragm. It goes inside a woman's vagina. It's used with some of this," Phoebe said, squirting a glob of spermicidal gel into the diaphragm. "This kills the sperm in a man's semen, so the semen can't fertilize a woman's egg."

We handed around various kinds of birth control, which the girls looked at and discussed with outright curiosity. We showed them a dental dam (a thin piece of latex that prevents bacteria and viruses from being transmitted from oral-vaginal contact), acknowledging that in a group our size, it is possible that one or more of them will become sexually involved with a woman. When Phoebe pulled out a bunch of bananas and began tossing us each a foil packet with a condom in it, everyone started laughing.

"Grab a banana," Phoebe instructed, "and open up your condom."

"Hey, mine is a rainbow one," Gabriella said when she opened the packet.

"I want one of those," April said.

"You can have mine," Libby offered, tossing her foil packet across the room.

"You've got to practice with these things," Phoebe told them.

"No peeling your bananas," Sarah interjected.

"You're going to unroll the condom over your banana, but make sure you leave a little extra room as you begin." Phoebe unrolled a condom over the yellow banana, leaving an empty inch at the top. "When a man ejaculates, his penis releases semen. It's the thick white liquid we talked about earlier. The condom is used to prevent it from entering the woman's vagina, which protects her from STDs and pregnancy."

"After the man has an orgasm, his penis will become limp, so it's important to make sure he holds on to the condom or it can come off inside the woman's vagina," Maisie added.

"But it's not just birth control that keeps you safe," Katy said. "It's mostly what kind of relationship you have with a person. Sex is a pretty big deal, not just because you can get pregnant, but because of how you can end up feeling," Katy warned the girls.

"We recommend that you wait until you are at least eighteen before you have intercourse, and we hope you'll wait until you are in a committed relationship," Phoebe said. All the mothers nodded in agreement. "Having sex is a serious responsibility. It's not just about physical pleasure; lots of emotions go along with sex, and you need to be grown up enough to handle them, and consider your partner's feelings, too."

"We really hope you'll go slowly, that you'll listen to what feels right to you and choose your partner carefully," Katy reminded them again.

....

As they became older teens, the daughters in our group bene-fited from explicitly addressing issues of desire and sexuality with their mothers early on. We saw our girls develop romantic rela-tionships, each in her own time, choosing partners who were kind and respectful. In the context of loving, ongoing relation-ships, some of them decided to have sexual relations, and before they did, they came to us, their mothers and their *comadres*, for support and advice. At sixteen, April became serious with her boyfriend, Raphael, and spoke with Maisie about setting up an appointment for birth control with their family doctor, which Phoebe drove her to. At age seventeen, Marisol told Katy that things were getting serious with her boyfriend. Katy later told the other mothers about her conversation with her daughter: "All of your voices were right there. Mari remembered our conversation about sex from five years ago, and she said, 'Phoebe said this, and Maisie said that,' and we were able to talk completely openly about her being ready to have sex in her relationship and her getting birth control." While some of our daughters did not wait until the age of eighteen to have intercourse, our recommendation helped them hold off until they were prepared to make a thoughtful decision based on their own desires.

Women's sexuality exists within the opposing borders of our desires and the threat of sexual coercion. The urge to protect our daughters is valid, but it can push us to the side where sex is viewed as a danger and our job as mothers is to ward off any harm. We'll get to that—in the next year, as our girls begin to gain more independence, the focus will be on how to prepare them for a world that can be unsafe. But now, in the security and comfort of their homes and families, *before* they have their first intimate relationships, our daughters will benefit most from learning the basics of sexuality, within the rich terrain of knowing and expressing their own desires.

·······················

CHAPTER THIRTEEN

Teaching Safety and Freedom

Thirteen Years Old—Gaining Independence

It's official. She's arrived! A teenager, at last! At least that's what she's probably thinking. Your own reaction may be more like: Already?

Girls at thirteen are like sponges, absorbing the world outside their families as never before and trying to figure out how they fit into it. Perhaps they notice that jocks seem pretty cool and think maybe athletics will be their ticket for fitting in, or they see that the kids they like all seem to be in the school orchestra. Many wonder if being sexy is the way to get what they want. Images of sexy young women loom so large that some girls completely lose perspective. When we point out ads we find objectionable, our daughters may think, *What's the big deal?* As they develop curvy women's bodies, their experiences in the world change. Do you remember how it felt when boys and men started looking at you in a new way? Was it exciting? Scary? Annoying? Titillating? For many girls it's a mix of emotions.

Thirteen-year-olds notice women's different modes of negotiating the world, and they observe how their own different choices get varying results. Having your large breasts ogled when you wear a skimpy top may be fun when you're at a dance, but when a teacher stares at your chest but never calls on you in chemistry, it doesn't feel very good. Telling your lunch-table friends that you don't like how they make fun of another girl's clothes may produce an uncomfortable silence at the time, but feel great when one of them later tells you privately how glad she was that you spoke up. Dieting may feel empowering when others comment on your new svelte body, but it's debilitating when you're starving, with a raging headache. It may be fun to get high or drink booze with your friend—until you're going home on the bus, some guy starts rubbing up against you, and you find you can't think clearly.

As our daughters begin dating, hanging out with groups of teens, or driving around with older friends and siblings, they are launching themselves into a scene we're not generally privy to, but which often poses greater risks than they've encountered before. At thirteen, girls can be sassy, brave, passionate, and playful. It's a creative time, as they jump with gusto into a whole new world of freedoms and challenges. Your daughter has already handled numerous obstacles successfully. She bravely walked into school with braces on her teeth; negotiated a conflict with a friend; tried out for a role in her school play; or answered all the questions on a tough exam. She may already (and we hope she does!) have great confidence handling herself in the world. So while it's important to acknowledge the dangers of being a female, we also want to recognize her capabilities and resourcefulness. Maintaining the balance between naming the very real dangers that women face and strengthening your girl's inner resources is the goal this year.

Thirteen-year-olds are still naïve about many of the dangers inherent in being a woman. By sixteen or seventeen, girls will be much more savvy about how to have the freedom they want while minimizing risks. By seventeen, many know girls who are sexually active and use birth control carefully and others who do not. They have likely seen girls unintentionally get pregnant, with all the emotional and physical consequences. They have witnessed mutually loving and respectful relationships as well as relationship violence among their peers. At thirteen, however, acknowledging the risks they are now facing often feels overwhelming, so they often deny the dangers to themselves.

Teenage girls may drink alcohol (and drive), smoke cigarettes, use illicit drugs, abuse prescription medications, buy compulsively, shoplift, diet endlessly (often with serious health consequences), have bad relationships. Kids do these things for the same reasons as adults: They think they'll be increasing their pleasure in life. The reality is that, over the next few years, our girls will take risks as they explore new territory, and we want to help them minimize the danger as they do so.

At thirteen, the ability to think abstractly and flexibly is just beginning to develop, which means it can be difficult to reason with our daughters. When they're sixteen and seventeen, we'll be able to have far more thoughtful discussions about how to negotiate potentially dangerous situations. This means our aim for thirteen is to introduce the concept that the world is not always a safe place, while developing their safety skills and drawing on the support of other girls and women in order to help them move through it feeling free and strong.

As we offer strategies to develop these skills, we also teach them that the world isn't *just* risky—it's a lot of fun. This year, it's especially important to alternate adventurous, fun-filled activities with topic-oriented meetings. Even in a single meeting, try to balance serious topics with fun. You might spend less than an hour of a two-hour meeting on heavy-duty issues. (But even getting to yell "NO!" at the top of your lungs in a self-defense exercise can be fun!)

We must also recognize that the world our girls are entering may feel a bit like a foreign land to us. While every generation faces similar issues—sex, drugs, alcohol, relationship violence—these issues play out differently for each. The fact that we don't completely understand what it's like to be a teenager today is partly why it can be so difficult to parent. We need our daughters to tell us what their lives are like in order to stay connected, which can be difficult when they are inclined to close off.

Already, the sphere of a thirteen-year-old's friends has a powerful influence. It may seem that your daughter doesn't need you—or at least she thinks (or acts as if) she doesn't need you. Not true. You still have a strong influence on her, which can be strengthened by a community of like-minded *comadres*.

How Safe Is It to Be a Girl Today?

As we discussed in Chapter Two, the answer to this question is: not very safe. Just consider this alarming statistic from the federal Bureau of Justice Statistics: Every two-and-a-half minutes, a woman is raped in this country. For a mother, it's even more alarming to read that young women are four times more likely than any other group to be victims of sexual assault.[1]

Dating violence also scares us. In 2005, Liz Claiborne, Inc., sponsored a study on teen dating abuse, which found that:

- One in three teenagers report knowing a friend or peer who has been hit, punched, kicked, slapped, choked, or physically hurt by a partner.
- One in four teenage girls who have been in relationships have been pressured to perform oral sex or engage in intercourse.
- Eighty percent of teens regard verbal abuse as a "serious issue" for their age group.
- Twenty-four percent of fourteen- to seventeen-year-olds know at least one student who has been the victim of dating violence, yet 81 percent of parents either believe teen dating violence is not an issue or admit they don't know if it is an issue.
- Of the women between fifteen and nineteen who are murdered each year, 30 percent are killed by their husband or boyfriend.[2]

Another factor affecting girls' safety is the influence of drugs and alcohol. Many teenagers are unaware that drinking alcohol makes them more likely to participate in risky behavior such as drunk driving, having unprotected sex (potentially resulting in HIV infection, other sexually transmitted diseases, and pregnancy), and taking illegal drugs.[3] Mothers need to figure out their stance on drugs and alcohol and explain it to their daughters before they become an issue (something we will discuss later in the chapter).

The statistics are indeed terrifying, and can make you feel paralyzed. But you aren't! We'll explain how to balance your daughter's desire to be free in her world against the dangers that exist, without triggering her resentment of you.

For Mothers Only

We've all been affected by the hazards inherent in being female, though our experiences may vary widely. Many of our lives have been touched by violence, and most of us don't feel the same freedom that men do. Whether or not you have other mothers with whom you can safely talk, you can ask yourself:

How did my mother support my safety and freedom when I was a teenager?

What are my strategies to know my own strength and stay safe?

How has violence against women and girls affected my life both directly and indirectly?

How am I supporting my daughter to feel bold and powerful in the world?

What helps her know her own strength?

Especially in relation to sex and violence, we need to examine our own issues in order to protect our daughters effectively. Otherwise, we'll overprotect, underprotect, or just feel so scared that we don't do anything.

Suppose that when you were an innocent thirteen-year-old, you went home with a boy after school and ended up having sex with him. During the next week, news of this got out, and you were branded a slut. What strategies will you use when your daughter turns thirteen? Will you get upset and ground her for life? Will you feel it's inevitable that she'll be victimized as you were? Or suppose you were in an abusive relationship. You don't want that for your daughter, but you aren't sure how to teach her to avoid it. Here are some ideas we recommend considering with other mothers before you begin to talk about safety and risk-taking with your daughter.

Starting with stories of strength. It's difficult to acknowledge our fear as we begin thinking about our daughter's safety, for it's deeply distressing to contemplate them being hurt. Some of us try to protect our girls (and ourselves) by denying that there are risks. Others pull into ourselves, restricting our own lives and our daughter's. Some of us turn to men for protection; others become trained in the martial arts. We may put on extra weight, hiding under layers of clothes, or we may become anorexic, eliminating womanly curves because it feels safer to be less visible.

It can be hard to recollect painful memories or even stories friends have told us of bad experiences. We can feel scared or angry that any of us has been raped, physically or emotionally abused, sexually harassed, or violated in any way, and we can also feel angry when we recognize how we restrict ourselves to try to stay safe.

For these very reasons, it's best to start by focusing on who and what help us feel *free* and *strong* in the world. Thus we begin the year by challenging the idea that women are weak and need protection by sharing stories of times we were strong and capable and able to overcome adversity, and by engaging in physical activities together. (Our group of moms and daughters had a great time hoisting a heavy canoe on top of a car for a fun-filled day on the river.) Women—and men, too—sometimes feel like children who just want a big strong mom or dad to scoop us up and fly us to safety. But women are also strong and competent and able to take care of ourselves.

Strengthening stories of survival. The topic of safety and freedom inevitably brings up memories of the times we *weren't* safe or free. Our own experiences of assault or harassment have a powerful effect on us and on our mothering. At the Mother-Daughter Project, we find it helpful to focus on *what helped us get through* those painful times. The compassionate support of other women is invaluable, and the more trust you feel in a group, the more upsetting or personal the material you can share. With a subject as powerful as trauma, it's essential to proceed gradually, both when we explore our experiences individually and when we share them with others. We recommend using the following questions.[4] Bring to mind and describe a time and place in which you feel particularly safe and free. Then ask yourself:

In that situation of safety, what skills and values of mine were present?

Have those skills and values helped me get through a time when I didn't feel safe? How?

What were the effects of that difficult time on my life? What helped me deal with or overcome any negative effects?

A safe, supportive way to share painful material with a group is to start by writing or reflecting on the questions above, or if you prefer, drawing a picture that captures your responses. You might want to begin with a minor incident that is not too painful. One woman then chooses to share her responses. When she finishes, each person notes one thing she said that is moving and why.

Next, the group brings to mind and shares with her a positive image or metaphor of her strength and survival. For example, "When you explained how you held on to your value of kindness to others despite being treated cruelly yourself, I had the image of you rising up like a bird out of a forest fire carrying precious seeds to plant in a better place."

Do the same for each woman as she shares her story. Once you have created an empowering survival story about a minor incident, you can use the same questions to explore more painful experiences. In our mothers' group, Sarah, a nurse, described a previous verbally abusive relationship, explaining that she was able to leave it because she "couldn't stand the idea of my girls thinking that that was all they deserved."

Over the course of the year, we focused many discussions on this issue. If you have no one with whom you can safely talk about safety and violence—particularly if you have been abused or believe your partner is being abusive—you may find it useful to get professional help. We often feel shame when we are unable to extricate ourselves from an abusive relationship. Reaching out for help can lessen our shame and increase our ability to have healthy relationships.

Exploring how our own experiences influence the kinds of messages we give our daughters, and hearing other mothers' stories widens our understanding as we each approach issues of safety and freedom with our daughters. While one mother won't allow her thirteen-year-old daughter to go to the mall without adult supervision, another may be perfectly comfortable allowing her daughter to hang out for hours there with her friends. Both are appropriate within the context of each family.

Talking to Our Daughters: Intuition and Saying "No!"

Discussions about violence against women may be the most challenging ones we have with our daughters. If you think talking about sex is tough, wait until you take on this one. Needing to have these discussions pains us—but we know that denying danger puts our girls at greater risk.

While there are many practical strategies for helping thirteen-year-olds stay safe, we begin the conversation by talking about intuition. We believe that a fundamental way to ensure our daughters' safety is to teach them to listen and respond to their intuition and learn to say "No!" with strength and conviction. We want them to understand that intuition is a useful tool *before* we acknowledge that the world can be an unsafe place for women. In this way, we begin the whole discussion with the idea of empowerment—rather than start by feeding fear.

Just as we have every other year, we build slowly as we prepare our daughters for this difficult subject. We want to strengthen their ability to intuit and self-reflect because we know that listening to the small voice deep within has gotten many of us safely out of tight jams. We want our daughters to know their own boundaries and have a clear sense of when their personal space is violated. At thirteen, our girls aren't as independent as they'll be at sixteen—they're not out driving around or taking mass transportation at night by themselves if they live in a city—so we can begin explaining intuition within the safe context of home. Intuition is a tool for feeling more self-assured in a world that can seem frightening. What's more, learning to listen to the inner voice of intuition is a foundation for all the more specific safety practices and the basis for developing a sense of one's personal boundaries. It will serve your daughter in other areas of her life as she grows into an independent woman.

You can explain to your daughter that intuition is an inner

sense of knowing, which can manifest as physical sensations or as emotions. In fact, our bodies can sense danger even when we are not consciously aware that any exists. According to Gavin De Becker, leading expert on predicting violent behavior and author of *Protecting the Gift: Keeping Children and Teenagers Safe (and Parents Sane)*, depending on the situation, intuition can communicate as:

- Nagging feelings
- Persistent thoughts
- Dark humor
- Anxiety
- Curiosity
- Hunches
- Gut feelings
- Doubt
- Hesitation
- Suspicion
- Apprehension
- Fear[5]

We use exercises like "Teaching Boundaries and Personal Space" below to strengthen our daughters' intuitive awareness. (You can find more resources for developing intuition in the bibliography.) Even if you aren't part of a regular mother-daughter group, some of these exercises are best done in a group. Most mothers are desperate for information on keeping their daughters safe, so getting a temporary group together should not be difficult. With a friend, write up and distribute flyers at a school event or post in your neighborhood, library, community center, or house of worship, inviting mothers with teenage daughters to an introductory meeting for a six-series Mother-Daughter Project session on "Staying Strong, Staying Safe." Using this chapter as a guide, meet several times first as mothers to explore personal histories, then choose and plan activities to do with your daughters.

Developing Awareness and Personal Boundaries

As a prelude to strengthening intuition, you can work to develop courage. We've taught our daughters to be "good girls," polite to adults, and thoughtful of others. This has served them (and ourselves) well, but now it's time to challenge some of the "good girl" training. If someone isn't nice to them, violates their boundaries, bullies, or in any way threatens or disrespects them, they need to know that they aren't required to be nice back. But learning to speak up for oneself, especially to an unfamiliar adult, is a skill that our girls need to learn and practice, especially if they're shy to begin with. Debbie and Mike Gardner, authors of *Raising Kids Who Can Protect Themselves*, define courage as "standing up to someone or something that can hurt you." Whether you're choosing not to drink a beer when it's handed to you at a party or summoning the guts to fight an attacker, it helps to practice developing courage. Here's an exercise to try when you and your daughter are out in public.

Courage coach.[6] Some girls rely on their parents to get directions, order a meal, and ask for assistance in finding something in a store. This exercise consists of sending your daughter into a situation where she needs to ask for help. Have her go into a store and ask: "Could you tell me where I'd find the shampoo?" Tell her you'll be right there as backup if she really gets stuck. You might start with a less threatening situation and work up to more difficult tasks.

Teaching boundaries and personal space.[7] This exercise is designed to heighten your inner senses and increase your natural sense of your personal boundaries. Gather in a large circle. One girl/woman is "it" in the center. A volunteer begins to approach her, coming from different angles, in either quiet, stealthy, or loud and obnoxious ways. Whenever she feels that her space is being violated, she calls out "Stop!" Each person takes a turn stalking into the space of the one who is "it." Keep approaching until she says "Stop!" (Note: If someone is unaware of her boundaries and never says "Stop!" you might help her by talking about how it generally feels when someone is "in your face." Would it feel different if it were someone you didn't know? Does gender or age or size make a difference?)

The second part of the exercise is the same, except that this time, the person in the center closes her eyes. When she *feels* as though someone has entered her personal space, she calls out "Stop!" Repeat several times with the same girl being "it." What differences do you notice between having the eyes open and closed?

Make sure that everyone, both moms and daughters, takes a turn being "it." It's important for the girls to hear that their mothers have clear boundaries and can say a loud, firm "Stop!"

You can adapt this exercise to do one-on-one with your daughter. Start by discussing when she feels as though someone is invading her space, perhaps by standing too close. What can she do about it? She can say "No." The point is to reinforce the fact that she's entitled to own her own personal space—and to tell someone else to back off.

It's my money. Part of learning to say no is being able to express anger appropriately. Anger is a difficult emotion for many women, and we often avoid voicing our dissatisfaction. It's a powerful lesson to hear our mothers express anger without resorting to name-calling or physical aggression. The following exercise generally doesn't lead to anger, although sometimes it does trigger a strong reaction.

One girl or mother (Player 1) puts a twenty-dollar bill under her foot. The job of Player 2 is to beg, wheedle, lie, annoy, harass, or do whatever it takes to verbally convince Player 1 to give her the money. Player 1's job is to stand firm on her twenty dollars. With increasing verbal insistence, others can join in and try to convince her to give it up.

Now add physical intimidation (no hitting, please). Two or more can gang up on Player 1. Your job is to continue harassing until she yells a loud "No!" at least once, though repeatedly is better. (Many girls find this easier to do than their moms. Make sure everybody takes a turn.)

Broaching the Subject of Physical Safety

After working on intuition and physical boundaries, you can begin to tell your daughter about the dangers present in the world. Girls need to know about relationship violence, date rape, rape, and murder. According to Gavin de Becker, teenagers are the most victimized segment of the population (and the least likely to report a crime).[8] We don't like having to tell our daughters that the outside world isn't always safe for them, but doing it as part of a group makes a huge difference. If you talk to your daughter alone, without the backing of others, it's far easier for her to dismiss your advice. "You're just paranoid!" was Renée's daughter's favorite line. Or "You've just listened to too many bad stories because you're a therapist." (She's got something there!) Hearing other women talk about these dangers made it difficult for her to completely dismiss her mother's concerns. If you aren't part of a mom-daughter group, use books as your backup authority. Give her a chapter from one of the books in our bibliography about personal safety. The two of you can read the chapter, or the whole book, together. (Don't randomly search the Internet, which is full of misleading information.)

Talking About Drugs and Alcohol

An important element of teaching daughters about their increasing freedoms and concurrent responsibilities is to clearly let them know where we stand on such issues as alcohol, drugs, smoking, and premarital sex. This is not the time to be lecturing: Girls naturally hate this and tune out. Generally they are already getting alcohol and drug education in school. Ask them what they've learned about these subjects. Get them to teach you. Sometimes they know more than us about the latest street drugs, and we can better tailor our discussions if we know what they already know, and what we're really up against. We specifically bring up the subject of illicit drug and alcohol use here because it's so predominant a factor in sexual violence against women.

In some families, a glass of wine with dinner or an occasional beer is acceptable for an older teenager. In other families, the rule is "No alcohol until you are legal." In our group, we had one important rule that we all agreed on, and repeatedly told our girls: "If you are ever at a party and kids are drinking or using drugs, NEVER get into a car when the driver has been drinking or doing drugs. If you need a ride home, any time of the day or night, even if you're the one who made a bad choice, *do not drive home.* We'll come get you and you will not be punished. You can expect a long conversation about your choices and how you're going to negotiate future decisions, but our most important consideration is for your safety."

If you do have to deal with an incident of drug or alcohol use, the next day—after you've calmed down and the effects of the substance have worn off—is the time to talk. Get your daughter to tell you what worked about the choices she made and what didn't work. Now you have an opening to talk about her values, your values, and how she's going to make decisions in the future. (The bibliography lists some useful resources that describe signs of a drug problem and provide suggestions on how to talk to your daughter about drugs and alcohol.)

Talking About Violence Against Women

Toward the end of the year, it's time to share the hard news that violence against women, especially teenage girls, is rampant. Before we spoke to our daughters about how violence has directly affected our own lives, we started a discussion about rape by watching the movie *Antonia's Line*, in which a young, mentally handicapped woman is raped by her brother. It's difficult to watch, but offers an avenue for beginning to explore this terrible subject. We acknowledged feelings with simple comments: *That was difficult to watch. Why do you think something like that would happen? Has anybody ever confided in you about rape?*

When we finally directly addressed the subject of violence against women later in the year, they were already standing on firm ground. We introduced the issue of safety by asking: *Has someone ever given you the creeps, made you feel naked or uncomfortable? Maybe your heart started pounding or your stomach was in knots. Can you describe a time when you listened to your intuition and took care of yourself?* When asking questions like these, give girls an opportunity to respond fully. It's important to validate how each girl listened to her intuition.

Having the opportunity to talk about a scary situation someone has been in is valuable. If a mother or daughter has a story to tell, encourage her to role-play it, choosing whomever she wants to play the antagonist, giving her lines and actions. First, have her role-play the story as it actually happened. Then re-create it, this time having her respond in the way she would have liked to. This exercise is quite effective and often allows someone to feel empowered instead of victimized.[9]

While you talk to your girl, stay alert so that the language of fear doesn't overpower you. As Debbie and Mike Gardner point out in *Raising Kids Who Can Protect Themselves*, we often use language that gives our daughters the message that they need to be protected rather than a message of empowerment. Think about using some of these short, strong messages:

You can do it!

Just use your head!

Get out of there!

You'll handle it!

Make it happen!

You're strong!

You're resourceful![10]

These brief assertions are the language of being brave. Use them as a way of thinking about yourself as well as your daughter.

Finding the balance between caution and confidence is difficult. Through straight communication and proper preparation, we can strengthen our girls' intuition. We can foster self-confidence. We can teach them the warning signs of danger. They can learn a martial art. But they may still be harmed. Ultimately, we can only do our best to prepare them for the realities of being a woman. Then we have to let go.

Coming Up with Specific Safety Rules

Brainstorming with a group of mothers or women friends can help you come up with more real-life tools that will help your daughter negotiate life as an adult woman. The rules you adopt for your daughter will depend on whether you live in an urban, suburban, or rural area, as well as on many other factors. For specific safety tips, you can go to www.prepareinc.com. Helpful books include *Protecting the Gift* and *The Safe Zone: A Kid's Guide to*

Personal Safety by Donna Chaiet and Francine Russell (for children seven to twelve).

Here's a list of strategies we developed for our own daughters to use in situations such as going to a party or concert or traveling in an unfamiliar area.

- Go with someone you know and trust. Keep in touch with them once you arrive.
- Have a backup plan for getting home. This can include a bus schedule, an adult who is willing to pick you up, enough money to pay for a cab and the phone number of the cab service, a safe house within walking distance. Know where a telephone is or who has a cell phone (make sure it works at the location you're in).
- Have an escape plan, and be aware of exits before going in.
- Listen to your intuition. If you get a creepy feeling, pay attention and take appropriate action.
- Know that using drugs and/or alcohol increases your vulnerability.
- Gather information before or as you arrive to evaluate a situation.
- Tell someone where you are going and when you plan to be back.

And here are some general rules that all parents would agree with:

- Never get into a car with a stranger.
- Never tell a stranger where you live.
- Don't give out private information over the Internet.

A June 2001 survey reported that one out of five children who uses the Internet regularly is solicited for sex.[11] Most frequently solicited were girls between twelve and fifteen. A basic rule that will help you negotiate your daughter's use of the Internet, from Gavin De Becker: "Don't include anything in a Web site that you would not be willing to post on the bulletin board of every supermarket in every city in America."[12]

Here are some safety tips from self-defense educators Marla BB and Nancy Rothenberg [13] that you can teach your daughter to use if she finds herself in a potentially dangerous situation:

- Breathe deeply.
- Stay aware of your surroundings.
- Clear your mind of worry (you don't want to be preoccupied), but do focus.
- Notice sensations in your body (if you are in true danger, your body will respond).

Mother-Daughter Group: Avoiding Abusive Relationships

Talking to our daughters about our own past experiences with abusive relationships was difficult, but sharing such experiences can actually make them easier for us to shoulder. Speaking in a group makes girls and moms both feel more comfortable. We began by reminding our girls that we talked to them about getting their period and about sex long before these things were likely to come up for them.

"Okay," said Sarah, "we hope none of you will ever be in an abusive relationship, but we want you to know the warning signs, not only for yourselves, but possibly to help your friends." Then she revealed that she herself was in an abusive relationship for five years and it was very difficult to get out of it. This startled the girls to attention.

Next we imagined a couple of scenarios. "Let's say your boyfriend throws a fit because you're planning to go out with your girlfriends instead of him. What would you do?" Sarah asked.

"I'd tell him to take a hike," Gabriella, Maisie's daughter, said. She put her hands on her hips, sitting up a bit straighter. "That's stupid. Of course I'm going to spend time with my friends. If you don't like it, too bad," she said with authority.

"I'd tell him that I'm always going to spend time with my girlfriends and it's no big deal," Maggie, Sarah's daughter, added.

The next scenario was: "Imagine that one of your friends was with her boyfriend and he started getting rough with her, pushing her around. What would you do?"

"I'd tell him he can't get away with that stuff. Then I'd tell her to get the hell away from him," Marisol, Katy's daughter, said.

"Yeah, and if you were my mom, she'd be going right up to him and yelling in his face, 'Cut it out!'" Gabriella said with a laugh.

After a long conversation about avoiding abusive relationships, Sarah told the girls, "The bottom line is that you never deserve to be hit and you never deserve to be called names or controlled by anybody else."

Phoebe explained the strategy she developed to feel that she was dealing with her husband as an equal. "Paul is much taller than me—and he weighs twice as much as I do. So sometimes I stand on a chair when I talk to him. I need to be able to look him straight in the eye. And usually when we're disagreeing about something, we sit down to make things more even."

Then Libby described her early, abusive marriage, and how, when she finally left her husband after he hit her, her mother got angry at her for leaving, saying, "That's just the way men are. Your father pushed me down the stairs once." "I don't think my father was particularly abusive," Libby added, "but he was a very big man and he controlled in part by his size and in part by his attitude."

Shared in the group, our individual experiences appear in a larger context, which helps our daughters make sense of them. They see that it's not just a question of their own mother making a stupid choice. It's the experience of many women, often the very women they have come to know and respect. When Libby's daughter, Vanessa, said, "I don't want to hear that about Grandma and Grandpa," Sarah, not Vanessa's mother, can ask her why.

"They're old and Grandpa is going to die soon. I don't want to think of him that way," Vanessa exclaimed.

"But Vanessa, it's true of Grandpa and it's true of everybody. We all have our good points and our bad. Most of the time Grandpa was a kind and loving man, but when he grew up, men were king of the castle. This made him think he could push Grandma around," Libby then explained.

....

If you're not in a group, one option is to use a news story as an opening for this type of conversation. You can explain that abuse may be common, but it's never acceptable. Emphasize that women and girls who suffer abuse are not at fault. This is also an appropriate time to consult *Saving Beauty from the Beast* (see the bibliography), and show her its list of behaviors (unfortunately ones that are fairly common among teens) that are warning signs of a bad relationship, such as calling you names, trying to prevent you from seeing your friends, and flirting with other girls to make you jealous.

Have Fun, Too!

Thirteen-year-olds love getting out in the world and seeing new things, so make sure to plan exciting, adventurous activities to do with your daughter. Balance safety talks and exercises with bold—maybe even a bit wild and risky—ideas, and choose some that make the girls feel brave: roller-coaster rides, tubing on a river, climbing a steep mountain with a great view, an adventure at a rock climbing wall. How about stock car races or a rodeo? Take city girls to the country for outdoor adventures like kayaking, whitewater rafting, hiking, and mountain biking. Country girls can visit the city and go to a neighborhood of art galleries or on walking tours. Take a nighttime trip to Chinatown, where everyone tries something strange and new to eat. Riding the subway, hailing a taxi, street musicians—all are new and exciting to a country girl.

These experiences can be grist for later conversations about safety and freedom, and they nurture your relationship now. In the meantime, keep up the low-key, at-home opportunities to connect, like watching movies together (you could rent a film like *Erin Brockovich* that features a brave female character) or making homemade pizza with your daughter and her friends. Conquering the wide world is exhausting, and she needs (and wants, even if she won't admit it) plenty of down time.

And then your daughter turns fourteen. She'll venture forth more and more without you at her side, perhaps start dating. The lessons you share on safety and freedom will better prepare her as she moves into the world with more independence.

CHAPTER FOURTEEN

Speaking Her Heart and Mind

Fourteen Years Old—Establishing Values

Big changes are blowing in! At fourteen, girls are still going through huge transformations—maturing physically, intellectually, emotionally, socially, and spiritually. The process is exciting, but uneven. While some girls reach puberty at ten, others do not mature physically until fifteen or sixteen. While some fourteen-year-old girls' intellectual and emotional development proceeds gradually until late adolescence, others have a sophisticated understanding of life that can shock us. But the vast majority flip-flop back and forth as their thinking becomes more complex, they learn to handle their emotions, and their bodies mature. Girls at this age seek recognition of their rapidly developing selves but usually lack the skills or self-awareness to clearly articulate the big changes going on outside and in.

Beginning in early adolescence and continuing right into adulthood, girls are figuring out who they are and in what they believe, and it's not an easy process. They try on different identities and explore different values, sometimes in rapid succession. Dressing as a goth one week and a jock the next is not a trivial exercise—it's part of the work of identity development and self-knowledge. In a few years, girls will be making important decisions about their lives, like what kind of education and careers they will pursue and what kind of long-term love relationships they want. They will need to know whom they can trust, who gives good advice, and who has their back. Does my coach care about my future as an athlete or just about my game stats this season? Is my teacher encouraging me toward a career in theater because of her own unfulfilled dreams or because I have what it takes? Does my boyfriend really love me? Is smoking weed really no big deal? While the occasional fourteen-year-old is clear about these things, most are in the midst of sorting it all out.

Especially as they enter high school, teenagers "are under great social pressure to abandon their families, to be accepted by peer culture and to be autonomous individuals," says Mary Pipher in *Reviving Ophelia*.[1] Unfortunately, their peer culture may glorify violence, endorse buying your way to happiness, and equate sex with love. Mothers who stay connected to their daughters can help provide another view.

At this age, many girls are intensely preoccupied with their bodies and acutely aware of the constant evaluation of their appearance by others. As the pressure to conform to a certain idealized type increases, girls may try to become the Perfect Girl, some as early as middle school and others in high school. They may try to be skinnier than thou; set their sights on being popular and getting into the *in* crowd; experiment with alcohol, drugs, and sex if they are part of a crowd of kids who think that's cool. Yet girls at this age also try to stay true to their authentic selves by gravitating to things they enjoy, maybe joining the school chorus, a sports or debate team, bonding with a small group of like-minded girlfriends, or studying hard to excel in school.

Daughters also try to figure out who they are by defining themselves as both different from *and* similar to their mothers. The emphasis at this age is on differentiating oneself from the parent of the same sex, while also continuing to share many of the same values and characteristics. That means you're likely to find yourself under the variously judgmental and admiring gaze of an adolescent who has her own idea of an ideal mother and woman.

Sometimes, no matter how much you bend over backward to meet her needs, your best may not feel good enough to her. Your love and care mean a lot to her, but at fourteen she still takes it for granted; only occasionally will she notice something you've done for her and let you know she's grateful. It's helpful right now not to expect your daughter to explicitly express her appreciation of you—instead she may be showing you anger as she realizes that you are a fallible human being. In early adolescence, girls are just beginning to recognize that their mothers aren't all-powerful. Even as they fight for independence, it comes as a blow to realize that mommy can't keep them completely safe, hard as we may try.

Add to this complicated scenario the fact that fourteen-year-olds are subject to rapid, extreme mood changes. The volatility, intensity, and instability of their feelings often leads to unpredictable behavior. In fact, a synthesis of studies of adolescence by the National Academy of Sciences found evidence that adolescents experience far more intense emotions than adults.[2] This is a time of continuous negotiation of the relationship between mothers and daughters. One day your girl may act as if she's still a loving child; the next day she's diffident or full of rage. Her ability to think through risks is still developing, she hasn't yet mastered her impulses, and her reactivity to stress is high. Although riding this emotional roller coaster is challenging for girls and their mothers (and fathers as well), it offers girls the opportunity to practice how to manage strong emotions while staying connected with those they love. Emotions, along with intellect, give us information we need to make wise decisions, and fourteen-year-olds are still early on the learning curve.

Why do we so often hear about adolescent girls fighting with their mothers? Sharon Lamb, a psychologist who has studied girls and anger extensively, writes in *The Secret Lives of Girls* that "Because middle-class girls in our culture are not permitted to be angry, they go to great pains to deny, suppress, mask, or hide it."[3] Consequently anger can reveal itself in self-destructive ways, as when girls cut themselves, gossip, exclude others, or withdraw emotionally. Often, however, they aim their secret anger at their mothers. "The mother-daughter relationship is particularly charged," Lamb explains, "because mothers teach their daughters to suppress anger and because they themselves have been taught to suppress anger."[4] Both girls and their mothers may feel enormous guilt when anger erupts, primarily because neither has learned how to accept and handle it and use it constructively.

Learning to have compassion for ourselves when we do express anger inappropriately helps us avoid self-judgment and shame. Acknowledging intense feelings and taking a break until you can express your anger constructively provides a model for your daughter as she learns how to voice strong feelings. As Lyn Mikel Brown reminds us in *Raising Their Voices*, "What is important is that we recognize the *potential* power of anger if and when it is heard, understood, and engaged in dialogue."[5]

Remember, it's perfectly normal for your more womanly looking fourteen-year-old to think and act like a child. Interestingly, researcher Louann Brizendine has found that the physical changes of early puberty can actually slow down other aspects of girls' development, perhaps because of the difficult challenges of suddenly being seen physically as a woman while remaining emotionally a girl.[6] Remind yourself that your girl is still growing up, learning how to handle the intricacies of becoming an adult woman, and desperately in need of your guidance.

Losing "Voice"

In the 1990s, Carol Gilligan, Lyn Mikel Brown, Mary Pipher, and other psychologists articulated how girls in early adolescence suffer a loss of self, which these experts describe as a loss of "voice." By *voice* they mean "the voice of courage to speak one's mind."[7] As girls encounter in their own lives the effects of racial prejudice, economic inequality, and discrimination against women and girls, they often stifle their anger and succumb to the

Perfect Girl paradigm. At the Mother-Daughter Project, we strive to counter these influences by encouraging our girls to recognize and name the social factors that suppress their voice and undermine their well-being. We urge them to keep expressing the full range of their thoughts, feelings, and desires, just as they did before adolescence made them self-conscious.

Learning to express one's opinions and to actively create meaningful experiences for oneself are powerful voice lessons. One way to foster our girls' voices is within the safety of a mother-daughter group. Here they can express their likes and dislikes and stand up for their own individuality—whether that means jumping onto a table and shouting "I love math games!" or trading a hoard of teen magazines. The group is the place to get their unique needs met, even when they have trouble articulating these needs clearly. As girls practice expressing their likes and dislikes among peers, they're also asserting preferences that are the same as and different from those of their mothers. A group can comfortably contain these types of differences so that they don't become sources of conflict or disconnection, allowing all members to find a way to meet their needs mutually.

Keeping up with your daughter's rapid changes while working to instill good values and communicate your own feelings can be challenging, especially since she may have trouble sharing the changes going on in her life. Sometimes our daughters want to protect us from knowing just what their lives are like right now. They're certain we'd be appalled (and we may well be) to learn about behavior common among today's teenagers. Keeping lines of communication open can help us stay informed, however, which can help us guide our daughters when they are receptive to us.

This year, you can focus on helping your daughter strengthen her own voice in the world and become an active agent for getting her needs met. At the same time, you can clarify your own values and voice, so you can best respond as your daughter moves into an increasingly complex world.

Setting Your "Mothering Compass"

What can we do to strengthen the values we hold dear for our daughters as outside influences increase? Articulating our own values helps us make sound parenting decisions. Our "values" are the things we care most about. They might include respect, love, truth, generosity, connection, fairness, security, freedom to be oneself, and so on. None of us are mothering solely by tradition or by what comes naturally. Rather, we are making individual decisions—consciously or subconsciously—about how best to parent. Luckily, we each have a mothering compass to guide these decisions. This compass is set by our values. At the Mother-Daughter Project, our true north is the place where girls and mothers are flourishing and have the closeness they want and need.

To discover how your own compass is set, begin by considering which moments of mothering have particular resonance for you.

In your journal or with a friend or group, vividly describe a moment of mothering that stands out for you—whether it felt particularly good or particularly difficult. Then consider:

What value can be seen in that moment?

Can this value be seen in other areas of my life?

Did I have to overcome anything to hold on to this value in my mothering?

What does this say about my commitment to this value and about my success in bringing it forward?

Telling Our Success Stories

When we feel we're not measuring up—perhaps we're acting short-tempered or impatient or feeling hopeless—the story we need to hear is how we're *already* succeeding in mothering, in big ways and small. It can be difficult to remember ways in which we *are* mothering according to our values because, for many of us, our worries about our daughters or our perceived shortcomings dominate our thoughts—but making the attempt can revolutionize our thinking and our self-respect. For example, bringing to mind how hard you are working to stay connected with your daughter (such as not taking it personally when she cancels her breakfast date with you, but, instead, offering to drive her across town to a friend's so you can have time with her), and observing the ways she may be thriving in her academic or social life, can strengthen your feelings of success, which can energize you to keep at it.

These days, in the face of alarming headlines and frightening news about teenagers, it might feel counterintuitive to focus on success, and you may wonder whether doing so would put you at risk of wallowing in weak-minded complacency and neglecting issues that threaten you. Actually, telling stories that inspire us makes us stronger. We don't ignore our failures to live up to our best intentions, but grounding ourselves in our achievements makes it easier to face these shortcomings and do better. Seeing how far we have already come energizes us to persevere toward our goals.

It helps even to recognize our brief moments of connection with our daughters. When Vanessa was fourteen and she and her mother, Libby, were in a contentious phase, we asked Libby to describe a happy moment with Vanessa. "The other night we were in the car on the way to pick up a friend of hers, and Vanessa asked what music I'd like to listen to. It's a small thing, but I felt she was appreciating my giving her a ride by considering my taste. We mutually decided on Stevie Wonder and then had a nice conversation with music we both enjoy in the background. I value being considerate, and that was there in that moment."

You can also find inspiration and confirm your values by watching others parent. Seeing a mother and her teenage daughter deep in conversation in a booth at a favorite diner reminds you that you value this type of intimacy. Watching a friend comfort her cranky three-year-old evokes your own value of patience.

To recall examples of your own successes, choose a value elicited by answering the questions above, then ask:

Who or what inspires me to persist in trying to live by this value?

Was there a time when it seemed like I might not be successful in manifesting this value in my mothering? What helped me hold on?

What difference does it make to my life now that I remain committed to this value?

Getting Clear on Difficult Subjects

Some subjects—sex, drugs, and alcohol, for example—are quite uncomfortable and hard to think about as they pertain to our daughters. So is Internet use, an increasing problem as kids get involved in chat rooms, surf for porn, or read the alienated writings of others. But if we don't figure out where we stand on these issues in relation to our children, no one else is going to step in and do it for us.

Take alcohol, for example. It's illegal for a minor to drink alcohol, but where do your values lie? Do you say absolutely, unequivocally, *No way?* If you discover that your daughter has been drinking, do you ground her? Or do you think that kids learn how to handle alcohol by having an occasional beer or glass of wine at home? Perhaps you experimented with alcohol yourself as a teenager with no ill effects, so you think, *Kids experiment. I did it. She'll do it. It's just being a teenager.*

Maybe your answer is "No way." In that case, when your daughter says, "Nobody else's parents are calling Carrie's parents about her party. Why do you have to?" you want to be able to express that value clearly, so she knows why you insist on making sure that parents will be home supervising, to prevent pot or alcohol from being used at a party.

We guide our daughters by being authentic ourselves. Kids are quick to pick up on hypocrisy. If we're telling them one thing and doing another, they'll see it. In our efforts to achieve this kind of consistency, it's extremely helpful to have support as we clarify our own positions on these issues before bringing them up with our daughters. If you don't have a mother-daughter group, perhaps you have at least one friend you feel comfortable talking to. If not, think about joining an online community of like-minded women.

Talking to Our Daughters About Values

When teenagers' behavior contradicts every value we hold dear, we can use the power of a mother-daughter group to reinforce those values. In our group, we encourage our daughters to actively resist some of the messages being promulgated by the media. Starting at age ten, we repeatedly ask: *Who is benefiting from that message? Whose needs are being served?*

Most girls will challenge their mother's values at one point or another. You can also back up your views by exposing your daughter to your favorite books and documentaries on hard-hitting topics. In our group, we watched excerpts from documentaries such as *Spin the Bottle: Sex, Lies and Alcohol* (available through your library or from the Media Education Foundation), which offers a different version of reality from that of many "reality" TV shows, about the power of alcohol advertising and its negative consequences for teenagers and young adults. Another documentary, *Tough Guise*, about media images of masculinity, stimulates questions about stereotypes of what men should be like. A third film, *The Strength to Resist: The Media's Impact on Women and Girls*, shows the effect of advertising on women's self-esteem. If you feel strongly about any documentary films you have watched with your daughter, consider talking to faculty or administrators of your daughter's school about introducing media education as part of the curriculum. We recommend that you preview any documentary you plan on showing your daughter to make sure its message, language, and situations are what you deem appropriate for her at this age.

I feel; I'd do. This exercise encourages girls to think about where they stand on issues and to clarify their values.

Before the meeting, two or more mothers prepare flash cards bearing two series of incomplete sentences. The first series should be sentences like: *When I see a good friend light up a cigarette, I feel . . . When I'm walking through my neighborhood and I see someone drunk or high on drugs, I feel . . . When I see girls calling one another names or fighting in school, I feel . . . When I'm at a concert and I hear a guy putting down a girl, I feel . . .*

Pair up each girl with a mother (not her own). In each pair, Person 1 reads the sentence; Person 2 completes it. Person 1 repeats back what she heard Person 2 say. (This is called mirroring or active listening.) Person 2 can ask for further clarification if an answer is unclear. "I don't know" doesn't qualify as an answer. Then reverse roles, with Person 2 reading the sentence and Person 1 completing it.

If a sentence evokes a lot of feelings, be sure to allow time for the story behind the feelings to be told.

The second series of questions is designed to elicit strategies to help a girl extricate herself from a difficult situation. Examples: *When I'm at a party and I know that everybody is getting too drunk to drive, what I would do is . . . When I'm sleeping over at a friend's house and her older brother and his friends come in high, I'd . . .*

After each pair has responded to each incomplete sentence, the entire group forms a circle. Now each mother describes how the girl she interviewed would feel and what strategies she would use for handling each situation. Last, each girl describes the feelings and strategies of the mother she was paired with.

Generally this exercise provokes a lively discussion. Write your sentences about issues that your daughters are dealing with right now, as well as about issues you expect to arise shortly. This will deepen the conversation.

If you are not part of a mother-daughter group, you can still trigger conversations about important issues by watching TV shows together. Renting a DVD of an old series (it's harder for girls to have enough distance from current programs to relate to them critically) like *Buffy the Vampire Slayer* offers openings to talk about difficult subjects, such as a boyfriend being mean. Later you can ask, "How do you think she felt when he said . . . ?" Or "How did you feel when he did such and such?" Or "What did you think about that interaction between Buffy and her mom?" Start with her thoughts and feelings, but make sure you share yours as well. She wants to know them.

Time to Assess the Mother-Daughter Group

As our daughters move into high school, they grow busy with extracurricular activities, jobs, and increasing time spent with friends, which often conflict with our time together. They are also now developing their own resources and taking on more responsibility for creating a community that supports them. If you are in an established mother-daughter group, it's time to ask whether the girls still value attending.

This year, at a mother-daughter meeting we ask everyone: *What is and isn't working for you in the group?* Although the mothers know that we want to continue meeting with one another, regardless of what the girls decide, we also want them to begin making a commitment to the group independent of us.

When to assess. Anytime one of your girls begins to question her involvement in the group is a good time to address the subject with the other mothers before doing a general assessment with the group. Libby raised the issue when she told the other mothers she wasn't sure if Vanessa wanted to continue. Maisie acknowledged that April, too, had been expressing some ambivalence. Both girls wanted more time to spend with their school friends, and April wasn't such a fan of sitting around and talking but liked it when the group went out and did activities together. Talking just among the mothers helps you brainstorm which of your daughter's needs are not being met. Often girls can't articulate what's missing or what they need in order to feel more comfortable, but mothers who have known them for years can come up with ideas for how the group can address more of every girl's needs. The mothers can also voice any problems they themselves might be having with the group, so that their needs can be taken into consideration as well.

We recommend that from this year on, each year begin with a formal assessment: what's working, what's not working, hopes and dreams for the group, and a particular goal that all can share for the year. You can assess during the summer before the start of the school year or at the first meeting in the fall. When you meet with the girls, acknowledge that you know their lives are getting busier, and explain that their commitment to the group is essential for the group to be effective for everybody.

If you are not part of a mother-daughter group, you can assess your daughter's situation more informally, but be sure to keep track of what is important to her about your relationship. Hanging out with mom may no longer be cool, but she still values you and wants desperately to have a good relationship, even though she may seem to be doing nothing but pushing you away these days. Don't be discouraged. Make a commitment to follow through with that once-a-month special activity that you both enjoy.

Group evaluation. We have found Marshall Rosenberg's approach to speaking and listening, which he calls "Nonviolent Communication," useful for teaching our daughters to express their needs effectively during evaluations.[8]

With everyone sitting in a circle, and one mom facilitating, we introduce two basic concepts: *Everyone's needs matter* and *If we listen carefully and connect empathically with others, we can find strategies that work for everyone:*

- Use I-statements: *I feel . . . I enjoy . . . I want . . .*
- No comments or judgments about someone else's feelings.
- Everyone's wants get put on the table.

Evaluating how the group is and isn't meeting the girls' needs is critical, for at fourteen you can begin to move to a more cooperative model. Instead of being generated only by the mothers, the group will now be created by everyone.

Brainstorming Your Group's Wish List

Girls care passionately about their lives and need outlets for speaking their minds, especially when they come up against external constraints that thwart self-expression. It's extremely difficult for a teenage girl to stand up to the pressure of conformity and voice an opinion different from her peer group. But a safe, nurturing environment like your mother-daughter group provides the opportunity for girls to practice saying what is in their minds and hearts.

Gather all your members. For this meeting, everyone must be present so that each person's ideas and desires are represented.

Use a large pad of newsprint that everyone can see. One person volunteers to be the scribe, and two mothers act as coleaders. As quickly as possible, *brainstorm a list of all the activities you think would be fun and/or meaningful to do together.* A road trip across the country. A month working in an orphanage in China. The sky's the limit! Brainstorming means allowing all possibilities to surface, without censoring. The coleaders should make sure that every person contributes an idea. This ensures that all participate in setting the direction the group will take over the next few years.

Once you have generated a long list of activities, sort them into categories. We ended up with five categories: traveling, social activism, recreation, challenging topics, and creative projects. After further discussion, we prioritized political activism.

The next step is to look for opportunities to clarify our values and find which ones we share. Libby, a lawyer, brought up a reproductive-rights march to be held in Washington, D.C., triggering an intense discussion of unwanted pregnancy and abortion, and the difficult choices women sometimes have to make. Some of us are unequivocally pro-choice. However, Katy said, "I think women need to be able to choose, but abortion is a painful choice. It's always unfortunate, even when it's the right choice for someone."

We reminded the girls that we prefer that they wait until they are much older and in a committed relationship before they are sexual with a partner. We told them that sometimes women are forced to have sex, or they make a poor choice and have unprotected sex, but in that case there is the possibility of the morning-after pill. And we talked about the huge responsibility we take on when we choose to be sexually active.

Eventually the group decided to go on the march. Some chose not to participate, for a variety of reasons (one girl was going to be traveling across the country to see her father; one mother supports the right to choose but would not choose abortion herself and felt uncomfortable marching for it). But we did come to a consensus that we all value a woman's right to choose. If we didn't have this consensus, we would not have attended this march as a group.

The march itself made a powerful impression on the girls. Here were thousands of women (and some men), all believing strongly that women should have the right to make decisions about their own bodies. As Amy said, "I'm really glad the mom-daughter group went together. I feel strongly about this issue, and knowing the moms were standing with us to fight for our reproductive freedom felt really important to me." For your own group, choose a project dear to all of you. For example, community service offers endless possibilities for mothers and daughters to spend meaningful time with other mothers and daughters. You could organize a one-day event such as cleaning up a local park or playground or an ongoing activity such as dog walking for an animal shelter. Or you could develop a list of useful resources for your group, such as Web sites that support the needs of girls. Don't be surprised if you inspire other people in the community to get involved.

If you don't have a mother-daughter group, brainstorm issues that matter to your daughter and you. Once you know what she cares about, link that value to a form of action. Again taking community service as an example, the two of you might volunteer in a soup kitchen once a month, act as a joint big sister to a girl in need, or visit the elderly in a nursing home. Working together on a concern that you both share will bond you, even though tensions sometimes run high. If you're thinking, "Who's got time for something like this?" consider how much more time would be lost if you and your daughter lose your connection.

Unplanned pregnancy is only one of the issues our group tackled as we clarified our values. You and your daughter will be addressing many difficult subjects over the next few years, from drugs and alcohol to the friends she chooses to how she spends money. Asking about these subjects and listening carefully to what she says will teach you about the young woman she's becoming. And as you address difficult subjects head on, rather than obfuscating or avoiding them, you teach by example. Even as you work through tough issues, remember that you are not simply trying to keep your daughter safe and instill healthy values. You're also sharing the joys of being an adult woman— thereby teaching what being a woman means and what a healthy mother-daughter relationship is like. A powerfully effective way to do this is to have fun together.

Too often, as the needs of school and peers dominate and tensions arise, mothers and daughters find fewer opportunities to enjoy each other's company. Gone are the childhood evenings of reading books together or playing board games. But a once-a-month outing together or meeting with other girls and mothers (or just one friend and her mother) sends the message that you want to take the time for fun activities. Even if your daughter goes through a period of active resistance, keep choosing activities you know she enjoys that you can share. (We've been careful to choose activities that cost little or no money so that no one would be put on the spot financially.)

As girls grow up, each year can take you further into challenging and provocative issues—ones that can have a direct impact on their futures. As our daughters' sophistication about the world increases, along with their ability to reason and think abstractly, our discussions together take on greater depth and breadth. We have entered the years of the subtle transition from child to adult. Articulating her values and establishing her voice prepares a girl to start considering what living a satisfying life will mean to her as a woman, an issue we will take up in the next chapter.

CHAPTER FIFTEEN

Earning Money and Wielding Power

Fifteen Years Old—Looking Ahead

At fifteen, our girls' identities are crystallizing. Beginning to negotiate the world more independently, they are getting jobs, spending their own money, and wanting to make more choices about their lives. Making choices entails learning how to acquire the power that will allow them to have real options in their lives as they become adults.

Girls pick up ideas about power from many sources: the media, teachers, family, books, and the subliminal messages they get from us, their mothers. Embedded in our culture are tremendous biases about women's relation to power and also to money, which is so closely connected to power. One well-known example is the fact that women's work—both paid and unpaid—is valued less than men's.

This year it is important to begin bringing these subliminal biases about women, money, and power into the light so that as our daughters move into adult life, they will better understand how their particular social context affects their life choices. We want them to be able to create their lives from a position of self-respect, self-awareness, and power. At this age, girls begin to think seriously about what comes after high school: college, a job, traveling, or community service? Although the immediate world of friends and school preoccupies them, when we ask about the future they wonder what kind of work they will do when they grow up and whether they'll even be able to support themselves. It's both thrilling and scary for girls to contemplate being adult women, especially when they consider the challenge of learning how to take care of themselves in all ways: emotionally, socially, spiritually, physically, and, of course, fiscally.

Fifteen-year-olds typically have little experience with money; most of their discretionary funds come from parents with perhaps a little extra from odd jobs such as babysitting or from birthday and holiday gifts. By the time they are seventeen, many more kids are earning money and choosing how to spend it. After seventeen, our girls will be immersed in the world of money, and they'll sort out their relationship to it much more independently of their parents.

Many teenagers are acutely status-conscious and vulnerable to the message that money is your ticket to the good life—to the world of fashion, status colleges, vacations, concert tickets, sports events. Teens judge themselves and their parents based on material possessions and equate personal worth with money. The central questions a fifteen-year-old grapples with are *Who am I? And who are you? Are you a loser or a winner?* Sometimes they see success and financial success as one and the same.

Although it's critical to teach girls about working toward achieving financial security, giving your daughter new yardsticks to measure a "good life" helps her sort out her values and enables her to recognize the many choices available for creating the life she wants. Asking questions such as *Can you describe the happiest woman you know? What are the qualities of her life that make her happy? What kind of relationships does she have that sustain her? What kind of work does she do?* will give her an expanded idea of what it means to be a fulfilled adult woman.

The goal of this year is to support our girls in learning how to have the power to create the most meaningful lives they can. Money is one way we get power in our lives, but, of course, it's not the only way. Learning that people have many resources to draw upon, including friends, family, and community, and that people at all income levels enjoy their lives—not just the wealthy—can inspire our daughters to look at the concept of success more broadly.

However, talking directly about money is still one of our culture's biggest taboos. Many of us grew up with parents who believed that you don't talk about money, not even to your children. We're a practical group of women, and we want our daughters to know how to balance a checkbook, use debit and credit cards, avoid debt, and negotiate the best salary they can. But we also know that talking about money is far more complex than that.

One thing we teach our daughters is to recognize the impact of their socioeconomic status and their gender on their lives. At fifteen, girls are creating an identity within their own social network. Think of the labels kids give themselves and each other: nerd, geek, preppy, jock, druggie. They have a sense of how they fit into a world that feels pretty separate from their parents' world. However, this teenage world is affected by the values and culture of the larger community, and the status of a girl's family within that community has an enormous influence on her understanding of life. Before speaking to our daughters, therefore, we examine the interrelated effects of socioeconomic status and gender in our own lives.

Mothers Talk About Work and Status

Our hopes for the future were shaped indelibly by the social situation we grew up in, yet its influence was often invisible as we grew up. To make it visible, we begin by reflecting on our varying backgrounds.

Autobiography exercise.[1] A very illuminating tool is writing a history of your mother's education, work, and income. This is an exercise to do by yourself to understand the impact of your own family history in shaping your understanding of money and power and your beliefs about what you wanted and were capable of doing in the world.

Write down your answers to the following questions:

Did your mother have the same access to career choices as your father?

What kind of work did your mother do, paid and unpaid? How was her work valued inside and outside your home?

How did your mother balance paid employment and caring for you and your siblings?

Did your mother have equal access to decisions about how money was earned and spent?

Who was the breadwinner in your family? Who handled the money/paid the bills?

What kind of choices did your mother make about how she spent her time? Was there a discrepancy between your parents in this respect?

In what ways was your mother accorded power and status in your family? Was it different with your father?

What did your family value most about your mother? How did income and career status influence your understanding of your mother's worth within the family?

What kinds of decisions did your mother have authority to make? Were you aware of a difference in authority between your mother and father?

What do you believe your mother felt most proud of about herself?

What about your mother made you feel proud?

What would you guess your mother felt the most shame about in relationship to money and her status?

Did your mother have a different socioeconomic background from your father?

If you like, you can dig even deeper by answering the questions again for different generations of women in your family.

You may want to share the results of this exercise in a mothers' group. We like to go around the circle one by one, each giving a synopsis of what she learned about her family and herself. Allow time for each listener to say what family story resonated with her.

Be aware that sharing information about money and education, particularly among people with different socioeconomic backgrounds, is not easy. It can mean addressing disparity in our lives and acknowledging the effects of factors such as race, intelligence, disabilities, income level, types of communities you belong to, and family situation (for example, one- versus two-parent households).

If you prefer not to share this information with a group, you can use it by answering these questions for yourself:

How has your family background influenced your thinking about money and getting your financial needs met?

What were the advantages and disadvantages of your socioeconomic background?

How did it affect your sense of yourself as a woman in the world, and does it still affect you now?

How did your mother have power in her life? Was her ability to make her own decisions hindered by a lack of money or opportunity?

Do you think you or your mother were limited in career choices or in access to money and power?

How did money and power affect your mother's sense of self-worth? Your own sense of self-worth? How do money and power affect your relationship with your daughter? Your hopes and dreams for her? Her own sense of self-worth?

What information and skills do you and she need in order to address money and power issues effectively?

Understanding the influence of our social and economic background reveals how this factor influences the *type* of dreams we create for our lives and the choices we make. Two books that are useful resources to help you manage money are *Prince Charming Isn't Coming: How Women Get Smart About Money* by Barbara Stanny and *Nice Girls Don't Get Rich: 75 Avoidable Mistakes Women Make with Money* by Lois Frankel.

Mothers Talk About Being Female

It's equally important to look at the influence of gender. Women have been and are treated differently from men in the work world, and the phrase that encapsulates this difference in treatment is "sexual discrimination." Its effects range from the ways we are subtly or not so subtly steered into certain types of careers to the wage gap that still exists.

For generations women were in an inferior social position, especially in relation to money and power. Usually financially dependent on men, they were educated to believe that they couldn't function effectively in the world of work. Even though women today have far greater access to careers that were closed to our mothers or grandmothers, this long history of myths about our nature continues to affect us and our daughters.

When Maisie was a teenager, she didn't think much about having to support herself as an adult, assuming her husband would provide financially, at least while they were raising young children. Although she went to college and studied to become a teacher, she assumed that her career, like her mother's, would be secondary to her husband's. "That worked fine as long as I was married, but the minute I got divorced I saw how that myth hadn't served me," Maisie says.

According to Evelyn Murphy and E. J. Graff in *Getting Even*, women working full-time make seventy-seven cents to every full-time male dollar, and that for African American or Hispanic women, the wage gap is even greater.[2] Add to that the impact of care-giving for children and elders, and the lifetime wage gap between men and women widens. Money lost during the peak years of caring for children has financial consequences for the rest of one's life.[3]

Despite media stories about women "opting out" of the workforce to stay home and raise their children, current statistics show a very different story. The Bureau of Labor Statistics reports that approximately 70 percent of women with children under eighteen work outside the home. According to Women Work!, the National Network for Women's Employment, 70 percent of families are headed by two working parents or a working single parent, and the vast majority (84 percent according to U.S. Census Bureau statistics) of children who live with one parent live with their mother.[4] Single moms are worse off than other women, making only 69 percent of a single dad's dollar (even counting the average three thousand dollars a year that half of them manage to collect in child support).[5]

It's not easy to explain this to our daughters, but they need to understand why it's so hard to find that magic balance between meeting the needs of home, family, and finance. Our social system is not set up to provide care for children, the elderly, or the disabled, so most of those needs are met by women, in an ad hoc way. This unpaid caregiving provides real value to society and can be personally satisfying, but at present it is done at a personal cost to families—and it's women who pay the heaviest price.[6]

Women and men make trade-offs when they become parents. By and large men trade off time with their children while women trade off financial security. "I made trade-offs when I was younger. I had time with my kids by not working outside the home for twelve years, which was great," Maisie told us in a mothers-only meeting. "But now, when my girls are teenagers and I wish I had more time for them, I'm working hard to just make ends meet. I still believe that money isn't nearly as important as other stuff, but you need money, too."

Many young women see how overworked their mothers are and long for their own lives to be easier. Yet our mother's model is often deeply embedded, and unless we think consciously about it, we can find ourselves following in her footsteps. Even when we choose a different path, it's sometimes in reaction to our mother's choices. Our task, then, is to become as conscious as we can about our own choices so that we can teach our daughters to think consciously, too.

Either in your mothers' group or alone, write down your responses to the following questions:

In your family of origin, who taught you about money? What did you learn?

Was there a woman other than your mother whom you saw as a model of a balanced, happy life?

How did your mother balance work, caring for you and your siblings, and home life in general?

How did your father balance these same things?

Did you see either of your parents engaged in activities that gave them joy and nourished their spirit? If so, describe.

If you are in a group, go around the circle and one by one answer the first question. The other members should reflect back to the speaker either what resonated with them or increased their understanding of her life choices. Continue through all the questions, allowing room for the discussion to take off in whatever ways are most meaningful for all of you.

Shame. Another effect of the power differential between men and women is to promote shame in women.[7] As our group talked about money and power in our lives, we recognized feelings of shame in ourselves. After separating from her husband, Maisie felt shame at her inexperience at getting a good teaching job and supporting herself financially. Libby thought that generations of women in her family had felt shame: her great-grandmother at being abandoned by her husband and left destitute to raise children, her grandmother at working with her husband on the farm until she became a teacher, and then her mother for becoming a farmer's wife. Recognizing the influence of these earlier generations helped Libby sort through her own choices and the message she was handing on to Vanessa.

At fifteen, your daughter is challenging who you are and the kind of choices you've made. She may be holding you up against a Supermom ideal. If you are still holding a secret shame deep within, you will be vulnerable to her criticism when you don't live up to her expectations—and to passing on your shame, particularly shame about just being female. To combat shame, we need both to acknowledge the pain we've experienced and also see what's heroic in our lives—our accomplishments, even ones that might not be culturally valued but are real nevertheless.

Naming our accomplishments. Women are good at making do. We'll stretch a dollar. We'll hunt out the best child care for our children. Some of us give up full-time, demanding careers to stay at home until the kids are in school. Others work part-time. We work nights so we can be home with our kids during the day. We work the equivalent of two full-time jobs, one at the office, the other caring for home and children. Many of us will also look to our partners to share the family/work load, just as we're sharing the financial load.

These are the things we tell our girls, who learn about being an adult woman by observing us. Watching a movie like *The Calendar Girls* (in which a group of middle-aged English women pose naked for the annual calendar of the Women's Institute as a means of raising money for a hospital—don't worry, it's only rated PG-13!) together can be the jumping-off point for a discussion about women, choices, and money. Our girls are interested in how we ended up where we are—the kinds of jobs we have, the ways we balance work and personal lives, the messages we got growing up about being supported financially versus being on our own. We don't lecture, but our storytelling grabs their attention.

Unlike Maisie, who began having babies when she graduated from college at twenty-one, Phoebe, a professor of anthropology, followed a straight line through college and graduate school. She had Amy while she was getting her PhD. Between school and child care, she had no time for herself for years. "It put a terrible strain on me and my marriage," she reported. "But we got through it. Now my life is great. I've got tenure, I make a good living doing work I love, and I've got flexibility, particularly in the summer when I have more time for my kids. At this point, I'd have to say all my hard work has paid off."

Creating a Vision of the Future with Your Daughter

The following two exercises focus on creating dreams for the future, then figuring out practical measures to make them a reality.

Visions of the future. One of the first building blocks in creating the life we want is articulating what's important to us. You can begin your discussion by asking your daughter to create a vision for her future. Naturally the vision a girl has at fifteen is likely to change radically as she grows up, but this exercise conveys the principle that she can actively create her life. You can do this exercise either alone with your daughter or in a group.

The leader tells everyone to close her eyes and take a few deep breaths. When all are quiet, she gives a "writing prompt": *Imagine your life twenty years from now. Thinking of things that bring a smile to your face!* This is a signal to brainstorm by writing down phrases or words, even doodling—anything that comes to mind. Everyone brainstorms for ten minutes, then reads the results to the group. Here are some of our girls' results:

Maggie: Worldwide travel; a glowing face; doing what I do really well; I have enough money to do what I want; a deep community of women.

Vanessa: Travel; content; kind of famous—scientist, doctor, soccer player; do what I do well; enough money to give to others; good friends.

Marisol: Travel everywhere and see everything; good job; creative writing; well known; music; long-term relationships; making art; self-supporting.

Amy: Do something that makes a difference; doing things seriously with commitment but also doing it well in a playful way; community; long-term intimate relationship; good health insurance.

Developing a budget. Now that you've come up with great things you want to do, it's time to imagine how to support these dreams materially. It's important to know where your money goes. The next exercise is designed to foster your daughter's awareness of the expenses currently involved in supporting her, whether or not she pays for them directly.[8]

Pair up each girl with a mother (not her own). List the following categories: clothing, entertainment, education, food, hobbies, special events, savings, and philanthropy. Then ask: *What percentage of each of these categories do you pay? What percentage do your parents pay? How much money do you think you spend each month in each of these categories? If you don't know how much money you and your parents spend on any one category, estimate what you think would be reasonable for a girl your age.*

Even if parents pay 100 percent of a girl's expenses, this exercise will help her realize that she'll soon be making these types of decisions herself.

You can do a version of this exercise alone with your daughter. Ask her what careers she thinks she may pursue. Start with at least three possibilities. Then you can both find out more about these lines of work. Read books, search for Web sites that describe jobs and typical salaries, and talk to friends and colleagues to find a mentor (preferably female) who will talk to her about a potential career. Your daughter can even interview the mentor, using a list of questions about how she balances work, self-care, intimate relationship, friends, and children (if she has any). It's a big help for your daughter to hear the creative ways that women create meaningful lives.

Learning About Money

Drowning in credit cards. Within a couple of years, our daughters will be bombarded by offers of credit cards with fabulous incentives. Choosing carefully and knowing how to handle credit cards responsibly is crucial for young adults. According to a 2004 report, there has been a sharp rise in credit card debt among eighteen- to twenty-four-year-olds in the United States, so that "the average credit card indebted household in this age group spends nearly 30 percent of its income on debt payments."[9] Explain to your daughter the concept of interest and late fees and provide some calculations of how quickly credit card debt can accumulate. Many teens think that credit comes free.

Here's an exercise that will help develop your daughter's ability to evaluate credit card offers. For a couple of months, all the mothers collect credit card offers that come in the mail. Be sure to include solicitations that offer frequent flyer miles or "thank-you gifts." (If you aren't getting regular offers in the mail, you can easily request credit card applications online.)

Pair everyone up, and hand out at least a dozen offers to each mother/daughter pair. Give them ten minutes to choose the "best" offer. As they decide, they should keep these questions in mind:

What goes into your decision making? How do you determine the best offer for yourself? What are the loopholes you need to watch out for?

Now reassemble as a group, and have each pair make the case for their chosen offer. It's time for a sales pitch. How are you going to convince the others? Each pair gets two minutes for their presentation.

In the discussion that follows, you can ask: *Who benefits from credit cards? What do you know about the practices of the company you were supporting? Who may get hurt from using credit cards?* Make sure each mother shares one thing she's learned about using credit cards responsibly (or not using them at all and why).

To do this exercise alone with your daughter, show her your stack of credit card offers and tell her you are considering switching cards. Say you'd like her help to figure out which offer is best. Talk her through the decision-making process. (You can do the same thing when it comes time to open a checking account.)

Take your daughter to work. It's not enough just to encourage our girls to have bright dreams. They also need role models and support to discover the paths they can take to realize those dreams. When Marisol started imagining herself as a journalist or writer, Katy and the other mothers talked about different paths women they knew or had read about have taken to accomplish that dream. Encourage your daughter to talk to you about her dreams. Maybe right now they seem like pipe dreams to you—"I'm going to be on the women's Olympic snowboarding team" or "I'm going to be a photojournalist for *National Geographic*"—but she's beginning to set her sights. Don't discourage her.

Finding mentors and looking for examples of women who have realized their goals provide guides for those paths. With that in mind, the Ms. Foundation initiated Take Our Daughters to Work Day in 1992 (now revamped to include sons).[10] Dreaming big is fun, but helping her learn the steps to take to realize her dreams is equally important. You may not know much about engineering, for example, and have little idea of how to support her in that career, but lots of people know exactly what it takes. If you know an engineer (man or woman), have your daughter go to work for a day with that person and get a taste for one aspect of engineering. Web sites such as www.braincake.org can help, too.

Mother-daughter camping trip. Modeling what women's lives are like for our daughters means balancing work and play. Our mother-daughter group tackles a difficult subject one month and sets off together for an adventure the next. We enjoy camping trips. Whatever you choose, plan at least one activity this year that involves preparatory work as well as fun.

When the mothers get together to plan this trip, we start by looking at all the hidden steps involved. We want our daughters to recognize and appreciate what it takes to make things happen. There are lots of ways to do this with just about any activity. When we meet with our daughters, we discuss sharing the work and expenses. Each mother-daughter pair will shop and plan for one meal. We figure out what equipment we'll need—kitchen supplies, tents, sleeping bags—and how to share resources so that the trip is affordable, especially if anyone in the group has never gone camping (and thus doesn't already own camping gear). Then, once we reach our campsite, we make sure that the girls are equally involved in the work of setting up tents, starting fires, getting water, and other tasks.

We've learned that the best way to introduce the subjects we want to discuss on these outings is in casual conversation. At some point, usually when we're all sitting around the fire in the evening or around the picnic table at breakfast, we begin a discussion. This summer, four of our six girls have summer jobs. Gabi is waiting tables and Maggie is working full time as a carpenter's assistant for her dad. Marisol has been working as a telephone solicitor for a computer company. Vanessa is lifeguarding at a local pool. Amy and April, both still fifteen, have busy social lives but no paid employment other than an occasional babysitting job.

Over breakfast, Phoebe asks, "We were wondering, what are the most important things you've learned about money and power and women?" (Other possible questions: *What have you specifically learned about money, power, and women from your mother and other women? Have you learned something similar or different from your dad or other men?*)

Marisol says she's learned that "time is money and money is time. Like when you work, you are paid for your time. And when you are working, you are giving up that time to get money." Vanessa chimes in that her job is boring, but she likes having her own money and having the financial freedom to decide what clothes to buy.

Marisol then shifts gears slightly, wanting to know how you can find satisfying work. "Last year I thought I wanted to be a journalist," she says, "but this year I'm not so sure."

"That's a good question," Phoebe says. "I think one thing that helps is letting yourself dream big." Dreaming big, she explains, is about not being limited in our thinking because of race, gender, or the income level in which we grew up. Dreaming big is about imagining you can create the life you want, not simply in terms of money, but also in terms of intellectual stimulation, quality of life, and work/life balance.

Coming to see oneself as an active agent in creating one's life represents a major shift in perception. For instance, Maisie describes how she worked with her former husband to build a house. After they split up, she used her construction skills working part time on a carpentry crew. Recognizing that she'd always been financially dependent on men spurred her to want to own a home and support her daughters herself. When she learned about a run-down house nearby, Maisie leaped at the chance to buy it. She got help from Sarah to calculate the financing, borrowed money for a down payment, and got a mortgage. With the help of friends, a hired crew, and her daughters, she bought and renovated her small house.

If your group isn't interested in camping, think of another activity you'd enjoy: an all-day excursion to a city to go exploring, or a day in the country if you have city girls. Using public transportation offers more opportunities for planning and research. Have the girls determine the logistics. How will you get there? What will it cost? What would be an equitable way to pay for the day (assuming that at least one mother-daughter duo has less discretionary money than others)?

If you are planning an activity for just you and your daughter, you'll need to exercise some vigilance in order to not slip into your familiar roles—you are her mom and are used to doing a lot for her. You can explicitly tell her that you want her to learn how to make good things happen in her life, and this often involves hidden work. Taking your daughter out for an entire day can feel special—just be sure that she helps plan it. Think about coming up with a budget for the day. Tell her "Here's what we have to spend. You decide how we're going to spend it." But remember, this is not a test. Help her think through in advance all the things you'll need money for: meals, entrance fees, transportation. You want to be sure you have money left to get home at the end of the day!

Discussion Questions for Daughters and Mothers

Starting when your girl is fifteen, look for opportunities to bring up issues of money and power. For example, we used the news that Michelle Bachelet was elected Chile's first woman president in January 2006 to talk about women in politics and to speculate on the changes that would happen in the girls' lifetimes as women take on more leadership positions.

The following questions can guide your discussions of money and power with your daughter:

What do you need money for in your life?

What needs do you feel are important to satisfy but that cannot be purchased?

How do you feel when you make your own money?

What kinds of responsibilities come with having to make financial choices?

We don't necessarily ask questions like this directly, because we know we'll likely lose the girls' interest, but we keep them in reserve, and they sometimes come up spontaneously in various conversations. Thus when Vanessa says she's thinking of taking lifeguard training, Maisie and Katy, who were both lifeguards as teenagers, describe the pros and cons of the job. Vanessa is tentative about her ability to shoulder that much responsibility, but once Maisie and Katy assert their confidence in her, she confides that her real motivation is to buy the clothes she likes and pay part of the cost of visiting a friend in Mexico next year.

Vanessa is learning a lesson in empowerment. She's recognizing her desire to earn money to make independent choices. She's discerning that there are different ways to go about that, one of which is to get training that increases the amount she can earn. By committing to contribute to her Mexico trip, she's also learning to negotiate with her parents. She's moving from passively participating in her life to actively taking responsibility for working independently toward a goal.

Whether our girls have families with many financial resources or live with a struggling single mother, they have choices available to them. Some adolescents make terrible choices, often in open rebellion against parents, unmindful of the potential long-term consequences. They can base their identity more on what they don't want than what they do want in their lives. Our focus is therefore to help our daughters learn to make choices that will enable them to create the lives they want. We teach them that money is only one way to get power in life, since power also comes through the kind of relationships we have and the communities we create.

We also help them develop compassion for the choices we and their grandmothers made in balancing motherhood, work, and personal lives, and we teach them about discrimination of all kinds and how to resist it. We strive to be positive role models, since we understand that they identify with us, and seeing us as whole women propels them to believe in themselves and envision themselves as powerful young women who can create fulfilling lives of their own. These lessons increase their confidence and sense of self as they begin to take steps toward leaving home and living on their own in the coming years.

CHAPTER SIXTEEN

Growing Roots and Wings

Sixteen Years Old—Testing New Boundaries

For many girls, sixteen means increased independence as they learn to drive a car or get a job, and begin to make choices about where they want to go and how they want to spend their own money. As they get their first taste of adulthood, they are able to start laying claim to what will be their mature identity, and to start to think about their path in life. They are better able to articulate what values they want to live by, and whom they love. While, for the most part, they are not yet making many concrete plans for the future, at this age, a girl is catching a glimpse of who she wants to be when she is a fully grown woman, and she is starting to contemplate how she might achieve her goals. The road she chooses may be straightforward or circuitous, but either way, she wants and needs the support and encouragement of caring adults. Her focus is moving from the self-absorption necessary for creating a sound initial identity in early adolescence to an increased openness to the wisdom and assistance of others, including her parents.

At sixteen, many young women are better able to care for others and be more empathic than when they were younger. In this capacity, they may recognize that their mothers are not their personal servants (at last!) but people who appreciate a kind word as much as anybody. (Then again, she may also feel she knows everything about life and ignore you.) Mother-daughter mutuality can gradually increase as daughters achieve greater capacity for both intimacy and autonomy. Moments of connection with our girls at sixteen may be brief, but can be deeply gratifying.

At sixteen, friends will be central to her life. Teenagers work together with their group of peers to figure out what adult life is going to look like for them. Moving from childhood to adulthood, adolescents make a transition from fulfilling their emotional and relational needs primarily through their parents and families to having their intimate partners and friends be their primary sources of love and succor. We adults want to impart our knowledge and experience to our kids, but they still have to decipher much for themselves, and they look to friends to help them sort it all out. As developmental psychologist Terry Apter notes, "Our choice of friends—and who choose us—helps to mark out our place in the social world and give us a reading on who we ourselves are."[1] As Maggie said at a mom-daughter group recently, "You moms taught us about everything—you pretty much have it covered—but then we get to figure out how we want to deal with it ourselves. So we talk to our friends."

Sixteen-year-olds often form strong friendship connections and look for satisfying romantic relationships. Given the opportunity, they socialize endlessly. When friendships are scarce, the grief that sixteen-year-olds feel can be painful to witness. Mothers cannot completely alleviate our daughters' loneliness for friends or a partner, but, just like when she was younger, we can help by acknowledging that loneliness is painful, reminding her of satisfying friendships she had in the past, and letting her know that we have faith that she will one day find a group of friends and a partner who love her for who she is. (It's okay if she rolls her eyes when you say this—she still hears it and it makes a difference.)

Sixteen is also a busy year. Daughters are often more sleep deprived than their mothers. Many teens feel overloaded by schoolwork, relationships, an after-school job, concerns about the state of the world, and anxiety about the future. Drawing on all their experimentation at fourteen and fifteen, our daughters are also working hard at figuring out how they can do what they love—whether snowboarding or lying on the beach or writing short stories—while still keeping an eye on what is rewarded socially by their peers and financially by society in general. Although she probably has a stronger sense of self than when she was an early adolescent, a young woman is still vulnerable to the demanding expectations of Perfect Girl, which can trap her into believing that only the superthin, supersuccessful, or superrich deserve love and happiness. Moms and dads play an important role in reminding our daughters that the things they may value most in life, such as a loving partner, a chance to do meaningful work in the world, motherhood, or a loving community of friends, are unrelated to income bracket, body mass index, or what is the college *du jour*.

Renegotiating Rights and Responsibilities

Society has decided that sixteen-year-olds can have certain privileges (even if they aren't all ready for them): In addition to legally driving and getting jobs (in many states) they are usually navigating public transportation by themselves and socializing with friends in unsupervised situations. Greater independence involves greater risk. While the tendency of teens to engage in risky behaviors is often described negatively, it can be clarifying to remember that young people are actually wired to take chances—the National Institute of Mental Health's brain imaging studies have shown that the prefrontal cortex, which controls judgment, reason, self-control, and planning, does not fully develop until early adulthood.[2] In addition, since a teenager can't know whether or in what ways she will succeed in life, *every step she takes* feels risky—from applying for a job, to striving to be the first one in the family to go away to college, to coming out as gay. Taking risks, large and small, is part of identity formation. During this process your kid may try on a thousand different hats including clothing and hair styles, religions, foods, vocations, music preferences, sleeping schedules, sleeping locales, social activism, academic achievement, academic underachievement, and so on. While obviously we don't condone behaviors that are outright dangerous or self-destructive, we encourage parents to be thankful and not just worried that our teens take more risks than the average middle-aged adult.

While sixteen-year-olds may take greater risks than they did at fourteen and fifteen, they often take better care of themselves. They might actually make enough time to study for their tough English exam without being prodded or arrange to go on the pill *before* having sex with their boyfriends—but not always. Again, it's important to remember that just because your daughter may look 99 percent grown up, she's not there yet. Negotiating privileges, like using the family car or establishing limits, such as curfews or attending unchaperoned parties, take the active ongoing involvement of parents—she still needs your guidance in a big way. This period of testing the waters of adulthood while still living under the caring gaze of parents is of critical importance for teenagers and helps them transition effectively into independent adults. At sixteen, our daughters are striving to be mature and competent when they are at school, work, among their friends, on their teams, and doing other extracurricular activities. Home is where they can let down their guard and show the tired, vulnerable, or cranky child inside the body of a developing woman. (Especially after finishing a big exam or paper, at sixteen, Amy loved having a "pajama day," when she would lie on the couch all day reading her younger sister Eliza's fantasy books, watching old movies, or making collage art, admitting that she was grumpy and whining for Phoebe to make her rice pudding.) When they make a miscalculation at this age (which they are bound to do on occasion), parents are still there to help them pick up the pieces. When, at sixteen, April couldn't find a summer job, she was grateful that Maisie "hired" her to paint their house.

Looking ahead, in a few short years, our daughters will take on the full rights and responsibilities of adulthood. By eighteen or nineteen, most young women expect to make key decisions about their lives: where to live, what education to pursue, how to support themselves, and with whom to be intimate—sometimes in consultation with mom, sometimes not. Often becoming an adult means leaving home. Leaving home is among the most emotionally intense experiences for mothers and daughters. It's a time of increased freedom for *both* mothers and daughters, and both feel a mix of emotions, excited and scared, worried and relieved. Sometimes both feel completely ready for the transition, but not always. While the first months after a daughter leaves home can be intensely poignant for a mother, most also find themselves excited about their new freedom and independence.

When a daughter reaches adulthood, whether she lives at home or on her own, our relationship with her changes, as it of course should. We still love her just as much as we ever did, but she is in charge of her life. As she assumes responsibility for herself, she also gains the right to make her own choices; as we parents are freed of responsibility for her, we lose the right to make choices for her—but still we worry. Will she get caught up in drugs or a bad relationship? Might she have an unwanted pregnancy? Will she continue her education? What if she gets married too young, or doesn't get married at all? Will she drive herself too hard and make herself ill, or will she give up her dreams too easily when the going gets rough? A central concern in these questions is: *Have I prepared her adequately for the world?* While our young adult daughter cares very much about what we think, and we can influence her more than we might imagine, we cannot control her. It takes time for both mothers and daughters to get familiar with this new world order, and emotions can run high on both sides. At eighteen or so, on the edge of adulthood, mothers and daughters sometimes can get drawn into feuding about every little thing as they find a new balance in their relationship. Being open about the fact that you are both in a time of transition and acknowledging that this can be challenging for anyone can reduce this tendency. We'll discuss navigating the issues surrounding your daughter leaving home in more depth in the next chapter.

Adapting, Guiding, and Reaching Out

While a daughter is still sixteen, we can start the process of actively negotiating our rapidly changing relationship with her as we prepare her for the independence of adulthood. How do we do this? Through their work synthesizing three hundred reviews of research and practice, A. Rae Simpson and colleagues at the Harvard Project on the Parenting of Adolescents conclude in *Raising Teens* that a hallmark of success is being able to adapt one's parenting to a teen's constantly growing abilities and changing needs. She and her panel of adolescent experts advocate that parents *monitor and observe* their older teens but with "less direct supervision and more communication, observation and networking with other adults"[3] and *guide and limit* them, upholding "a clear but evolving set of boundaries, maintaining important family rules and values, but also encouraging increased competence and maturity."[4]

Maisie put these ideas into practice parenting sixteen-year-old April. She observed that some of April's friends were smoking marijuana daily (both from the smell of their clothing and their own self-reports), and she worried that April would get drawn into regular use as well, which went against Maisie's values and hopes for her daughter. Raised in a home in which heavy alcohol use was a problem, as an adult, Maisie made the personal decision not to drink or use drugs and enforced a "no drinking, no drugs" policy in her home. April understood and had always respected that rule. But once the winter sport season was over and basketball practices ended, April got home from school at 2:30 in the afternoon, hours before her mother. Maisie was worried she might start using marijuana during that time. She wanted to reestablish limits—so one evening when just the two of them were home, Maisie shared her concerns with April and April agreed not to smoke in the house, but she didn't want to talk to her mother about what she did elsewhere. Maisie immediately reached out to her network of other mothers for help.

April felt comfortable speaking one-on-one with Sarah, who was particularly close with their whole family. She arranged to meet April at home after school one afternoon, and asked her what the effects of marijuana use were on her life and helped her evaluate if those effects were desirable to her. While not admitting any drug use, April acknowledged that her grades had suffered that spring, which wasn't what she wanted, as she hoped to go to the University of Connecticut, hopefully on a basketball scholarship. Together she and Sarah brainstormed how April could fill the boring, lonely hours after school. April decided to start training for the cross-country running team. Acting as a kind of comother, Sarah fulfilled another parenting task recommended by the Harvard project, to *model and consult*, providing teens "ongoing information and support around decision making, values, goals and interpreting and navigating the larger world."[5] Maisie modeled a drug-free life as Sarah offered decision-making support to April. While briefly sharing her own thoughts about the risks of heavy marijuana use, which included young people losing touch with their aspirations, missing out on educational opportunities, and interfering with sound relationships, Sarah directed her conversations with April around *April's* values and goals.

As much as parents want to influence them, teens make many choices based on their own evaluations of what is best, some of which won't jibe with ours. When our girls are sixteen, our task is passing the reins of decision making to them while keeping them as safe as we can. It may be something as simple as checking whether they've got enough money with them to grab a bite to eat before they head from school to work. Parents can be involved, such as reminding teens to get their homework and laundry finished in a timely fashion, but we don't need to do the work for them. As we guide them to take responsibility for themselves, it is most effective to ask how well their choices are working *for them*. And it is most productive if our primary means of influence can shift from enforcing consequences to dialogue and persuasion. When a daughter has her own job and money or no longer lives at home, we will have little power to enforce consequences, and, more important, respectful dialogue is a more effective way to encourage and influence her. Our daughters care intensely about their parents' good opinion of them even if it doesn't always appear that way.

Older teens generally want to hear parents' frank opinions—we just need to recognize that they have increasing power to make the final decisions themselves. (Practically speaking, you can't ground them for life!) It's fully appropriate and necessary, however, to set limits with our sixteen- and seventeen-year-olds, such as not letting a daughter drive to parties after she comes home one night drunk.

Creating a Strong, Caring Support System

Networking with other parents is a key recommendation of the Harvard Project on the Parenting of Teens, which specifies that as parents *provide and advocate* for their teens, they should make available "not only adequate nutrition, clothing, shelter and health care, but also a supportive home environment and a network of caring adults."[6] Along these lines, after their initial conversations, Sarah checked in with April regularly, and was pleased to discover that April was running in the afternoons and doing better in school. At the same time, Maisie was able to set aside time in her busy schedule just to hang out with April after school once a week, and the two of them started running together.

As mothers, we can make a huge difference in our daughter's

life by helping her clarify her vision for her own life while providing the structure and support she still requires as a sixteen-year-old. Her interest in figuring out what's meaningful to her and deciding which values should guide her gives us an opportunity to thoughtfully anticipate the momentous changes that are coming. At the Mother-Daughter Project, we are guided by the intention of helping our daughters have deep roots in the communities that love them and the values that they cherish while growing strong wings of vision, courage, determination, and skill that will take them as far as they dream of going. To honor our dual goals of staying connected with our daughters as we encourage them to fly, we chose *roots and wings* as the theme for the year.

Mothers Thinking About Change

Our own experience of growing up affords some perspective on what it means for our daughters to become adults, and all the complexities that entails for us and them. Over the course of the year, in a journal or among other mothers, we can ask questions like:

What hopes and dreams did I have as I became an adult?

How did my community and the wider culture support or discourage my hopes and dreams?

How did my mother support my hopes and dreams as I made the transition to adulthood? What worries did she have?

How did our relationship change at that time? What did I like about our relationship then? What would I have liked to be different?

We can then clarify our hopes and fears as our daughters become adults.

What are my hopes for my daughter as she becomes an adult? What worries me?

What are her hopes and dreams at this time? What worries her? What kinds of support would be helpful to her?

We have found our mothers' group to be an invaluable support when our daughters were fifteen to seventeen years old. As daughters gradually take on the rights and responsibilities of making adult decisions, other moms can offer fresh insight on how to balance limits and freedom. This is a tender period for many women—we're happy that our girls are gaining independence, although we may be feeling some growing pains ourselves. In our group, as the girls grew up, branched out, and had less time for get-togethers, the moms, in fact, became closer. Today we trade anecdotes and advice about our children, and like always, support each other as mothers and as women speaking frankly about our own lives.

Maisie came to moms' group one day in the fall of 2005 thinking about her teenage girls and the fact that she was a newly single woman. "I'm grieving buckets every day," she said. "I miss David"—the girls' former stepfather. "Here I am at forty-two remaking my life. The girls are good, but it's intense. Last weekend when Gabi and April were hanging out with their friends in the living room, Gabi comes up to me and asks, 'Mom, was I a mistake?' And I said to her, 'Honey, you aren't a mistake! You are a fabulous person, and I love you so much.' But she says, 'No, Mom. What I mean is, was I a *mistake*, you know . . . ?' I suddenly realized that the kids have been talking about withdrawal as birth control. So I said to her, 'Yes, you absolutely *were* a mistake, and no, it does *not* work to pull it out, and I want everyone in this room to know where we keep the condoms.'"

The other mothers cracked up. Katy caught her breath and asked, "Did you really say she was a mistake?"

"You bet I did. She knew what I meant. But it isn't fair, I was such a nerd in high school, and my kids are into everything, while my sister, who was totally wild, has these four *angelic* children."

"It sure isn't fair," says Katy. "I was one of those wild kids, and Marisol is the easiest, nerdiest kid (and I mean that in the nicest possible way) you could ever hope to have."

"What rules do you all have for your girls nowadays?" asked Phoebe. "The other day Amy wanted to know if she had a curfew, and I said, 'No. I just need to know where you are, who you're with, and when you're going to be back, and no drugs.' And Amy said, 'M-o-o-o-m. We don't do drugs.' Her gang doesn't—so, no curfew. But does that make sense?"

"I need to know where Vanessa and her friends are going, and there are definitely times when I say 'you need to be home by midnight,'" said Libby.

"The girls are at an age now where they are making their own choices," said Sarah. "But they still look to us. I don't give Maggie a curfew, but I do tell her my opinion. Maggie said she was going to get a ride home from a party with her friend Clara, and I told her that Clara was the last person I would want her to drive with. After the party, Maggie came to me and said, 'Mom, you're so right, she did drink a lot.'"

"April is just sixteen," said Maisie, "and she wants the freedom that Gabriella has at eighteen, but she's not ready for it, so I have to have a curfew for her. I am doing what I can, but I agree that our influence at this age is limited."

Katy looked at Maisie and brought the conversation back around. "So, Maisie, is there anything we can do for you now, at this time of re-creating your life?"

"Yes," she said, looking around our small circle of women. "You can do this."

As Maisie says, mothering sixteen-year-olds is intense. The encouragement and insight of other mothers of teenage kids refuels us as we strive to nurture our daughters' well-being in their exciting but risky world, and take care of our own complicated lives as well.

Strengthening Roots and Wings with Mothers and Daughters Together

At sixteen, your daughter will be busy with everything—waiting tables, trigonometry, concert choir, hanging around with her friends, softball, driver's ed, college entrance exams, finding a cozy spot to be alone with her sweetie (maybe all in the space of a week)—so you may need to be creative in finding opportunities to spend meaningful time with her. Maintaining connection during her transition to adulthood paves the way for ongoing closeness and mutuality among adult daughters and mothers and enhances your ability to reach her when she needs help. As we've discussed, sixteen-year-old girls want to be with their peers all the time, so mother-daughter time often means including her friends, whether from her primary social circle or from your mother-daughter group. And since your daughter likely is quite distracted by her own life, we'd suggest that you include the company of other mothers for yourself.

Catching your breath together. Sixteen-year-olds often run themselves ragged, and sometimes they need to be reminded to slow down and relax, especially after a big exam. Lying around watching a video, eating a leisurely brunch together, doing an at-home pedicure, and other soothing activities are restorative for mothers and daughters alike, one-on-one, or with friends. Summers and school vacations offer a chance for more ambitious outings, like going to the beach, amusement parks, concerts, road trips, and other activities that are purely fun.

Catching up with each other. When sixteen-year-olds are at home, they are typically consumed with schoolwork, talking with friends on the phone and IM, and e-mailing, but your daughter still gets hungry, so mealtimes can be a time to connect. Take her out to lunch or dinner and ask what's on her mind. She may feel like talking about her personal life or she may not, but either way, despite her response, she appreciates your respectful interest. Feeding your daughter and her friends is also an important way for a mother to stay current with what her daughter is doing and feeling, and vice versa. When your daughter and her friends break from band practice or cramming for a chemistry exam to wolf down some dinner, join them in the kitchen and ask *her friends* what's going on in their lives and how they're feeling. The other girls will feel honored by your interest, and your daughter can follow their lead and tell you what's she's doing and how she's feeling, too. In a mother-daughter group, make "checking in" a part of every gathering: Going around the circle, each person (mothers and daughters alike) can say what's up in her life. Offering to give her a ride to a friend's house or to an activity can also be a time to catch up with each other. There's nothing like the easy conversation that can happen during a car ride.

Showing up for each other. Many girls have spent the last few years or more mastering a sport or art or other interest that she loves. You can honor their accomplishments and help them grow their wings by showing up for games, performances, and other events that are important to them whenever it's possible in your schedule. Several of the girls from our mother-daughter group love to perform, and when they were sixteen and seventeen, we scheduled group outings to see Maggie perform African dance, Amy do West Coast Swing, Gabi thrill us as Clytemnestra, and Mari sing in *Annie*. We also cheered as Vanessa played midfield in soccer and April led her team in three-point shots in basketball.

Reflecting on Becoming an Adult

Explicitly addressing what it means to become an adult can deepen your daughter's roots and strengthen her wings. She will likely appreciate it if you schedule periodic conversations to talk about giving her more rights to make her own decisions (like what time she comes home on weekends), based on her demonstrated ability to handle them (such as telling you where she is and when she will be home) and match those increased rights with greater responsibility for herself (such as doing her own laundry and keeping her room clean). Flexibility is the order of the day. If her active school, sport, and social schedule makes it hard for her to consistently walk the dog or do the dishes, negotiate with her to find household responsibilities that match her varied schedule and prepare her for independence, like putting gas in the car and buying her own shampoo.

It's easiest on parents if her new responsibilities primarily have consequences for her and not the whole family, like no clean clothes for *her* because she didn't do *her* laundry. You can make eating a home-cooked meal contingent on helping with the dishes afterward or finding her favorite foods in the fridge a privilege based on doing the grocery shopping. While she may complain at first, her desire to be more mature will help her step up to the task if you continue in a low-key way to let her know it is expected of her. (Life will also be easier if you let things slide on occasion, such as allowing her to run out of the house without clearing the dinner table because she's about to miss her ride to the school musical.) In the context of talking about practical issues, ask what her hopes and worries are about reaching adulthood, getting a real job, moving out, or going to college. If your daughter is uncomfortable speaking one-on-one, bring up the topic of impending adulthood with her friends. As you serve pancakes to the five bleary-eyed girls who slept over after the dance, ask what it's like for them to be approaching graduation, or how they feel about their older friends leaving home. Even if your own daughter says nothing, she gets the benefit of hearing and thinking about what it means to become an adult.

In an ongoing mother-daughter group, you can address issues

of impending adulthood explicitly. Choose a timely word or phrase as a prompt that has particular relevance to your girls, such as *becoming an adult* or *leaving*, and invite everyone to write or draw whatever comes to mind for fifteen minutes. Each daughter and mother is then invited to share what she created with the group (with the option to pass), and after she does, everyone says one thing that moved her or resonated with her about what was shared. You can do this two or three times over the course of the year, in between lighter activities.

When our group did this activity, the secure and familiar setting of the group allowed moms and daughters to directly explore the emotionally charged concept of leaving in a way that felt both open and safe.

Vanessa, Libby's daughter, was the first to read her response:

"Leaving. It seems nowadays everything is changing. When the thought of someone leaving your life forever comes up it makes you realize how much you love that person. Beth left. So many of my friends will be leaving next year."

Someone handed her a tissue. "I didn't know this was going to be so heavy . . ."

"It's okay," one of the moms said, "keep reading."

"And then I'll be leaving," she continued. "I don't like change. I especially hate leaving. What if I leave and go to the wrong place? What if I leave at the wrong time? What if someone leaves forever and you aren't ready for them to leave? When my grandpa died last year, it made me wish I had done so many things differently. I don't like having to change and I don't like losing touch with the people I love. I don't like saying good-bye."

Everybody grabbed for the tissue box. "So," quipped Phoebe after blowing her nose, "anyone moved by anything they heard?"

"I resonated with the part where you said what if I go at the wrong time or to the wrong place," said Maggie, Sarah's daughter. "It's hard to leave if you don't know whether you're going to like where you're going."

"I could relate to the part about your friends leaving," said Amy, Phoebe's daughter.

It was Maggie's turn next:

"Leaving seems to have such a negative connotation. When I first hear the word, I think of all the sad parts of my life that I associate with leaving. Mostly I think of my dad. Then I think of my sister, Kay, and how much I miss her now that she lives on her own in another city. But I also think of what can change for the positive when they leave. Since my sister left, I can love her more easily. When people leave, hopefully they are going to find something more fulfilling. My sister found her pride when she left. She found self-confidence and love. Leaving offers new opportunities. But does the person being left have the same opportunities as the person leaving? Is it okay to leave someone even if it hurts them?"

"The part about leaving being associated with your dad," said Marisol, Katy's daughter, "I relate to that."

"I was moved by how you noticed what your sister got by leaving," said Amy.

After everyone offered a thought, Libby read:

"I am leaving a time in my life focused on home and family. I'm leaving a solid, familiar place and I'm not exactly sure what this new phase will bring. I hold a vision of living with Aaron and Vanessa more like three adults, cooperatively, less like parents and child—where we figure out a new way to be in relationship to one another, one that is easier and more pleasurable to all of us."

After the group shared responses to Libby, Phoebe read:

"For me leaving home to go to college was like diving over the rainbow. When I was young I thought that because I was fighting with my mother all the time we weren't close—but now I see we were fighting *because* we were close, and we were trying to reconcile our differences. It wasn't until years later that I realized that the reason I felt so happy flying off was that home felt like a rock-solid place that I could always return to. So I would say that the other half of leaving is having a place *to* leave—leaving is the space between the new adventure and what stays the same."

The last young woman to read was Amy, the most private of the daughters. "I'm not going to read what I wrote, I'm just going to paraphrase." She glanced at her paper. As she tried to speak, she started to cry.

"Just go ahead and cry while you're talking," said Katy.

Amy nodded and said through her tears, "The first thing I think of about leaving is that so many of my friends are leaving for college. I'm lucky to have a really great, close group of friends, but most of them are seniors, and they are going away. I've been feeling so happy and relieved for them as they are getting accepted at the colleges that they want to go to, but it feels hard to be the one who is left behind . . ."

Her voice catching, she continued, "And then I'll be the one leaving. And I'm thinking more about what I'll be leaving behind, like my sister. When I go, she'll be the one left behind, and my family, and everything else. So all that leaving feels really hard." She paused for a breath. "But at the same time, maybe leaving will be good. It's hard, but it leads to things that are really great."

"Well, I relate to every single thing you said," said Vanessa.

"Me, too," said Maggie.

"I was moved by what you said about how happy and relieved you are for your friends getting into college, and how hard it is to be left behind," says Katy.

"I resonated with your awareness of who you will be leaving behind, like your sister, Eliza," said Sarah.

"What moved me most," said Phoebe, Amy's mother, "was when you said that even with all the sad parts of leaving, you know that leaving will bring you great things. Even more than how much I will miss you when you go, I want you to have those great things."

As our girls reach sixteen and seventeen, our relationships

can deepen as they achieve greater capacities for self-reflection, communication, and empathy. At the same time, our daughters are moving more and more fully out into the world as women. Mothers are letting go—but not of our daughters—we're letting go of our day-to-day responsibilities for them. We cannot control our grown-up daughters, but we can love them and be as close to them as ever.

CHAPTER SEVENTEEN

Flying Toward the Future

Seventeen Years Old—Becoming a Young Woman

At seventeen and eighteen, a young woman is often taking her first concrete steps toward manifesting her destiny. Being an independent adult feels more real as her plans evolve from hopes and musings into action. While she looks to her mother and other supportive adults for advice and support, a young woman of seventeen is often keenly aware that she is making life-changing decisions about how and where to direct her talents and energies and wants to have final say on her choices. Her plans take all kinds of forms: A high school senior may be throwing herself into college entrance exams and applications with dreams of becoming a teacher or doctor, trying to book a cross-country tour with her band, or considering the logistics of what it might take to establish her own home and family with a mate. Her conclusions about what is best for her may or may not match ours as she decides the initial course of her life, such as going to college across the country or leaving high school without her diploma.

Letting go, not of our relationships with our daughters, but of having control of their lives, can be one of the hardest parts of this stage of parenting. If we demand they follow our preferences, a young woman's focus can be drawn into opposing us instead of evaluating the risks and benefits of their plan. As they try to convince us of why their choice is right, it can increase parents' anxiety—which may lead us to an even more polarized stance. When Maggie, who was going to be eighteen in a few months, shared with her mother her plans to bike from village to village in Brazil during a trip this summer, Sarah, forty-nine, had concerns for her safety. At first, Maggie brushed them off as excessive and unknowledgeable. Rather than try to force Maggie into a plan she didn't agree with, Sarah suggested she gather more information and weigh the risks herself. After speaking with an American woman who worked at an NGO in Brazil and learning that female travelers are assaulted with some frequency there, Maggie dropped the bicycling idea and focused on finding another way to create a travel experience that would still bring her in touch with the land and the people but with more security. If we respectfully ask teens to share their reasoning, we enter a dialogue that fosters mutuality and we have a better chance to positively influence their lives.

For many teens, senior year is both exciting and scary. Some of our daughters will be confident and exuberant as they make their bid for independence, ready to jump into the rights and responsibilities of young adulthood, while others are cautious and frightened. Some of our daughters will make few plans, preferring to wait until after they finish high school to decide what comes next, taking full advantage of this last year of being their parents' responsibility. Just like a toddler who clamors to let go of her mother's hand to walk across the room by herself then rushes back to the security of mom's arms, at seventeen, a young woman often alternates moving toward independence with a return to reliance on her parents when she reaches the edge of her comfort zone. Maybe she'll choose her own doctor and attend an appointment by herself, but then she'll ask mom to call the insurance company to negotiate coverage for the acne medicine she prefers. That's okay. What's easy and what's difficult about becoming an adult is different for each of our daughters. Gradually taking on more responsibility in those areas where she feels secure, and being comfortable to ask her parents for support, is an important way she strengthens her knowledge and ability to make larger and more successful forays into adulthood. As researchers Susan Jekielek and Brett Brown in their 2002 report *The Transition to Adulthood* for the nonpartisan, nonprofit organization Child Trends explain, "This transition can be a period of growth and accomplishment, especially when youth have the resources they need to navigate this process, such as community connections and a stable family that can provide guidance and financial assistance if needed, and access to education and experiences that provide a foundation for learning, life skills, and credentials."[1] In our experience with the Mother-Daughter Project, we have seen that when a young woman knows she can rely on her mother for needed emotional and practical support, she feels more sure-footed and can pursue her aspirations more freely and with greater confidence.

Each young woman has a unique learning curve in becoming an adult and each mother has her own unique journey as she transitions from raising a teen to relating to an adult daughter. The time a daughter leaves home is often rife with emotions for mothers. Whether she leaves home at eighteen to go to college, at twenty to take a job after community college, or at twenty-four to get married, losing daily contact with our daughters can be among the most poignant and, indeed, wrenching experiences of our lives. It's difficult to know in advance what it will be like for us, as mothers often experience a whole range of emotions, including sadness, joy, relief, loneliness, freedom, boredom, and pride. These feelings can be more intense when it is our first, last, or only child who is leaving. When we no longer have children living in our homes, we will experience dramatic changes in the nature of our daily lives, which we may either relish or dislike. There's no question: It's a watershed moment in the life of a parent.

As mothers and daughters negotiate their changing balance of intimacy and autonomy on the cusp of a girl's adulthood, many intense emotions can arise—but we can honor those emotions by communicating them to our daughters and working toward greater mutuality. While giving her a foot rub after her long shift of waitressing, you could tell her how you are proud that she is working, excited for the opportunities the next year will bring, and sad when you think about how much you will miss her. Most daughters will appreciate your authenticity and perhaps even respond by sharing their own mix of feelings. This year we are forming the foundation of our future relationship as adults, a relationship between two women who share a rich history and have powerful emotional claims on each other, a relationship that will continue for the rest of our lives.

During your daughter's senior year in high school she doubtless will be busy and not have as much time to pursue organized activities with you. As when she was sixteen, we suggest being flexible and seeking low-key ways to hang out when it is convenient for both of you. Acknowledging the issues surrounding her increasing independence, while being together in a relaxed way while she is growing up but still at home offers the opportunity to begin to create the mutual connection we want as our daughters gradually transition to the greater freedom and responsibility they will have after graduation.

Emancipated, but Still Needing Support

At eighteen, a young woman is legally emancipated to make her own decisions about her body and her life. She can vote, open a checking account, accrue credit card debt, rent an apartment, be tried as an adult in a court of law, get married, consent to surgery, tattoo her skin, pierce her tongue, or go skydiving. And yet, although they have the rights of adults, many of our daughters want and expect us to provide them with significant financial support, regular guidance, and a home base through their early twenties. When Maisie, a teacher, who had started parenting immediately after college, broached the topic of selling her house and fulfilling her dream of joining the Peace Corps after April graduated from high school, neither April, sixteen, a junior in high school, nor Gabi, eighteen, a senior, liked the idea one bit—at least not for a few more years. They both wanted Maisie to stay right where she was during their early adulthood. "I want to be able to come home on college breaks to my own bed," said April. "At least for a year or two." In SuEllen's experience of working with college women, she found that the first years in college go more smoothly when daughters can count on ongoing emotional support from and connection with parents who respect them as young adults but who still provide them with the comforts of home. Maisie decided to hold off on the Peace Corps but explore doing short-term projects such as helping redevelop schools in New Orleans.

When adult children live at home, whether year-round or just for a few weeks during college vacations, positive relations are supported by negotiating in advance what their rights will be. It is challenging for mothers and daughters to change their accustomed ways of relating from that of an adult supervising a minor to two adults living together. It's not always easy to do so, but it helps to try to think of the household negotiation as one among housemates, in which the same general rules apply to everyone, from cleaning up after oneself to having the freedom to stay out late if one wishes. Relationships can also be eased by defining in advance what a grown child's *responsibilities* will be, such as taking college courses or doing yard work in lieu of rent, if she's still living at home, as well as consequences if she doesn't hold up her end of the bargain, such as losing access to the car, meals cooked by mom or dad, or the password needed to log on to the family computer—or if problems persist, being asked to move out. When grown children come home on breaks, it likewise helps to establish the rules of sharing the house right from the start to avoid falling back into accustomed roles. Perhaps you'll offer three or four days of indulgence and recovery from finals during which nothing is asked of your daughter, letting her know that by day four or five she'll be back on the chore chart for dishes and vacuuming like everyone else in the house. In addition, be fore-warned that she will likely want to spend as much or more time with her friends than with you—offering to cook for her and her friends is a useful strategy to spend time with her.

Many parents contribute financially to their adult children who have left home, such as helping to pay for college. We suggest be-ing clear in advance about who will be paying for what, who is re-sponsible for any debts, and what kind of say parents will have about their daughters' lives while they are at least partly financially responsible for them. Keep in mind that a pocketbook makes a poor lever for getting our adult children to do what we think is best for them. Our experience as psychotherapists has shown us that the relational costs are very high when parents make paying tuition contingent on controlling the details of their daughters' or sons' lives, such as choosing a particular career, making dean's list, or constraining their social lives. Our children want us to be proud of them and often want our advice, and we are much more effective at persuading them by sharing our thoughts and experi-ences with them than by coercing them with money, which can poison parent-child relationships with resentfulness and, often-times, deceit. Nonetheless, if a daughter gets into significant trou-ble, such as developing a serious drug or alcohol problem, and our efforts to help and persuade her are ineffective, there are times when withdrawing financial support (or taking action to get her into a treatment facility) may be necessary for her well-being.

Even if they are hundreds or thousands of miles away, young adult daughters generally feel strongly connected to their moth-ers and families. When home appears to be stable and everyone is well, daughters might not give it much thought. Their focus is on their own exciting new lives. But if there is change or trouble, such as parents moving to a new city or divorcing or the death of a family member, young adults experience as much or more worry and grief as when they were living at home with their parents. Their worry is compounded if they don't have regular contact or aren't sure of exactly what is going on. Don't assume that it is best not to "worry" your daughter with significant news such as her father moving out or starting medical treatment; she is more likely to feel hurt and left out. You both may benefit from sharing grief and concerns, and you can avoid burdening her by letting her know that you have local sources of support, and encouraging her to find the same.

Cell phone use has dramatically changed the kind of contact all of us can have with one another. After Amy's best friend, Peggy, who was a grade older, left for college, the two still spoke on the phone almost daily just like they used to, since it was no more expensive to call across the state than across town. Many college women speak daily with their mothers via cell phone. How much and what kind of phone contact feels right is different for each mother-daughter pair and can be negotiated by them to fit both their needs and preferences, which will change over time. Regular calls home from your daughter are not a sign of immaturity or unhealthy dependence; they are a sign of intimacy and connection between a mother and daughter who are also enjoying greater freedom and autonomy. Our experience as psychotherapists shows us that mothers and daughters both benefit from close, loving, mutually supportive relationships with each other throughout their adult lives.

Life After Launching

The transition from parenting a teen daughter to sharing a mutually satisfying adult relationship with her is often long and gradual. Like all relationships, adult mother-daughter relationships require care and communication. While our path is eased the earlier we begin, it is never too late to nurture our relationships with our daughters—or with our mothers. Even if our relationships have been characterized by distance or tension, recommitting to our intentions to foster loving connection allows us to seek even brief moments of mutuality and help them grow. As people, we grow and change over time, and so must our relationships. We can orient ourselves to how we can nurture our evolving relationships with adult daughters by asking:

> Can I describe a moment of connection with my daughter since she has become a teenager that felt good to both of us? What quality that we both value was present in our relating?

> When my daughter no longer lives at home, would I like to continue to have that quality in our relationship? What form could that take? What would help us have the opportunity to experience that way of connecting with each other?

As discussed, when our children leave home, we may grieve the loss of daily contact with our daughters and the daily satisfactions of mothering as we simultaneously enjoy new freedoms and possibilities. It can be helpful to refresh our awareness of what gives our lives meaning as we prepare for this new phase of life.[2] We can ask:

> Can I describe a time or era when I felt especially happy and fulfilled in my life? (This could range from last week to decades ago.) When do I feel best nowadays? What quality that is important to me was present at those times?

> Why are those qualities or experiences important to me? Are they linked to hopes or aspirations I have for my life? If so, what might they be?

> Are those hopes or aspirations linked to important commitments or values that I hold? If so, which?

> What would it look like if those commitments or values were more fully expressed in my life? What would that mean to me?

Who would be supportive of such developments in my life? What would it take for those developments to be possible? What would be the first step in making those possibilities a reality for me?

What other hopes and aspirations do I have for this new phase in my life? Who supports and nurtures them in my life?

What We Have Learned at the Mother-Daughter Project

It's been ten years since we began the Mother-Daughter Project and launched our first mother-daughter group. Our own daughters are at the end of high school, on the cusp of adulthood themselves. Our journey of mothering our adolescent daughters is coming to a close as our journey of nurturing our adult relationships begins. We love and admire the young women our daughters have become. Soon they will fly out into the world, following their dreams, supported by the love of their mothers and a whole community of women.

The ideas, activities, and relationships that the Mother-Daughter Project has generated have taught us a great deal about girls and mothers, and have made an enormous difference in both our lives and the lives of our daughters. Together we have celebrated being girls and women and stood up to and challenged the assumptions that can harm us. Perhaps most significantly, we have successfully bucked the notion that girls must separate from their mothers in order to grow up.

Instead, we have seen how cultivating the deep bond of connection between mothers and daughters facilitates the growth and development of each. Feeling safe in the knowledge that they are loved makes it easier for girls to individuate and venture forth into the world. Daughters want close, loving, and mutually respectful relationships with their mothers, even when they differ in important ways or make different choices as girls and women.

Holding on to the idea that mother-daughter connection is good for girls powerfully supports healthy mother-daughter relationships. When, as occurs in all intimate relationships, mothers and daughters have troubled moments together, the belief in connection is a potent healing force, as it was for Libby and Vanessa and all the mothers and daughters in our group. The idea of connection, along with encouragement and advice from other mothers who also valued it, helped Libby stay the course and find ways to nurture her relationship with Vanessa through the episodes of high conflict that cropped up during Vanessa's teen years. "Even when she's yelling that she hates you, she still loves you," Phoebe reminded Libby during a particularly heated time with Vanessa. "Like the sun and the moon and back, she loves you." Understanding conflict as arising from the desire for greater understanding helped Libby and Vanessa shake off the idea that they just couldn't get along or that they were somehow personally at fault.

What Libby and Vanessa came to know is true of all our daughters: They love us, even when they are furious with us, just like we love them, to the sun and the moon and back again. Girls value connection just as much as mothers. When we asked April what she valued most about being in the mom-daughter group, she said, "Being able to get along with my mom. Other kids talk about hating their moms, but for me, my relationship with my mom is like having an understanding between different generations."

Our explorations and experiences of mother-daughter connection in the Project were especially valuable to us as mothers in nurturing more understanding and textured relationships with our own mothers. While simply becoming mothers ourselves illuminated the realities of our mothers' lives to us in profound new ways, responding to and discussing the Project's questions about our mothers deepened and enriched our awareness of how much our mothers loved us when we were young and how much effort they put into manifesting that love, sometimes against great odds. Even those among us who had difficult relationships with their mothers in the present were able to remember those moments in childhood when we felt close. All of us felt more compassion for our mothers—and were better able to accept ourselves.

When we speak with other mothers about the Mother-Daughter Project and our close relationships with our girls, we've heard again and again, "Wow. That's incredible! You mean my daughter and I can stay connected?" As a result, mothers are reaching out to their daughters in new ways. SuEllen's friend Marguerite Winter, forty-three, an obstetrician, had been increasingly distressed by her twelve-year-old daughter Sierra's distance and rude remarks to her and was unsure how to nurture their relationship—or if it was even possible. Armed with news of the Project's success, Marguerite decided to invite Sierra to go away, just the two of them, for a long weekend, and let Sierra decide what kind of trip would please her. While Marguerite loves hiking all day in the woods with a heavy backpack and camping under the stars, she discovered that Sierra preferred a city trip that included a pedicure at a day spa. The two of them had a blast, and it boosted their relationship at a critical moment. Now mother-daughter weekends are an annual event in their lives.

Girls Thriving

Every month we see evidence in our own mom-daughter group that a strong mother-daughter connection fostered by the ideas of the Project has helped our daughters thrive. Amy, April, Gabriella, Maggie, Marisol, and Vanessa are lively young women with their own thoughts and ideas about themselves, one another, and the world around them. Because of our ongoing bonds with them through adolescence, we have been able to help them discover and develop their unique gifts and resist girl-negating messages. With our guidance, they have honed their ability to ask critical questions. Will this choice I'm contemplating serve me? How are my values similar to or different from those of my friends, my parents, or my teachers? We witness how the Mother-Daughter Project has helped them cultivate authenticity—the self-knowledge and confidence needed to live according to their most cherished values. Watching our daughters develop skills and confidence to face the challenges that may come their way reassures us mothers. No guarantees, of course, but we feel assured that we have given our daughters roots and wings that will serve them well as they strike out on their own.

Mothers Thriving

As mothers participating in the Project, it has been a relief to have the opportunity to focus on our own needs in the context of raising our daughters. Acknowledging the demands on us and appraising the requirements of the ideal mother from the vantage point of our own values and experiences has helped us resist judging ourselves when we inevitably fail to meet Supermom expectations. Instead, we are freed to help both ourselves and our daughters define what it means for us to thrive and discover what helps us do so. We have seen how enhancing our well-being as mothers is not just good for us; it is good for our daughters, too.

....

Near the end of the first year of our mom-daughter group, Katy, thirty-six at the time, was beleaguered by the daily demands of wage-earning, homemaking, and single parenting. She was keenly aware of the gap between what she was able to do and what she thought a "good mother" should do and felt like a failure. She nearly quit the group, believing that she had little to offer. Maisie, thirty-two, was herself separating from Gabi and April's father, Richard, shifting her life from homeschooling her daughters to getting her first full-time teaching job, and she offered Katy particularly knowledgeable and empathetic emotional support and practical advice, which helped pull Katy out of her low. Katy stuck with the group and never looked back. Recently she reported that at the start of the Project, she was so focused on meeting the needs of her children, partner, coworkers, and others that she had no idea what she herself needed or wanted. Over the years, through her journal writing and conversations with other mothers, Katy gradually came to discover and value her own preferences and voice. Her new strength and clarity spurred her to retool her freelance window design business a few years ago to be more satisfying, flexible, and lucrative; to create a more fulfilling relationship with her new partner, Jeff; and to nurture love, art, kindness, connection, self-confidence, academic success, humor, and joy in her daughters, Kaili and Marisol, who are both growing up beautifully.

Mothers and Daughters Together

Katy's story is an example of one of the most meaningful discoveries of the Project: Far from being at odds, the well-being of mothers, daughters, and their relationships are interdependent and nourish each other. We found that simultaneously honoring the needs, hopes, and aspirations of both mothers and daughters was the surest road to helping our daughters and our relationships thrive. Katy's journey mirrors those of the rest of the mothers in the Project. Taking time to focus on ourselves as women in the midst of our hectic lives as mothers helped us to get back in touch with who we really are and to more closely align our parenting with our positive intentions. As our children grow up and we pursue new work, create new homes after difficult divorces, ask that more of our needs get met within our relationships, dance and hike and pursue our dreams, we, too, are coming more fully into ourselves as women. Our fulfillment as women offers our daughters compelling examples and energizes us to be fully present as mothers.

In our work to help mothers, daughters, and their relationships thrive, we have found that community is an invaluable resource. Mothers need other mothers. We're tired of hearing the endless call to muster for the "Mommy Wars" when we know that women support one another all the time as we balance family, work, and our personal lives. A strong network of support, whether family, friends, community, or religious groups, increases our ability to face the hardships that inevitably will come our way. In our group, we have all turned to the strength of our community to support our journeys as mothers and women. At the start of the Mother-Daughter Project, Phoebe, thirty-six, was an untenured professor with a two-year-old and a seven-year-old who was new in town and felt lonely, isolated, and exhausted. Her husband, Paul, was in graduate school at the time and overwhelmed with responsibilities himself. The mom-daughter group helped her create mutually supportive relationships with other mothers much faster than she would have been able to otherwise. By the time Amy hit age ten and felt alienated from her peer group at school, Phoebe felt supported by a community of women whom she deeply trusted to help her aid Amy.

In addition to easing our lives as mothers, a nurturing group or community is a powerful example for our daughters. Our girls have watched us turn to one another for comfort and support for over a decade, when a parent died, a child was hospitalized, a relationship ended, or an accident laid one of us up, and they saw how we helped one another grieve, plan, and move forward with our lives. Talking about what she got out of mom-daughter over the years, Maggie reflected, "I learned that adults keep learning. Hearing about the other moms making big transitions in their lives, like beginning a new job or relationship, has given me insight into the changes that are happening (and will happen) in my life." Vanessa remarked, "I learned that everybody needs support, including my mom. Sometimes it's been hard for her, having a teenager, but when she needed help, it wasn't a big deal to ask for it from the other moms."

Having relationships with other mothers and being part of an intentional mother-daughter community has been another great benefit for our daughters. Amy said at seventeen, "More than just a group of friends, mom-daughter has a purpose—to provide us support, give us information, and help us be successful. Because I've known everyone for so long, we're really close, and it's a place where I'm accepted, I don't have to hide anything." Marisol spoke about her appreciation of the unique opportunity the group offered her. "Mom-daughter group has always given me a sense of community. It's a place where I feel connected to other people that I share the same values with. Everything that we cover gives me insight into myself and other people. It's a place that's really safe and comfortable for me. It's one of the few places that I cry. At mom-daughter, I actually *feel* my emotions when I'm talking about them, while with my friends at school it's more detached. In mom-daughter I convey exactly what I am feeling."

Our Mom-Daughter Group Heads into the Future

In September 2006, we gathered in the basement party room at Pasta Paradiso, the same cozy Italian restaurant filled with candlelight and the scent of garlic bread and fresh pasta where we had celebrated our first year of meeting a decade earlier, to plan for our last year of monthly meetings. After we consulted menus and placed our orders, mothers and daughters concurred that our priority was to stay connected and caught up with one another's lives, even—or perhaps especially—as our girls prepared to leave home the following year. We decided to meet for dinner on the second Tuesday of every month—"Even if we're busy, we have to eat!" said Vanessa. We planned one last trip to the apple orchard. "It's our tradition," Maggie reminded us. The other girls chimed in, "Yeah, riding on the hay wagon," "Throwing apples," and "Don't forget eating cider doughnuts!"

"I would love help on my college entrance essays," said Marisol, and the other girls agreed. Most are in the midst of applying to college. We have encouraged our daughters to pursue education because we know that it gives them the best chance of future financial success as adults.[3] April, still a junior, was a good sport when the group decided to spend a meeting or two in the fall, offering feedback and encouragement on applications, and Maisie thought it would be good for her to start thinking about college early anyway.

"We should have a graduation for our group," said Amy. We all agreed. We decided to take one weekend away in the spring to celebrate and have a formal closure to our group—or at least this first stage of our group. At that ceremony, we plan to honor daughters and mothers one at a time, each of us sharing what we love and admire about her and what difference she has made in our lives. The girls have already begun talking about having reunions, a thought that makes us all a bit teary-eyed.

As we wait for our meals to arrive, we go around the table doing our customary check-in, during which each mother and daughter shares how she's feeling and what is up in her life. Maggie is taking on a heavy academic load in the fall so she can travel to South America in the spring with a group that includes her father, David. She is busy applying to college with an eye to major in international relations but still makes time for African dance. Her mother, Sarah, is content in her full-time nursing job, for the moment anyway. She notes she doesn't see as much of Maggie these days and anticipates even more time and freedom when Maggie leaves home, and is wondering what new adventures might tempt her and her husband of sixteen years, Dan.

Marisol is busy preparing for the ACT test, applying to college, searching for scholarships, attending honors classes in high school, and singing with the concert choir. Katy, forty-five, is excited by the new clients for whom she is designing store windows. She is busy with work, helping Marisol, raising Kaili, twelve, who is just beginning seventh grade, painting, and nurturing her relationship with their stepfather of eight years, Jeff.

April, sixteen, decided against fall sports so she can get an after-school job, but she hasn't found one she's excited about yet. She can't wait for basketball season to start. Her sister, Gabriella, eighteen, is working as a waitress at a local diner as she prepares Shakespeare monologues for her auditions to theater conservatories and finishes up the last requirements of high school.

When it's time for Gabi and April's mother, Maisie, forty-two, to check in, the waiter is still puttering in the corner of our private party room, so she announces in a very loud voice, "Well, I am having *great* sex these days." Our looks of incredulity turn to laughter as the waiter beats a quick exit from the room. We all love Maisie's free spirit. Maisie informs us that she is actually spending most of her time figuring out what she wants to do with the next phase of her life. Since she had her kids "bing-bang" right out of college, she is hankering for the kind of young adult freedom the rest of the mothers had in their early twenties before becoming parents.

Vanessa is a respected senior in high school with a wide network of diverse friends. She's cocaptain of her soccer team and an avid photographer. She and Libby, fifty-two, are getting along well these days, enjoying their trips to visit colleges, both close to home and not so close. Libby finds her work in family law continuously satisfying and is intrigued by imagining what life will be like for her and her husband, Aaron, when Vanessa leaves home.

Amy is taking advanced calculus and physics at a local college (along with the usual English and history classes at her high school), tutoring high school sophomores in geometry, and dancing salsa every chance she gets as she works on her college applications. She is also (blush) spending time with her boyfriend, Zach, a quiet, easygoing senior who shares her goofy sense of humor. Phoebe, forty-five, is relieved that although Amy, like usual, procrastinated getting her schedule in place until the last possible minute, has created a great fall schedule for herself, and is grateful that her daughter's first romance is with someone so kind and considerate. Phoebe is busy with research and teaching anthropology and is enjoying long conversations and bike rides with her younger daughter, Eliza, eleven, who is in her final year of elementary school, and more evenings out with her husband of twenty-four years, Paul.

We've all finished eating, the empty plates have been cleared, and the waiter has taken the check. It's time to go. "Can we do the rain thing here?" asks Maggie. *Of course we can,* we say. *We'll do it softly.* Phoebe starts with rubbing her hands together, and the swish swoops around the circle. Snapping, clapping, stomping, as we make a rainstorm crescendo and decrescendo, we mothers can't stop staring at the smart, articulate, confident young women we see in the circle, and they beam back at us. We did it. We banded together and beat the odds, and there is no doubt about it: Our daughters are thriving.

Each generation of women does their part in finding creative ways to protect and encourage their daughters. We would not have the opportunities we enjoy today if not for the courage and tenacity of our mothers and grandmothers who—despite their apparent flaws—also strived to make life better for girls and women. It is their legacy we draw upon as we seek to help mothers and daughters thrive, together, now, and into the future.

Appendix 1:
Creating a Mother-Daughter Group

Women have always sought the companionship and support of other women. We have gathered in kitchens, campuses, and playgrounds, cafés and factories, our places of worship. Prenatal classes segue into playgroups and babysitting clubs. Our female friends and relatives provide guidance and help us shoulder our burdens. The Mother-Daughter Project draws on and extends the relationship- and community-building that comes automatically to many women. You may already have a robust community that shares your hopes for your daughter and you, but if you don't (like many of us mothering today) here is how you can create one yourself.

Meet First as Mothers Only

Before bringing your daughters together, meeting first as mothers gives you time to get to know one another and create a common vision of your hopes for mothers and daughters. It is not necessary to agree on all the ways you parent your daughters, but for a group to work, members need to know and respect one another's values. You are building a community of women for your daughters to join. The trust you develop with one another will determine its strength.

Trust comes from experiencing that your group can compassionately hear your sometimes tender and difficult stories of mothering—and of being a daughter. Sharing frankly about your relationship with your own mother provides insight. Openly discussing the challenges you faced as a teenager and young woman can be a balm and helps you identify your strengths and vulnerabilities as your daughter negotiates adolescence. When you feel as if you have hit a dead end, other women can add their novel perspectives and help you see a way through.

There are many ways to start a group. Word of mouth is a common way to begin. It is not necessary to know another mother personally to ask her to join; she just needs to be a mother who wants to help and support her daughter as she grows up. In fact, bringing together women from different social groups or girls from several different schools can add a level of ease and provide a social haven when there are stresses in one's everyday circles. Posting a flyer at your library, house of worship, cultural center, or other community center is another way to form a group. (There is a sample flyer at the end of this appendix that you can use for this purpose.)

An ideal size for a group is four to six mothers. A group can be as small as two and larger than six, but the larger the group, the harder it is to establish the trust and comfort level needed to share true feelings about intimate topics, and it can become logistically tough to get everyone together at the same time. Groups can start online or be time-limited; they can meet monthly for an evening or biannually for a weekend. We found it easiest to create groups in which the daughters are all within a year or two of the same age. And it's never too late to start a group—whether your daughter is seven or eleven or sixteen.

Hosting the Introductory Meeting

It's your first meeting. Sit in a circle to help establish that you are peers. Start by introducing yourself and explaining that the intentions of the group are to help mothers and daughters thrive and stay close through adolescence. Share your own hopes for the group, or, if you want, read a passage from this book that captures those hopes. Then share the agenda for the meeting, which is as follows:

Introductions.

Begin by asking each mother to introduce herself, and tell the names and ages of her children, how she heard about the group, who she already knows in the group, and for how long. (Being clear about who already knows whom clarifies the social dynamics and helps everyone feel more comfortable.)

Sharing hopes for the group.

Invite each woman to share what her hopes are for the group, and write them down, preferably on a big piece of newsprint or a blackboard so everyone can see. Be sure to add your own! Here are some ideas to get you started:

Support one another as mothers

Build trust in a noncompetitive environment

Listen with an open mind and compassionate heart

Stay connected with our daughters

Explore and grow as women as well as mothers

Help our daughters grow up strong and free

Work toward mutuality in our family relationships

After everyone has shared her hopes, discuss them, and star the ones you all agree on. These are the goals that can guide your group.

Establishing group guidelines.

These are the nuts-and-bolts agreements, such as how often the group meets, that will help things run smoothly. Remember, the group should fit into the lives of the mothers, not the other way around. Here are some suggestions, but change them to fit your needs:

- Mothers meet once a month in a private location
- All mothers share responsibility for and leadership of the group
- Two women will plan and colead each meeting on a rotating basis
- Meetings will start with a check-in to share what's up in our lives as mothers, followed by a discussion, exercise, or activity selected by the coleaders
- Keep what's said in the group confidential
- Start and end on time
- Group decisions will be made by consensus
- Make sure every mother's voice is heard
- Set up a calendar of meetings six months in advance
- Membership in the group is closed (or will close by next meeting)
- Call the coleader if you can't come
- After six months of mothers-only meetings, mother-daughter meetings will begin

As you discuss group guidelines, encourage mothers to ask themselves, *What do I need to make this group work for me?* Be creative. What's important to you? Meeting in one another's homes or a neutral space, getting help with child care, bringing food to share or not? In our group, we had a *No cleaning, no apologies* rule because we wanted to make it explicit that we weren't meeting to judge one another's homes or to make more work for ourselves. Each group is unique. Acknowledging individual needs and differences will help foster a safe, nurturing environment.

Closing.

To encourage shared leadership, invite two mothers to volunteer to lead the next meeting, decide if you will be doing a reading beforehand, and confirm the date, time, and location. Create a name, phone, and e-mail list for group members. Often at this point, the idea of starting a group is so exciting that women will want to invite every mother they know to join! Be clear in the first meeting that mother-daughter groups work best when they are relatively small. If there is a lot of interest, we strongly suggest establishing two or more groups organized according to the daughters' ages.

....

As in any group, sticky issues can arise. Letting interested friends and acquaintances know that the group size is fixed and limited and encouraging them to start another group can allay a sense of being left out. Likewise, simply not talking about your group (unless asked) in front of other mothers protects their feelings. It's common in the first six months for some mothers to decide that a group isn't a good fit for them and drop out; if your group seems too small, you can invite other mothers to replace them.

The Next Five Mothers-Only Meetings

We suggest beginning every mothers' meeting with a check-in to see how each mom is doing and share what is going on in her and her daughter's life at the moment. It's a way to get to know and stay current with the other women, and it works best if you hold back comments and responses until every mother has checked in (reminded by the facilitators if necessary) both for expediency and to not get drawn into conversation before hearing from every woman. Then open up a general topic of discussion, either one that was predetermined, or something raised by a mother in her check-in.

The first section of this book can be used to spark conversation for the first six (or more) meetings after your introductory get-together. It is organized so that you can read one chapter in advance and then discuss it or respond to the suggested questions together at a meeting. The questions we pose in the second section on mother-daughter groups can be explored anytime before the general themes are shared with the girls.

If you use our questions in a group, we suggest the following format to promote balance in discussions and ensure that every woman's voice is heard.

1. Whoever is facilitating the meeting reads the questions, letting the mothers write them down, and then everyone takes ten or fifteen minutes to think, draw, or write a response.

2. One at a time, each woman who wishes to shares her responses while the other women just listen.

3. Going around the circle again, each woman shares one or two things that another mother said that are moving or pertinent and why.

4. Follow individual responses with a general, unstructured discussion. Many of the questions lend themselves to creating group goals or a group vision about topics such as "what it means for adolescent girls to thrive." It can be helpful to write out ideas on a chalkboard or big piece of newsprint, starring the ones you all agree with. Groups also benefit from creating a log of their meetings as a resource to refer to and look back on.

Taking Care of Your Group over the Long Haul

Mothers are the backbone of the Mother-Daughter Project and a group is only as strong and flexible as our relationships with one another. Once or twice every year it is helpful to discuss:

What's working for me in this group? What isn't?

What's working for my daughter? What isn't?

How can our group change so that all our needs can be met?

We have found that while not necessarily easy, these conversations are essential for group longevity.

The First Mother-Daughter Meetings

After mothers have been getting together for about six months, or whenever the moms all feel ready, it's time for your first mother-daughter gathering. The initial meetings should focus simply on having fun and getting to know the other mothers and daughters, then gradually add in activities that have more content, following the age-appropriate, year-by-year curricula we provide in Part II. You can start a mother-daughter group when your daughter is any age, but it's easiest to start when the girls are ten or younger because they are less self-conscious and can bond with other girls more readily. Older girls will become close, but be patient—it can take time.

Girls of different ages respond to different kinds of invitations. You can simply tell a ten-year-old-or younger that the two of you will be joining a mother-daughter group to have a good time, learn things about growing up as a girl, and make friends with other mothers and daughters, and she will probably be openly excited to join you. A girl who is eleven to fifteen will be *secretly* thrilled when you explain to her that now that she is getting so grown up, you want to find ways to stay connected with her and have a good relationship. You can tell her that hanging out and doing activities with other girls and their moms would be a fun way to stay close, and on the first get-together you're all going to: (choose an activity that the mothers know the girls in the group would like, such as going to the beach or having a "girls night in" to watch a movie they all love). At sixteen and older, your daughter will likely be pleased to hear that you want to understand her and stay close with her now that she's almost an adult, and that you would like to invite her to come with you to a gathering of other mothers and their daughters to relax and talk or do something fun together.

Sample flyer for starting a group

Come join us in cocreating a

Mother-Daughter Project Group
for mothers and their daughters

Mothers and daughters can do together what one mother alone cannot: create a lively subculture that simultaneously nurtures mothers, girls, and mother-daughter connection. —The Mother-Daughter Project

Join with a small group of women to explore how we can help one another nurture our daughters through childhood, adolescence, and into adulthood. The intention of our group is to support one another as mothers, nurture our relationships with our daughters, help them thrive as girls and young women, and welcome them into a community of women. Our goal is for each of us to shine in her own identity, not in any proscribed or limited one. We want our daughters to appreciate their many gifts, learn to use them wisely, and to emerge from adolescence full of their own choices and desires.

As our primary guide, we will use the book *The Mother-Daughter Project: How Mothers and Daughters Can Band Together, Beat the Odds, and Thrive Through Adolescence* by SuEllen Hamkins, MD, and Renée Schultz, MA. We will also draw on other resources that we each bring to make this project uniquely our own. To start, we will meet as mothers alone for six meetings, then we will add gatherings for mothers and daughters together.

When: Once a month, beginning _____
Where: Location
Time: Two hours; specify time
Who: Mothers who have daughters between the ages of _____
       and _____
Size: 5 to 7 mothers
Questions? Contact: Name, telephone number, e-mail address

Appendix 2:
The Moon Dance of the Body

A short, participatory musical theater dance
For mothers and daughters ages seven to ten years old
To joyfully teach about women's monthly cycles

Choose one mother to be the director, who holds a script, directs the action, and feeds the characters their lines. Another mother or daughter can offer technical assistance and help with singing or music.

Characters:

The MOON, adorned with white and black scarves, the time-keeper and originator of all the action

HORMONES, (also known as WOMANFIRE), which include estrogen, progesterone, follicle-stimulating hormone (FSH), and lutenizing hormone (LH), who offer help and guidance to all the other characters, adorned with scarves of any color

2 OVARIES, each holding a package of seeds or carton of eggs

BLOOD in the uterus, played by two or more dancers adorned with pink, purple, and red scarves

The CERVIX, played by two dancers creating an arch, adorned with white scarves.

(As the dance begins all is quiet. The center of the room is the inside of the uterus. The two dancers performing the CERVIX stand center downstage, the OVARIES stand on the far left and right, the BLOOD sits on the floor, and the HORMONES sit quietly amid them. The MOON is offstage.)

ENTIRE COMPANY (*Softly hums a gentle song everyone knows, such as "Twinkle, twinkle little star" [traditional], "Fireflies" [traditional], or "Nissa" [traditional], or play soft instrumental music.*)

MOON (*Enters draped mostly in the black scarf. Speaking to HORMONES*): Start to dance. (*HORMONES rise and begin to gently dance and wave their scarves as the humming continues.*) Dance around the ovaries, and choose one to get ready to release an egg.

HORMONES (*Dance around the ovaries, ultimately choosing one.*)

MOON: Tell the blood to begin to blossom.

HORMONES (*To the BLOOD*): Begin to blossom! (*BLOOD begins to wave their scarves.*)

MOON (*Reaching the darkest phase, the new moon, drapes the black scarf over her face, and speaks to the HORMONES*): Now I am the new moon. Tell the ovary to release an egg.

HORMONES (*To the designated ovary*): Release an egg.

MOON: Tell the blood to take care of the egg.

HORMONES: Take care of the egg.

OVARY (*Takes a seed or egg out of the package and hands it to the girls who are playing* BLOOD, *who stand up and pass it carefully among themselves as they continue to dance and wave their scarves.*)

MOON (*To the* CERVIX): Cervix, open wide and make lots of slippery mucous!

CERVIX (*Dancers create an arch and wave their white scarves.*)

MOON (*Uncovers her face and begins waxing, placing the white scarf over the black one*): Now I am waxing, getting larger. The cervix needs to close! (*The* CERVIX *closes and quiets again.*) Now is the time for the dance party! Everybody dance! (*Put on some great dance music like Aretha Franklin's "Respect" or sing a lively song together such as "Under the Full Moonlight" [traditional] and the* BLOOD *and the* HORMONES *dance!*)

MOON (*To the* HORMONES): Tell the blood to dance more wildly!

HORMONES: Dance more wildly! Dance with joy! (*BLOOD dances and waves their scarves more wildly, one of the dancers still holding the egg.*)

MOON: Now I am a full moon! It's time for the gateway of the cervix to open again! It's time for the blood to fly!

HORMONES: Gateway, open! Blood, fly! Fly! Fly out into the world! (*The* CERVIX *opens, and the* BLOOD *dances through the arch and all around the room.*)

COMPANY (*Sings together a river or traveling song everyone knows, such as "You Rolling Old River" [traditional] or "She'll Be Comin' 'Round the Mountain" [traditional].*)

FINIS.

Notes

Introduction

1. Elizabeth Debold, Marie Wilson, and Idelisse Malavé, *Mother Daughter Revolution: From Betrayal to Power* (New York: Addison-Wesley, 1993).

2. Michael White and David Epson, *Narrative Means to Therapeutic Ends* (New York: W. W. Norton, 1990); Jill Freedman and Gene Combs, *Narrative Therapy: The Social Construction of Preferred Realities* (New York: W. W. Norton and Company, 1996).

Chapter One: What Is the Mother-Daughter Project?

1. Susan Douglas and Meredith Michaels, *The Mommy Myth: The Idealization of Motherhood and How It Has Undermined All Women* (New York: Free Press, 2004); Judith Warner, *Perfect Madness: Motherhood in the Age of Anxiety* (New York: Riverhead Books, 2005).

2. Bureau of Justice Statistics, 2004. Table 4, "Personal Crimes, 1996–2002: Victimization rates for persons age 12 and over, by gender and age of victims and type of crime," www.ojp.usdoj.gov/bjs/; Efrosini Kokaliari, "Deliberate Self-Injury: An Investigation of the Prevalence and Psychosocial Meanings in a Non-clinical Female College Population" (PhD diss., Smith College, 2005); National Institute of Mental Health, "Eating disorders" (2005), www.nimh.nih.gov/publicat/eatingdisorders.cfm; National Institute of Mental Health, "Depression" (2005), www.nimh.nih.gov/publicat/depression.cfm.

3. Kathy Weingarten, *The Mother's Voice: Strengthening Intimacy in Families, 2nd ed.* (New York: Guilford Press, 1994); Judith V. Jordan, Alexandra G. Kaplan, Jean Baker Miller, Irene P. Stiver, and Janet L. Surrey, *Women's Growth in Connection: Writings from the Stone Center* (New York: Guilford Press, 1991); Carol Gilligan, *In a Different Voice* (Cambridge, MA: Harvard University Press, 1982); Jean Baker Miller, *Toward a New Psychology of Women* (Boston: Beacon Press, 1976).

Chapter Two: Daughters: Helping Our Girls Thrive

1. Craig Winston LeCroy and Janice Daley, *Empowering Adolescent Girls: Examining the Present and Building Skills for the Future with the "Go Girls" Program* (New York: W. W. Norton and Company, 2001), 34.

2. A. Rae Simpson, *Raising Teens: A Synthesis of Research and a Foundation for Action* (Boston: Center for Health Communication, Harvard School of Public Health, 2001), 62.

3. "Perfect Girl" was first coined by Lyn Mikel Brown and Carol Gilligan, *Meeting at the Crossroads: Women's Psychology and Girls' Development* (Cambridge, MA: Harvard University Press, 1992).

4. Claudia Mitchell and Jacqueline Reid-Walsh, "Theorizing Tween Culture Within Girlhood Studies," in Claudia Mitchell and Jacqueline Reid-Walsh, eds., *Seven Going on Seventeen: Tween Studies in the Culture of Girlhood* (New York: Peter Lang, 2005), 6. "Although not (yet) listed in the OED the word 'tween' is commonly understood to be a construction of the present day pertaining to a younger preadolescent and adolescent age group exclusively or almost exclusively female, possessing or defined by a distinct commodity culture."

5. Simpson, *Raising Teens*, 17.

6. Ibid., 60.

7. Ibid., 59.

8. Carol Gilligan, *The Birth of Pleasure* (New York: Alfred A. Knopf, 2002), 15.

9. Simpson, *Raising Teens*.

10. American Association of University Women Education Foundation, 1998, *Gender Gaps: Where Schools Still Fail Our Children* (Washington, D.C., 1998), 32. The *Philadelphia Inquirer* reports that among

local high school valedictorians in 2003, girls outnumbered boys two to one.

11. Anita Harris, ed., *All About the Girl: Culture, Power, and Identity* (New York: Routledge, 2004).

12. Melody J. Slashinski, *Girls and Science, Math, and Engineering* (Washington, D.C.: Girls Incorporated, 2004).

13. Mary Pipher, *Reviving Ophelia: Saving the Selves of Adolescent Girls* (New York: Ballantine Books, 1994), 23.

14. Gilligan, *In a Different Voice*; Carol Gilligan, Nona P. Lyons, and Trudy J. Hammer, eds., *Making Connections: The Relational Worlds of Adolescent Girls at Emma Willard School* (Cambridge, MA: Harvard University Press, 1990); Gilligan, *The Birth of Pleasure*.

15. A. Rae Simpson, *Raising Teens*.

16. Dale Kunkel, Keren Eyal, Kelli Finnerty, Erica Biely, and Edward Donnerstein, "Sex on TV," A Kaiser Family Foundation Report, 2005 (Publication 7398), www.kff.org.

17. Jay G. Silverman, Anita Raj, Lorelei A. Mucci, and Jeanne E. Hathaway, "Dating Violence Against Adolescent Girls and Associated Substance Use, Unhealthy Weight Control, Sexual Risk Behavior, Pregnancy, and Suicidality," *Journal of the American Medication Association* 286 (2001): 572–579.

18. Ibid.

19. Centers for Disease Control, Center for Injury Control and Prevention, "Intimate Partner Violence Fact Sheet, 2006," www.cdc.gov/nicp/factsheets/ipvfacts.htm.

20. Silverman, Raj, Mucci, and Hathaway, "Dating Violence Against Adolescent Girls," 572–579.

21. Efrosini Kokaliari, "Deliberate Self-Injury: An Investigation of the Prevalence and Psychosocial Meanings in a Non-clinical Female College Population" (PhD, Smith College, 2005), 127–129, 135–137.

22. Simpson, *Raising Teens*, 53.

23. *Morbidity and Mortality Weekly Report*, 2004. Centers for Disease Control, www.cdc.gov/mmwr/PDF/wk/mm5322.pdf.

24. Richard Maisel, David Epston, and Ali Borden, *Biting the Hand That Starves You: Inspiring Resistance to Anorexia/Bulimia* (New York: W. W. Norton and Company, 2005).

25. Howard H. Goldman, *Review of General Psychiatry* (Los Altos, CA: Lange Medical Publications, 1984), 464.

26. Anne E. Becker, Rebecca A. Burwell, Stephen E. Gilman, David B. Herzog, and Paul Hamburg, "Eating Behaviors and Attitudes Following Prolonged Exposure to Television Among Ethnic Fijian Adolescent Girls," *British Journal of Psychiatry* 186 (2002): 509–514.

27. K. Boutelle, et al., "Weight control among obese, over-weight and non-overweight adolescents," *Journal of Pediatric Psychology*, 27 (2002): 531–40; National Institute of Mental Health, 2005, "Eating disorders": www.nimh.nih.gov/publicat/eatingdisorders.cfm.

28. If your daughter is affected by anorexia or bulimia, we recommend *Biting the Hand that Starves You* (see note 24 above) as an essential guide to help you support your daughter in reclaiming her true self and shutting out the lies of anorexia and bulimia.

29. K. Boutelle, et al., "Weight control," 531–540.

30. Office of National Drug Control Policy, "Girls and Drugs: A New Analysis: Recent Trends, Risk Factors and Consequences" (Executive Office of the President, 2006), www.streetdrugs.org/pdf/girls_and_drugs.pdf.

31. The National Center on Addiction and Substance Abuse, "The Formative Years: Pathways to Substance Abuse Among Girls and Young Women Ages 8–22" (Columbia University, 2004), www.CASAColumbia.org.

32. Office of National Drug Control Policy, "Girls and Drugs."

33. Ibid.

Chapter Three: Mothers: Confronting the Myth of Supermom

1. Judith Warner, *Perfect Madness: Motherhood in the Age of Anxiety* (New York: Penguin Books, 2005).

2. U.S. Bureau of Labor Statistics, "Labor Force Participation Roles for Wives, Husbands Present by Age of Own Youngest Child 1975 to 2000" (U.S. Department of Labor, 2001), Statistical Abstracts Table No. 578.

3. Arlie Hochschild, *The Second Shift* (New York: Penguin Books, 2003), xxxviii.

4. Warner, *Perfect Madness*; Susan J. Douglas and Meredith Michaels, *The Mommy Myth: The Idealization of Motherhood and How It Has Undermined All Women* (New York: Free Press, 2004).

5. Hochschild, *The Second Shift*, xxiv.

6. Sallyann Roth and Richard Chasin, "Entering one another's worlds of meaning and imagination: Dramatic enactment and narrative couple therapy," in Michael F. Hoyt, ed., *Constructive Therapies* (New York: Guilford Publications, 1994), 189.

Chapter Four: Preventing Mother-Daughter Disconnection

1. Monica McGoldrick, John K. Pearce, and Joseph Giordano, eds., *Ethnicity and Family Therapy*, 1st ed. (New York: Guilford Press, 1982).

2. Personal conversation, International Narrative Therapy Conference, Oaxaca, Mexico, 2004.

3. Elizabeth Debold, Marie Wilson, and Idelisse Malavé, *Mother Daughter Revolution: From Betrayal to Power* (New York: Addison-Wesley, 1993), 25.

4. Ibid, 17.

5. Estelle B. Freedman, *No Turning Back: The History of Feminism and the Future of Women* (New York: Ballantine Books, 2002), 7.

6. Christine Bolger, "For the mothers of teenage girls, uncool is the way to be" (Northampton, MA: *Daily Hampshire Gazette*, April 27, 2003), c1. Susan Borowitz, *When We're in Public, Pretend You Don't Know Me: Surviving Your Daughter's Adolescence So You Don't Look Like an Idiot and She Still Talks to You* (New York: Warner Books, 2003).

7. A. Rae Simpson, *Raising Teens: A Synthesis of Research and a Foundation for Action* (Boston: Center for Health Communication, Harvard School of Public Health, 2001), 6.

8. Carol Gilligan, *In a Different Voice: Psychological Theory and Women's Development* (Cambridge, MA: Harvard University Press, 1982); Carol Gilligan, *The Birth of Pleasure: A New Map of Love* (New York: Alfred A. Knopf, 2002); Jean Baker Miller, *Toward a New Psychology of Women* (Boston: Beacon Press, 1976); Stone Center for Developmental Services and Studies, 1986–present, *Work in Progress* (Wellesley, MA: Stone Center); Kathy Weingarten, "The discourses of intimacy: Adding a social constructionist and feminist view," *Family Process* 30 (1991): 285–305; Kathy Weingarten, *The Mother's Voice: Strengthening intimacy in families*, 2nd ed. (New York: Guilford Press, 1997); Michael White and David Epson, *Narrative Means to Therapeutic Ends* (New York: W. W. Norton, 1990); Michael White, *Re-authoring Lives: Interviews and Essays* (Adelaide, Australia: Dulwich Centre Publications, 1995).

9. Barbara F. Turnage, "African American mother-daughter relationships mediating daughter's self-esteem," *Child & Adolescent Social Work Journal*, 3 (2004): 155–173.

10. Lori Lobenstine, Jessica Castro, Yasmin Pereira, Jenny Whitley, Jessica Robles, Yaraliz Soto, Jeanette Sergeant, Daisy Jimenez, Emily Jimenez, Jessica Ortiz, and Sasha Cirino, "Possible Selves and Pasteles: How a Group of Mothers and Daughters Took a London Conference by Storm," in *All About the Girl*, Anita Harris, ed. (New York: Routledge, 2004).

11. Carol Gilligan, Nona Lyons, and Trudy Hammer, eds., *Making Connections: The Relational Worlds of Adolescent Girls at the Emma Willard School* (Cambridge, MA: Harvard University Press, 1990).

12. Kathy Weingarten, *The Mother's Voice: Strengthening Intimacy in Families*, 2nd ed. (New York: Guilford Press, 1997), 194.

13. Janet Surrey, "The Mother-Daughter Relationship: Themes in Psychotherapy," in Janneke van Mesn-Verhulst, Karlein Schreurs, and Liesbeth Woertman, eds., *Daughtering and Mothering: Female Subjectivity Reanalysed* (London: Routledge, 1993), 116–117.

14. Elliot Currie, *The Road to Whatever: Middle Class Culture and the Crisis in Adolescence* (New York: Henry Holt, 2004).

Chapter Five: Finding a Common Ground: Developing Mother-Daughter Mutuality

1. Janet Surrey, "The Mother-Daughter Relationship: Themes in Psychotherapy," in Janneke van Mesn-Verhulst, Karlein Schreurs, and Liesbeth Woertman, eds., *Daughtering and Mothering: Female Subjectivity Reanalysed* (London: Routledge, 1993), 119.

Chapter Six: Creating a Community for Mothers and Daughters

1. A. Rae Simpson, *Raising Teens: A Synthesis of Research and a Foundation for Action* (Boston: Center for Health Communication, Harvard School of Public Health, 2001), 59.

2. Jennifer Baumgardner and Amy Richards, *Manifesta: Young Women, Feminism, and the Future* (New York: Farrar, Strauss and Giroux, 2000), 200.

3. Patricia Hersch, *A Tribe Apart: A Journey into the Heart of American Adolescence* (New York: Fawcett, 1998).

4. Lisa Foster, "Effectiveness of Mentor Programs: Review of the Literature from 1995–2000," prepared at the request of Senator Dede Alpert, Chair, Senate Select Committee on Family, Child, and Youth Development (California Research Bureau, 2001).

Chapter Seven: Celebrating Girls

1. For a thorough analysis of the impact of marketing, refer to Sharon Lamb and Lyn Mikel Brown, *Packaging Girlhood: Rescuing Our Daughters from Marketers' Schemes* (New York: St. Martin's Press, 2006).

2. Annie Rogers, excerpted from "The Development of Courage in Girls and Women," an earlier version of "Voice, Play, and a Practice of Ordinary Courage in Girls' and Women's Lives, *Harvard Educational Review,* Fall 1993, quoted in Elizabeth Debold, Marie Wilson, and Idelissa Malavé, *Mother Daughter Revolution* (New York: Bantam, 1992), 141.

Chapter Eight: Fostering True Friendship

1. Libba Bray, *A Great and Terrible Beauty* (New York: Delacourte Press, 2003).

Chapter Nine: Welcoming Cycles

1. Judy Grahn, *Blood, Bread, and Roses: How Menstruation Created the World* (Boston: Beacon Press, 1994).

2. © SuEllen Hamkins; used with permission of the author.

Chapter Ten: Learning to Love Our Bodies

1. Alvan Feinstein, "How Do We Measure Accomplishment in Weight Reduction?" in Louis Lasagna, ed., *Obesity: Causes, Consequences and Treatment* (New York: Medcom Press, 1974); Llewellyn Louderback, *Fat Power* (New York: Hawthorn Books, Inc., 1970); The Boston Women's Health Book Collective, *The New Our Bodies, Ourselves* (New York: Simon and Schuster, 1992); J. S. Garrow, *Energy Balance and Obesity in Man,* 2nd ed. (New York/Amsterdam: Elsevier/North-Holland Biomedical Press, 1978); H. J. Roberts, "Overlooked Dangers of Weight Reduction," *Medical Counterpoint,* 9 (1970): 15.

2. A highly recommended resource: Richard Maisel, David Epston, and Ali Borden, *Biting the Hand That Starves You: Inspiring Resistance to Anorexia/Bulimia* (New York: W. W. Norton & Co., 2005).

3. T. Mann, et al., "Are Two Interventions Worse than None? Joint Primary and Secondary Prevention of Eating Disorders in College Females," *Health Psychology* 16 (3) (1997): 215–225; C. Shisslak, et al., "Primary Prevention of Eating Disorders," *Journal of Consulting and Clinical Psychology* 55(5) (1987): 660–667.

4. Clarissa Pinkola Estés, *Women Who Run with the Wolves* (New York: Ballantine, 1992), 201.

5. Jane Gottesman, *Game Face: What Does a Female Athlete Look Like?* (New York: Game Face Productions, 2001). For additional inspiration, you can watch the movie *A League of Their Own*. For mothers only, it can be enlightening to watch the documentary *Playing Unfair: The Media Image of the Female Athlete*.

Chapter Eleven: Hanging Out and Having Fun (Shhh!) with Mom

1. Girl Scouts Research Institute in conjunction with Partners in Brainstorms, Inc., *The Ten Emerging Truths: New Directions for Girls 11–17,* (2002): 13.

2. A. Rae Simpson, *Raising Teens: A Synthesis of Research and a Foundation for Action* (Boston: Center for Health Communications, Harvard School of Public Health, 2001), 21.

3. Sharon Lamb and Lyn Mikel Brown, *Packaging Girlhood: Rescuing Our Daughters from Marketers' Schemes* (New York: St. Martin's Press, 2006).

4. "It is now not unusual for families to be headed by either a single mother or by two wage earners, and as much as 40 percent of young adolescents' time is unstructured, unsupervised, and consequently unproductive . . . Neighborhoods and communities—particularly inner-city, poor neighborhoods—are also increasingly less able to provide resources and services to the young, and school systems are often not organized to provide opportunities to learn and grow during the after-school hours" (National Research Council and Institute of Medicine, 1999; "Risks and Opportunities: Synthesis of Studies on Adolescence," Forum on Adolescence, Michele D. Kipke, editor, Board on Children, Youth, and Families (Washington, D.C.: National Academy Press).

5. Judy Schoenberg, T. Riggins, and K. Salmond, "Feeling Safe: What Girls Say" (Report, Girl Scout Research Institute, 2003): 10.

6. Simpson, *Raising Teens,* 40.

7. Ibid., 41.

8. Christina Robb, *This Changes Everything: The Relational Revolution in Psychology* (New York: Farrar, Straus and Giroux, 2006), xxvi–xxvii.

Chapter Twelve: Cultivating Desire

1. Sharon Lamb, *The Secret Lives of Girls: What Good Girls Really Do—Sex Play, Aggression, and Their Guilt* (New York: The Free Press, 2001), 27–28.

2. J. C. Abma, G. M. Martinez, W. D. Mosher, and B. S. Dawson, "Teenagers in the United States: Sexual activity, contraceptive use, and childbearing 2002," *National Center for Health Statistics* 23 (2004): 24.

3. Elizabeth Terry and Jennifer Manlove, "Trends in Sexual Activity and Contraceptive Use Among Teens," *Child Trends Research Brief* (2000), www.childtrends.org/store/prodpage.cfm?CategoryID=2.

4. According to Planned Parenthood, fewer than half of American public schools provide information about birth control. Planned Parenthood, "Teen Pregnancy and Sex Education Fact Sheet" (2005), www.plannedparenthood.org/news-articles-press/politics-policy-issues/abstinence-6236.htm.

5. *Adolescence and Abstinence Fact Sheet,* SIECUS Report, vol. 26 (1), Oct./Nov. 1997.

6. Lamb, *The Secret Lives of Girls,* 134–135.

7. Sharon Thompson, *Going All the Way: Teenage Girls' Tales of Sex, Romance, and Pregnancy* (New York: Hill and Wang, 1995).

8. Ellyn Kaschak and Leonore Tiefer, eds., *A New View of Women's Sexual Problems* (New York: Haworth Press, 2001), 206.

9. Barbara Huberman and Sue Alford, *Are You an Askable Parent?* (Advocates for Youth, 2005), www.advocatesforyouth.org/publications/frtp/askable.htm.

Chapter Thirteen: Teaching Safety and Freedom

1. Rape, Abuse and Incest National Network, Report of Bureau of Justice Statistics, *National Crime Victim Survey 2004,* www.rainn.org/statistics/index.html.

2. Liz Claiborne, Inc. Study on Teen Dating Abuse conducted by Teenage Research Unlimited, February 2005, www.loveisnotabuse .com/statistics/htm.

3. www.drugstrategies.org/keepingscore1999/teen.html.

4. We are indebted to Michael White for our understanding of healing and empowering ways to respond to trauma. Michael White, "Working with people who are suffering the consequences of multiple trauma: A narrative perspective," *International Journal of Narrative Therapy and Community Work*, 1 (2004): 45–66; Michael White, "Children, trauma and subordinate storyline development," *International Journal of Narrative Therapy and Community Work*, 3 and 4 (2005): 10–21.

5. Gavin De Becker, *Protecting the Gift: Keeping Children and Teenagers Safe (and Parents Sane)* (New York: Dial Press, 1999), 26.

6. Debbie Gardner and Mike Gardner, *Raising Kids Who Can Protect Themselves* (New York: McGraw-Hill, 2004), 5–6.

7. Marla BB and Nancy Rothenberg, *Private Communication*, 2006.

8. De Becker, *Protecting the Gift*, 192.

9. BB and Rothenberg.

10. Gardner and Gardner, *Raising Kids Who Can Protect Themselves*, 161.

11. Kimberly J. Mitchell, David Finkelhor, and Janis Wolak, "Risk Factors for and Impact of Online Sexual Solicitation of Youth," *The Journal of the American Medical Association*, 285 (2001): 3011–3014.

12. De Becker, *Protecting the Gift*, Appendix 7.

13. BB and Rothenberg.

Chapter Fourteen: Speaking Her Heart and Mind

1. Mary Pipher, *Reviving Ophelia: Saving the Selves of Adolescent Girls* (New York: Ballantine Books, 1994), 53.

2. Michele D. Kipke, ed., "Risks and Opportunities: Synthesis of Studies on Adolescence. Board on Children, Youth, and Families Commission on Behavioral and Social Sciences and Education" (National Research Council, Institute of Medicine, National Academy of Sciences, 1999).

3. Sharon Lamb, *The Secret Lives of Girls: What Good Girls Really Do—Sex Play, Aggression, and Their Guilt* (New York: The Free Press, 2001), 159.

4. Ibid., 162.

5. Lynn Mikel Brown, *Raising Their Voices: The Politics of Girls' Anger* (Cambridge, MA: Harvard University Press, 1998), 210.

6. Louanne Brizendine, *The Female Brain* (New York: Morgan Road Books, 2006).

7. Elizabeth Debold, Marie Wilson, and Idelisse Malavé, *Mother Daughter Revolution: From Betrayal to Power* (New York: Addison-Wesley, 1993), 94.

8. Marshall Rosenberg, *Nonviolent Communication: A Language of Life* (Encinitas, CA: PuddleDancer Press, 2003).

Chapter Fifteen: Earning Money and Wielding Power

1. This exercise was inspired by the work of Class Action: Building Bridges Across the Class Divide, www.classism.org/action_self.html.

2. Evelyn Murphy and E. J. Graff, *Getting Even: Why Women Don't Get Paid Like Men—And What to Do About It* (New York: Touchstone, 2005), 14.

3. Ibid., 26–27.

4. "Chutes and Ladders: The Search for Solid Ground for Women in the Workforce," *Women Work! The National Network for Women's Employment*, 2005, www.womenwork.org.

5. Murphy and Graff, *Getting Even*, 21.

6. According to the "1999 MetLife Juggling Act Study" produced by MetLife Mature Market Institute in conjunction with the National Alliance for Caregiving and the National Center for Women and Aging, the average caregiver loses upward of $659,000 over her lifetime in lost wages, lost social security, and pension contributions.

7. Brené Brown, *Women and Shame: Reaching Out, Speaking Truths and Building Connection* (Austin, TX: 3C Press, 2004).

8. This exercise was inspired by Joline Godfrey, *Raising Financially Fit Kids* (Berkeley, California: Ten Speed Press, 2003): 100–101.

9. Tamara Draut and Javier Silva, "Generation Broke: The Growth of Debt Among Young Americans, Borrowing to Make Ends Meet," Briefing Paper, 2004, Demos, www.demos.org/pub295.cfm.

10. www.daughtersandsonstowork.org.

Chapter Sixteen: Growing Roots and Wings

1. Teri Apter and Ruthellen Josselson, *Best Friends: The Pleasures and Perils of Girls' and Women's Friendships* (New York: Three Rivers Press, 1998), 27.

2. National Institute of Mental Health, "Imaging Study Shows Brain Maturing" (Source: Paul Thompson, PhD, UCLA Laboratory of Neuroimaging, 2004), www.nimh.nih.gov/press/prbrainmaturing.cfm.

3. A. Rae Simpson, *Raising Teens: A Synthesis of Research and a Foundation For Action* (Boston: Center for Health Communications, Harvard School of Public Health, 2001), 8.

4. Ibid., 9.

5. Ibid., 10.

6. Ibid., 11.

Chapter Seventeen: Flying Toward the Future

1. Susan Jekielek and Brett Brown, *The Transition to Adulthood: Characteristics of Young Adults Ages 18 to 24 in America* (The Annie E. Casey Foundation, Population Reference Bureau and Child Trends, 2005), 7.

2. Reauthoring questions such as these are informed by the work of Michael White, as presented at numerous conferences and workshops we have attended over the last decade, most recently: Michael White, "Advanced Workshop in Narrative Therapy," sponsored by the Family Institute of Cambridge, Cambridge, Massachusetts, March 21–22, 2006. See also Michael White, "Workshop Notes," www.dulwichcentre.com.au/Michael White Workshop Notes.pdf.

3. Jekielek and Brown, *The Transition to Adulthood*, 11.

Selected Bibliography

Books and Other Resources for Mothers and Daughters

Loving and Caring for Our Bodies

Angier, Natalie. *Woman: An Intimate Geography.* New York: Houghton Mifflin, 1999.

Boston Women's Health Book Collective. *Our Bodies, Ourselves: A New Edition for a New Era.* New York: Touchstone, 2005.

Caplin, Rachel. *I'm Beautiful Dammit!: Waging Your Own CurVolution.* Waco, TX: Terrace Publishing, 2006.

Lobovits, Dean, David Epston, and Jennifer Freeman. *Archive of Resistance: Anti-Anorexia, Anti-bulimia,* 2001, www.narrativeapproaches .com/antianorexia%20folder/anti_anorexia_index.htm.

Maine, Margo and Joe Kelly. *The Body Myth: Adult Women and the Pressure to Be Perfect.* Hoboken, NJ: John Wiley and Sons, 2005.

Maisel, Richard, David Epston, and Ali Borden. *Biting the Hand That Starves You: Inspiring Resistance to Anorexia/Bulimia.* New York: W. W. Norton and Company, 2004.

Nichter, Mimi. *Fat Talk: What Girls and Their Parents Say About Dieting.* Cambridge, MA: Harvard University Press, 2000.

Orbach, Susie. *Fat Is a Feminist Issue,* (rev. ed.). New York: Arrow, 1998.

Wann, Marilyn. *Fat!So?: Because You Don't Have to Apologize for Your Size!* Berkeley, CA: Ten Speed Press, 1998.

Enhancing Intuition and Communication

Bryson, Kelly. *Don't Be Nice, Be Real: Balancing Passion for Self with Compassion for Others.* Santa Rosa, CA: Elite Books, 2004.

Day, Laura. *Practical Intuition: How to Harness the Power of Your Instinct and Make It Work for You.* New York: Villard, 1996.

Gladwell, Malcolm. *Blink: The Power of Thinking Without Thinking.* New York: Little, Brown and Co., 2005.

Mariechild, Diane. *Mother Wit: A Guide to Healing and Psychic Development.* Berkeley, CA: Crossing Press, 1989.

Martin, Angela. *Practical Intuition: Practical Tools for Harnessing the Power of Your Instinct.* New York: Barnes and Noble, Inc., 2002.

Myers, David G. *Intuition: Its Powers and Perils.* New Haven, CT: Yale University Press, 2002.

Rosenberg, Marshall. *Nonviolent Communication: A Language of Life: Create Your Life, Your Relationships, and Your World in Harmony with Your Values.* Encinitas, CA: PuddleDancer Press, 2003.

Tannen, Deborah. *You're Wearing That?: Understanding Mothers and Daughters in Conversation.* New York: Random House, 2006.

Creating Community

Bolen, Jean Shinoda. *The Millionth Circle: How to Change Ourselves and the World—The Essential Guide to Women's Circles.* Boston: Conari Press, 1999.

Carnes, Robin Deen and Sally Craig. *Sacred Circles: A Guide to Creating Your Own Women's Spirituality Group.* San Francisco: Harper San Francisco, 1998.

Fluegelman, Andrew. *More New Games!: . . . and Playful Ideas from the New Games Foundation.* New York: Dolphin, Doubleday, 1981.

Hochman, Anndee. *Everyday Acts and Small Subversions: Women Reinventing Family, Community and Home.* Portland, OR: The Eighth Mountain Press, 1994.

Hughes, K. Wind and Linda Wolf. *Daughters of the Moon, Sisters of the Sun: Young Women and Mentors on the Transition to Womanhood.* Gabriola Island, BC, Canada: New Society Publishers, 1997.

Leondar-Wright, Betsy. *Class Matters: Cross-Class Alliance Building for Middle-Class Activists.* Gabriola Island, BC, Canada: New Society Publishers, 2005.

Le Fevre, Dale N. *Best New Games: 77 Games and 7 Trust Activities for All Ages and Abilities.* Champagne, IL: Human Kinetics, 2002.

Rohnke, Karl. *The Bottomless Bag Again!* Dubuque, IA: Kendall/Hunt Publishing Co., 1991.

Rohnke, Karl. *Silver Bullets: A Guide to Initiative Problems, Adventure Games and Trust Activities.* Dubuque, IA: Kendall/Hunt Publishing Co., 1984.

Sewell, Marilyn, ed. *Cries of the Spirit: More Than 300 Poems in Celebration of Women's Spirituality.* Boston: Beacon Press, 1991.

Stout, Linda. *Bridging the Class Divide and Other Lessons for Grassroots Organizing.* Boston: Beacon Press, 1996.

Zimmerman, Jack with Virginia Coyle. *The Way of Council.* Las Vegas, NV: Bramble Books, 1996.

Confronting Consumerism

Kilbourne, Jean. *Can't Buy My Love: How Advertising Changes the Way We Think and Feel.* New York: Touchstone, 1999.

———. *Killing Us Softly 3: Advertising's Image of Women* (Featuring Jean Kilbourne), DVD, directed by Sut Jhally. Northampton, MA: Media Education Foundation, Mediaed.org, 2000.

Lamb, Sharon and Lyn Mikel Brown. *Packaging Girlhood: Rescuing Our Daughters from Marketers' Schemes.* New York: St. Martin's Press, 2006.

Quart, Alissa. *Branded: The Buying and Selling of Teenagers.* Cambridge, MA: Perseus Publishing, 2003.

Schor, Juliet B. *Born to Buy: The Commercialized Child and the New Consumer Culture.* New York: Scribner, 2004.

Cultivating Desire and Sexuality

Barbach, Lonnie. *For Yourself: The Fulfillment of Female Sexuality,* rev. ed. New York: Signet, 2000.

Beck, Martha. *The Joy Diet: 10 Daily Practices for a Happier Life.* New York: Crown Publishers, 2003.

Choquette, Sonia. *Your Heart's Desire: Instructions for Creating the Life You Really Want.* New York: Three Rivers Press, 1997.

Domar, Alice. *Self-Nurture: Learning to Care for Yourself As Effectively As You Care for Everybody Else.* New York: Penguin Books, 2001.

Griffin, Carolyn Welch, Marian J. Wirth, and Arthur G. Wirth. *Beyond Acceptance: Parents of Lesbians and Gays Talk About Their Experiences*. New York: St. Martin's Griffin, 1996.

Kogan, Natasha. *The Daring Female's Guide to Ecstatic Living: 30 Dares for a More Gutsy and Fulfilling Life*. New York: Hyperion, 2006.

Lamb, Sharon. *The Secret Lives of Girls: What Good Girls Really Do—Sex Play, Aggression, and Their Guilt*. New York: Free Press, 2001.

Markova, Dawna. *I Will Not Die an Unlived Life: Reclaiming Purpose and Passion*. Boston: Conari Press, 2000.

Ogden, Gina. *The Heart and Soul of Sex: Making the ISIS Connection*. Boston: Trumpeter Press, 2006.

Tolman, Deborah. *Dilemmas of Desire: Teenage Girls Talk About Sexuality*. Cambridge, MA: Harvard University Press, 2002.

Weill, Sabrina. *The Real Truth About Teens and Sex: From Hooking Up to Friends with Benefits—What Teens Are Thinking, Doing, and Talking About and How to Help Them Make Smart Choices*. New York: The Berkeley Publishing Group, 2005.

Wolf, Naomi. *Promiscuities: The Secret Struggle for Womanhood*. New York: Random House, 1997.

Reveling in the Most-Feminist Era: Third-Wave Feminism

Baumgardner, Jennifer and Amy Richards. *Manifesta: Young Women, Feminism, and the Future*. New York: Farrar, Straus and Giroux, 2000.

Estrich, Susan. *Sex and Power*. New York: Riverhead Books, 2000.

Freedman, Estelle B. *No Turning Back: The History of Feminism and the Future of Women*. New York: Ballantine Books. 2002.

Guerrilla Girls. *Bitches, Bimbos, and Ballbreakers: The Guerrilla Girls' Illustrated Guide to Female Stereotypes*. New York: Penguin Books, 2003.

hooks, bell. *Feminism Is for Everybody: Passionate Politics*. Cambridge, MA: South End Press, 2000.

Smith, Barbara. *The Truth That Never Hurts: Writing on Race, Gender, and Freedom*. Piscataway, NJ: Rutgers University Press, 1998.

Facilitating Friendship

Apter, Terri and Ruthellen Josselson. *Best Friends: The Pleasures and Perils of Girls' and Women's Friendships*. New York: Three Rivers Press, 1998.

Goodman, Ellen and Patricia O'Brien. *I Know Just What You Mean: The Power of Friendship in Women's Lives.* New York: Simon and Schuster, 2000.

Jonas, Susan and Marilyn Nissenson. *Friends for Life: Enriching the Bond Between Mothers and Their Adult Daughters.* New York: William Morrow, 1997.

Gathering Inspiration for a Better World

Bolen, Jean Shinoda. *Urgent Message from Mother: Gather the Women, Save the World.* Boston: Conari, 2005.

Ellison, Sheila, ed. *If Women Ruled the World: How to Create the World We Want to Live In—Stories, Ideas, and Inspiration for Change.* Maui, HI: Inner Ocean, 2004.

Hewlett, Sylvia Ann and Cornel West. *The War Against Parents.* New York: Houghton Mifflin, 1998.

Robb, Christina. *This Changes Everything: The Relational Revolution in Psychology.* New York: Farrar, Straus and Giroux, 2006.

Wilson, Marie C. *Closing the Leadership Gap: Why Women Can and Must Help Run the World.* New York: Viking, 2004.

Nurturing Mental Health

Black, Claudia. *Changing Course: Healing from Loss, Abandonment, and Fear,* 2nd ed. Center City, MN: Hazelden, 1999.

Brown, Brené. *Women and Shame: Reaching Out, Speaking Truths and Building Connection.* Austin, TX: 3C Press, 2004.

Duerk, Judith. *Circle of Stones: Woman's Journey to Herself.* Philadelphia: Innisfree Press, 1989.

———. *I Sit Listening to the Wind: Woman's Encounter Within Herself.* Philadelphia: Innisfree Press, 1993.

Lerner, Harriet. *The Dance of Anger: A Woman's Guide to Changing the Patterns of Intimate Relationships* (reprint edition). New York: Harper and Row Publishers, 2005.

Maltz, Wendy. *The Sexual Healing Journey: A Guide for Survivors of Sexual Abuse.* New York: HarperCollins, 2001.

Miller, Jean Baker. *Toward a New Psychology of Women.* Boston: Beacon Press, 1976.

Managing Money and Wielding Power

Dominguez, Joe and Vicki Robin. *Your Money or Your Life: Transforming Your Relationship with Money and Achieving Financial Independence.* New York: Penguin Books, 1992.

Ehrenreich, Barbara. *Bait and Switch: The (Futile) Pursuit of the American Dream.* New York: Metropolitan Books, 2005.

———. *Nickel and Dimed: On (Not) Getting By in America.* New York: Metropolitan Books, 2001.

Frankel, Lois P. *Nice Girls Don't Get Rich: 75 Avoidable Mistakes Women Make with Money.* New York: Warner Books, 2005.

Godfrey, Joline. *Raising Financially Fit Kids.* Berkeley, CA: Ten Speed Press, 2003.

Murphy, Evelyn and E. J. Graff. *Getting Even: Why Women Don't Get Paid Like Men—and What to Do About It.* New York: Touchstone, 2005.

Nemeth, Maria. *The Energy of Money: A Spiritual Guide to Financial and Personal Fulfillment.* New York: Ballantine Wellspring, 1997.

Perle, Liz. *Money, A Memoir: Women, Emotions, and Cash.* New York: Henry Holt and Company, 2006.

Stanny, Barbara. *Prince Charming Isn't Coming: How Women Get Smart About Money.* New York: Penguin Books, 1997.

Tea, Michelle, ed. *Without a Net: The Female Experience of Growing Up Working Class.* Emeryville, CA: Seal Press, 2003.

Exploring Motherhood

Crittenden, Ann. *If You've Raised Kids, You Can Manage Anything: Leadership Begins at Home.* New York: Gotham Books, 2004.

Douglas, Susan and Meredith Michaels. *The Mommy Myth: The Idealization of Motherhood and How It Has Undermined All Women.* New York: Free Press, 2004.

Ellison, Katherine. *The Mommy Brain: How Motherhood Makes Us Smarter.* New York: Basic Books, 2005.

Garcia Coll, Cynthia, Janet L. Surrey, and Kathy Weingarten, eds. *Mothering Against the Odds: Diverse Voices of Contemporary Mothers.* New York: The Guilford Press, 1998.

Peskowitz, Miriam. *The Truth Behind the Mommy Wars: Who Decides What Makes a Good Mother?* Emeryville, CA: Seal Press, 2005.

Steinberg, Eden, ed. *Your Children Will Raise You: The Joys, Challenges, and Life Lessons of Motherhood.* Boston: Trumpeter, 2005.

Warner, Judith. *Perfect Madness: Motherhood in the Age of Anxiety.* New York: Riverhead, 2005.

Mothering Our Daughters

Brown, Lyn Mikel. *Girlfighting: Betrayal and Rejection Among Girls.* New York: New York University Press, 2003.

———. *Raising Their Voices: The Politics of Girls' Anger.* Cambridge, MA: Harvard University Press, 1998.

Brown, Lyn Mikel and Carol Gilligan. *Meeting at the Crossroads: Women's Psychology and Girls' Development.* Cambridge, MA: Harvard University Press, 1992.

Debold, Elizabeth, Marie Wilson, and Idelisse Malavé. *Mother Daughter Revolution: From Betrayal to Power,* 2nd ed. New York: Addison-Wesley, 1993.

Gilligan, Carol. *In a Different Voice: Psychological Theory and Women's Development.* Cambridge, MA: Harvard University Press, 1982.

Hersch, Patricia. *A Tribe Apart: A Journey into the Heart of American Adolescence.* New York: Fawcett Columbine, 1998.

Hughes, K. Wind and Linda Wolf. *Daughters of the Moon, Sisters of the Sun: Young Women and Mentors on the Transition to Womanhood.* Gabriola Island, BC, Canada: New Society Publishers, 1997.

Kashtan, Inbal. *Parenting from Your Heart: Sharing the Gifts of Compassion, Connection, and Choice.* Encinitas, CA: PuddleDancer Press, 2005.

Machoian, Lisa. *The Disappearing Girl: Learning the Language of Teenage Depression.* New York: Dutton, 2005.

Northrup, Christiane. *Mother-Daughter Wisdom: Creating a Legacy of Physical and Emotional Health.* New York: Bantam Books, 2005.

Parrish, Cindy L. *Heroic Girlz: An Educational Feature Film* and *Heroic Girlz Curriculum Guide,* 2006. Available through www.heroicgirlz.org.

Solomon, Rivka, ed. *That Takes Ovaries!: Bold Females and Their Brazen Acts.* New York: Three Rivers Press, 2002.

Ward, Janie Victoria. *The Skin We're In: Teaching Our Children to Be Emotionally Strong, Socially Smart, and Spiritually Connected.* New York: The Free Press, 2000.

Being Safe and Free

Bancroft, Lundy. *Why Does He Do That?: Inside the Minds of Angry and Controlling Men.* New York: Berkeley Publishing Group, 2002.

Bass, Ellen and Laurie Davis. *The Courage to Heal, 3rd ed.—Revised and Expanded: A Guide for Women Survivors of Child Sexual Abuse.* New York: Collins, 1994.

Chaiet, Donna and Francine Russell. *The Safety Zone: A Kid's Guide to Personal Safety.* New York: Morrow Jr., 1998.

Crompton, Vicki, and Ellen Zelda Kessner. *Saving Beauty from the Beast: How to Protect Your Daughter from an Unhealthy Relationship.* New York: Little Brown and Company, 2003.

De Becker, Gavin. *Protecting the Gift: Keeping Children and Teenagers Safe.* New York: The Dial Press, 1999.

Gardner, Debbie, and Mike Gardner. *Raising Kids Who Can Protect Themselves.* New York: McGraw-Hill, 2004.

Kraizer, Sherryll. *The Safe Child Book.* New York: Fireside, 1996.

Snortland, Ellen. *Beauty Bites Beast: Awakening the Warrior Within Women and Girls.* Pasadena, CA: Trilogy Books, 1998.

Resisting Substance Abuse

Black, Claudia. *It Will Never Happen to Me: Growing up with Addiction as Youngsters, Adolescents, Adults.* New York: Ballantine Books, 1987.

Cermak, Timmen. *Marijuana: What's a Parent to Believe?* Center City, MN: Hazelden, 2003.

Jay, Jeff and Debra Jay. *Love First: A New Approach to Intervention for Alcoholism and Drug Addiction.* Center City, MN: Hazelden, 2000.

The National Center on Addiction and Substance Abuse at Columbia University. *Women Under the Influence.* Baltimore: The Johns Hopkins University Press, 2006.

Wilmes, David J. *Parenting for Prevention: How to Raise a Child to Say No to Alcohol/Drugs.* Center City, MN: Hazelden, 1995.

Resources for Girls and Teens

Arnoldi, Katherine. *The Amazing "True" Story of a Teenage Single Mom.* New York: Hyperion, 1998.

Basso, Michael J. *The Underground Guide to Teenage Sexuality*, 2nd ed. Minneapolis, MN: Fairview Press, 2003.

Bell, Ruth. *Changing Bodies, Changing Lives*, 3rd ed. New York: Random House, 1998.

Brashich, Audrey D. *All Made Up: A Girl's Guide to Seeing Through Celebrity Hype . . . and Celebrating Real Beauty*. New York: Walker and Company, 2006.

Brooks, Susan M. *Any Girl Can Rule the World*. Minneapolis, MN: Fairview Press, 1998.

Drill, Esther, Heather McDonald, and Rebecca Odes. *Deal with It!: A Whole New Approach to Your Body, Brain, and Life as a Girl*. New York: Pocket Books, 1999.

Eichberg, Rob. *Coming Out: An Act of Love: An Inspiring Call to Action for Gay Men, Lesbians, and Those Who Care*. New York: Plume, 1991.

Goldman, Paula, ed. *Imagining Ourselves: Global Voices from a New Generation of Women*. Novato, CA: New World Library, 2006.

Gottesman, Jane. *Game Face: What Does a Female Athlete Look Like?* New York: Game Face Productions, 2001.

Haag, Pamela and the AAUW Educational Foundation. *Voices of a Generation: Teenage Girls Report About Their Lives Today*. New York: Marlowe and Company, 2000.

Harris, Robie H., illustrated by Michael Emberley. *It's Perfectly Normal: Changing Bodies, Growing Up, Sex, and Sexual Health*, 10th ed. Cambridge, MA: Candlewick Press, 2004.

———. *It's So Amazing!: A Book About Eggs, Sperm, Birth, Babies, and Families*. Cambridge, MA: Candlewick Press, 2002.

Heron, Ann. *Two Teenagers in Twenty: Writings by Gay and Lesbian Youth*. Los Angeles, CA: Alyson Books, 1995.

Hipp, Earl. *Fighting Invisible Tigers: A Stress Management Guide for Teens*, Rev. Ed. Minneapolis, MN: Free Spirit Publishing, Inc., 1995.

Parrish, Cindy L. *Heroic Girlz: An Educational Feature Film* and *Heroic-Girlz Curriculum Guide*, 2006. Available through www.heroicgirlz.org.

Shandler, Sara. *Ophelia Speaks: Adolescent Girls Write About Their Search for Selves*. New York: HarperCollins, 1999.

Weschler, Toni. *Cycle Savvy: The Smart Teen's Guide to the Mysteries of Her Body*. New York: HarperCollins, 2006.